EVALUATION FOR THE REAL WORLD

REAL WORLD

The impact of evidence in policy making

Colin Palfrey, Paul Thomas and Ceri Phillips

First published in Great Britain in 2012 by

The Policy Press
University of Bristol
Fourth Floor
Beacon House
Queen's Road
Bristol BS8 1QU
UK
Tel +44 (0)117 331 4054
Fax +44 (0)117 331 4093
e-mail tpp-info@bristol.ac.uk
www.policypress.co.uk

North American office:
The Policy Press
c/o The University of Chicago Press
1427 East 60th Street
Chicago, IL 60637, USA
t: +1 773 702 7700
f: +1 773-702-9756
e:sales@press.uchicago.edu
www.press.uchicago.edu

British Library Cataloguing in Publication Data
A catalogue record for this book is available from the British Library.

Library of Congress Cataloging-in-Publication Data
A catalog record for this book has been requested.

ISBN 978 1 84742 914 8 paperback
ISBN 978 1 84742 915 5 hardcover

Cover design by The Policy Press
Front cover: image kindly supplied by Patrick Hajzler
Printed and bound in Great Britain by Henry Ling, Dorchester
The Policy Press uses environmentally responsible print partners

Contents

List of tables and figures

Tables

Figures

Preface

In the UK the formal evaluation of public services has a relatively brief history. Discovering what impact various social policies, programmes and projects have had on the intended beneficiaries makes political and economic sense. Why, one might ask, has evaluation had such a relatively limited pedigree?

Part of the explanation could perhaps lie in the response from several medical practitioners in the 1970s and 1980s who considered the movement towards evidence-based medicine as an unwarranted assault on their professional wisdom and integrity.

Laboratory experiments testing the effectiveness of drugs for treating a whole range of conditions had been carried out for decades. However, the origin and nature of the evidence have often stimulated controversy. A prime example of this was the resistance to acknowledging the well-founded evidence that smoking cigarettes caused lung cancer. It was not only the vested interests of the tobacco manufacturers and retailers that proved obstructive. Some in the medical profession – many of whom were themselves smokers – continued to advocate smoking as beneficial.

Research findings that challenge conventional wisdom and traditional practices often cause consternation among individuals and groups who see their customs and practice as potentially under threat. For some, change can be very uncomfortable.

Nevertheless, in spite of initial opposition from some quarters, evidence-based medicine, with its emphasis on the randomised controlled trial as the primary, if not the sole, method of producing cogent evidence, became widely accepted as the 'gold standard' on which to base professional practice.

While evidence-based medicine focused at the outset on the effectiveness of certain drugs and other clinical interventions, politicians and civil servants in countries where health services were funded wholly or substantially by the state began to take an interest in the comparative costs as well as the impact of treatments on people's health. Such a consideration also had relevance where access to health services depended on an individual's ability to pay, often through health insurance systems.

Although academic articles and books began appearing in some numbers in the USA during the 1960s, there was little academic or political interest in formal evaluation in the UK until two decades later. It would appear that in the UK, for example, the formulation of a policy, particularly when enshrined in legislation, was deemed sufficient to ensure its full implementation and once implemented to have the intended effect.

However, it is highly probable that the movement towards evidence-based medicine impinged on the world of civil servants and politicians. Certainly with the Thatcher Conservative government in the 1980s questioning the value of the public sector in terms of its efficiency, major projects and initiatives – notably in the National Health Service – came under close scrutiny. Government spending on public sector services now had to prove its cost-effectiveness.

In the UK this concern with efficiency spawned a number of government documents directed at policy advisers. Politicians now needed to know 'what works' and at what cost. This emerging culture of evidence-based policy prompts the question of how evaluation research commissioned by governments influenced or even shaped central policy.

It is on this question that our book focuses. Given the plethora of learned articles and books on the subject of evaluation over the past 50 years or so, what evidence is there that evaluation research in its many manifestations – commissioned project evaluation, policy evaluation, theory-driven evaluation – has had an impact on public policy at central and more local levels? In short, how cost-effective has evaluation research been?

The book examines the possible reasons why academics, in particular, appear somewhat sceptical, if not despondent, about the outcome of their research-based findings. Those who make decisions about allocating taxpayers' money to a range of policies and their embodiment in programmes and projects, are not bound by any contractual arrangements to act on the results of evaluation research – whether this has been designed and delivered by academics or by research-oriented private companies.

We contend that the exploration of the impact of evaluation research on public policy is long overdue.

Acknowledgements

We are indeed grateful to Alison Shaw and colleagues at The Policy Press for the helpful advice, guidance and support offered during the preparation of the book.

ONE

Evaluation in the political and academic worlds

The primary purpose of this book is to *examine the development of evaluation and its impact on public policy.* This will involve a critical analysis of much of the evaluation literature generated mainly in the USA and the UK from the 1950s onwards. In particular, we shall be seeking published accounts of empirical research which has reported on attempts to identify clear evidence of a link between formal evaluation results and policy formulation. The text will also focus on the application of theory-driven evaluation to policy making.

Although discussions of data collection methods, research designs and the selection of criteria for evaluating policies, programmes and projects are included (Chapters Three, Four and Five), this book is not intended to be something akin to an evaluation handbook. These chapters contribute to the key theme of the book, which centres on the interface between the academic and political worlds.

We intend the book to be of interest and relevance to students engaged on a variety of courses at both graduate and undergraduate levels; to public sector personnel involved with implementing and/ or evaluating the impact of policies, programmes and projects on intended beneficiaries; and to various stakeholders, notably politicians, community leaders and non-governmental organisations.

Within the broad aim set out above as the primary purpose, the objectives of this book are to:

- trace the emergence of evaluation in the political and academic worlds;
- explore the concept of evaluation and its various interpretations;
- identify the potential opportunities and problems in a range of data collection methods and in the analysis of data;
- explain the development of evaluation frameworks;
- assess critically a range of evaluation criteria commonly used in evaluations;
- examine the role of economic evaluations;
- consider the extent to which academics have influenced the practice of evaluation;

- examine the nature of evidence and its use/non-use by decision makers;
- assess the impact of evaluation on the formulation of policy;
- offer suggestions as to the direction in which evaluation needs to travel.

The emergence of evaluation

The practice of evaluation as an aid to decision making at government level has a history of at least 50 years. Yet despite this, serious misgivings about the extent to which the results of evaluation research have influenced and informed policy making have formed a continuous theme running through the academic literature. If these misgivings are well-founded, the reasons for this disjunction between this particular form of applied research and its intended function must be analysed. However, it will also be important to examine the evidence for statements about the non-utilisation of evaluation findings. Does this apparent lack of connection between the results of evaluation research and their acceptance by decision makers stem from a mutual misunderstanding, or even mistrust between those who inhabit different cultural spheres: a dissonance between academia and the 'real world' of politics? Or is this too crude a distinction?

What do we mean by the 'real world'?

In the context of this book, the 'real world' resonates closely with that in which Hogwood and Gunn (1984) locate their discussion of how policies are formulated in the arena of political ideologies and pragmatism. 'Models' of the policy-making process remain just that unless they not only relate to how policies are made but are formed from data derived from research into actual case studies. Central to real world policy analysis and evaluation is the issue of 'rationality'. Some commentators, for example, contend that evaluation can and should lead to more rational decision making (Weiss, 1972). Yet the very concept of what is rational, we would argue, is contingent on the actual context in which any decision is being made. This consideration also features very prominently in the significant volume of literature on evidence-based policy (Davies et al, 2000; Duke, 2001; Walshe, 2001).

For this reason, an important feature of this book will be to discuss the nature of 'evidence' and why that evidence can legitimately be used or disregarded by those who have the power and authority to develop projects and programmes and to devise policies. A prominent theme in the literature on evaluation is that those commissioning the evaluations often appear to disregard the research findings and any resulting recommendations for action. Running through this book is an undercurrent questioning: 'are those who write about evaluation actually living in the real world?' In this sense – as we shall note later – the theses set out by Hogwood and Gunn (1984), Robson (1993), Gray (2004) and Bamberger et al (2006) occupy common ground. In the laboratory, in order to 'evaluate' the value to society of a new treatment or intervention, those who carry out the tests are working in a controlled environment: the trials are usually 'randomised' and 'controlled'. In the world outside the laboratory there are very few situations in which the subjects participating in the evaluation can be controlled. This phenomenon even applies to an extent in what Goffman (1968) described as 'total institutions' such as prisons and secure hospitals.

The 'real world' in which evaluation takes place is fraught with the possibility of encountering what might appear to be irrational decision making and unpredictable behaviour. In this book we are interested in exploring how experts on the subject of evaluation allow for such contingencies in their analysis of evaluation. In this context, the laboratory is the world of hypothesis and theory-building. The real world is where evaluators have to operate.

To what extent does our use of the term 'the real world' resemble the interpretation of other authors who have used the same phrase in the context of social research or evaluation? Hogwood and Gunn (1984) are somewhat reticent about their presentation of policy analysis in 'the real world'. The Preface to their book includes a brief explanation, stating that in much of the literature it is assumed that in the policy process 'the optimal decision will automatically be taken and enforced by a single, authoritative decision-maker. This literature fails to discuss the use and limits of policy analysis techniques in real-world political settings' (p v).

This approach resonates very clearly with our contention: that much of the literature on evaluation appears to ignore the hard truth about decision making – that not only political pragmatism but time and resource constraints limit the possibility of the 'best' option being followed. In fact, one of the key assertions made in this book is that there is very little evidence that writers on the subject of evaluation have ever carried out their own evaluations, so limited are the references to actual real-world evaluations within their expositions of theories and prescriptive advice as to how to conduct evaluations. This is certainly not to suggest that the world of academia lies outside the province of the 'real world'. We are merely expressing the view that the mutual benefits that could be secured between the ideas put forward by academic devotees of evaluation and actual examples of evaluated projects, programmes and policies are not made explicit in the voluminous evaluation literature. This results in texts that are strong on hypotheses and 'theories' but weak on evidence to support what amount to unfounded assertions and recommendations about how to conduct evaluations.

In the Prefaces to the first and second editions of his book, Robson (1993) claims to have undergone something of a revelation in his research as an experimental psychologist. This is because he no longer regards the experiment as necessarily the 'gold standard' for all research. He now advocates qualitative approaches as having 'an important place in the pantheon of research involving people' (p x). He now describes himself as a 'critical realist' (p xi). As a result of his 'conversion' his book on research methods is intended to encourage 'those who want to carry out "real world enquiry": research on and with people, outside the safe confines of the laboratory' (p xv). He argues that many real-world studies are evaluations because in research about people in real-life situations 'we are often seeking not simply to understand something, but also to try to change it' (p xvi). Increasingly, according to Robson, people in the helping and caring professions are being called upon to carry out evaluative and other 'enquiry projects'. This raises the question, which is relevant to our text, of whether the reports of evaluation studies carried out by people 'in the field' are accessible to the general public, or to the academic community only. Such reports are likely to have a circulation limited to the commissioners of the research and possibly the range of participants in the study. Robson concludes by accepting that the 'real world' is a questionable concept and is probably more appropriately described as a state of mind.

Gray's position is that research is not, nor should it be, the exclusive realm of academics (Gray, 2004). The purpose of his book is to help people working in commercial businesses, public sector organisations, voluntary services, professional networks, neighbourhoods and communities to 'design and carry out research' (p xvii). Gray conceives of the real world as that which lies beyond the boundaries of the laboratory or at least beyond the confines of the experimental and control group model of social research. He emphasises the importance and validity of qualitative research using designs and methods that allow a range of data collection approaches to be adopted. These include focus groups, individual interviews, action research and other means of capturing opinions on a range of public services. Gray's concept of the 'real world' closely resembles that held by Robson: that what might broadly be labelled 'social research' – because of its focus on people in their social environment – is rarely amenable to the randomised controlled group research design. Instead, the data required will have to be collected through qualitative research methods and at times by evaluators who work in the same environment. In essence, both Robson and Gray are defining the real world as the 'zone' beyond the laboratory and, by inference, that which operates outside the realm of academia.

The work by Bamberger et al (2006) displays a different orientation. While Robson and Gray deal with the broad area of what might be termed 'research on people, for people and often by the people', Bamberger and his colleagues address the issue of the inevitable constraints faced by evaluators. These are primarily: budgets, time, data and political pressures. No research project has at its disposal unlimited resources of funding and time available in which to complete the research. There might also be problems gaining access to the type, quality and quantity of data needed to carry out the 'ideal' piece of research. Bamberger et al discuss the various threats to validity that these constraints pose and how best to counter them. By doing so, they provide a welcome element of reality into what, we would argue, is a corpus of evaluation literature that to a large extent ignores the practicalities of evaluating projects, programmes and policies; practicalities that include having to respond to pressure from the commissioners of the research, to produce data that will suit budgets, time constraints and political commitments.

Rossi et al (1999) refer to evaluation as a real-world activity without enlarging on what they actually mean. If they are suggesting that evaluation is essentially founded on an empirical methodology geared towards informing decision makers, then we would agree, it surely is a real-world activity. However, if it is shown that such evaluations rarely influence policy making or policy implementation, then the question of whether there is another 'dimension' that reflects a much more subtle and complex relationship between 'evidence' and 'decision making' must be asked.

Evaluation in the political context

The emergence and development of evaluation as a formal, research-based activity has a fairly long history. Rossi and Freeman (1993) identify the 1930s as the starting point for evaluation research in the USA. In the 1940s monitoring the morale of front-line soldiers gained in importance and by the end of the next decade large-scale evaluation programmes were commonplace, for example in the field of delinquency prevention projects, public housing schemes and community organisation activities (Palfrey et al, 1992).

However, Shaw et al (eds) (2006), argue that in the USA there were several histories of evaluation, depending on the policy domain, for example education, welfare and economics. In the UK they refer to 'the policy research tradition' (p 9) as providing a stimulus for evaluation research. This tradition stemmed from the Fabians' impact on British Welfare State policy after the Second World War, with the new social policy becoming a distinct discipline within the social sciences.

During the 1960s evaluation research broadened from a programme and project focus to a growing concern with the process of policy making in the USA and the UK – see Suchman (1967) and Campbell (1969) – and by the 1970s, according to Weiss (1977), evaluation research had become a growth industry. Indeed, the corpus of literature on the practice of evaluation had become substantial enough for Care (1977) to produce a collection of readings.

In Britain, during the 1970s the evaluation of particular programmes directed by government policy concentrated on output measurements in a few areas of public sector activity – notably criminal justice, health services and education – to the extent that, by the 1980s, output measurement schemes were operating in 31 central government departments (HM Treasury, 1986 and 1987). During this period, the main instrument of measurement was a set of performance indicators (PIs) – an approach which was given impetus by the Audit Commission after its establishment in 1983 following the Local Government Finance Act 1982 (Palfrey et al, 1992).

During the 1980s, according to Henkel (1991), evaluation and the institutions through which it was carried out acquired a new and more sharply defined public profile in the UK. The government of the day identified evaluation as a significant component in the strategy to achieve the key objective of controlling public expenditure. The emphasis from central policy makers was on outputs, outcomes and the setting of targets and performance standards. 'Vigorous attempts were made to establish economy, efficiency, value for money, effectiveness and performance as incontestable values, essential to the sustainment of political order' (Henkel, 1991, p 12). The government newly elected in 1979 brought in a new approach to public sector accountability supplanting the traditional system of bureaucratic administration with what came to be known as 'the new public management' or 'managerialism' (Hughes, 1994; Ranson and Stewart, 1994). Clear objectives were to be set for public sector organisations and there was to be a 'systematic evaluation of programmes' (Hughes, 1994, p 58). The programmes related not only to local authorities and other public bodies but also to central government, in order to determine whether resources were being used in an efficient and effective manner.

In a document published in 1992, the government made it clear that evaluation was central to the planning and provision of services:

> It is government policy that all Cabinet papers proposing new policies should state clearly what is to be achieved, by whom, at what cost and how the policies are to be measured and evaluated. (Department of the Environment, 1992, p 3)

As far as the government was concerned, the main purpose of evaluation was to improve on existing policies. Although some forms of evaluation had been done previously by civil servants, the new approach was to be more systematic and comprehensive. Internal evaluation was to continue, particularly in the initial design stages, and civil servants would assist in the commissioning of research by outside bodies and in collaborating with them in progressing the evaluation. Apart from evaluation research studies, the government in the 1990s and into the 21st century introduced a range of systems set up in order to ascertain whether certain public services were meeting targets and required standards of performance. Audits, inspections, reviews, inquiries and accreditation bodies relied heavily on PIs as their main criteria for assessment.

Central government's enthusiasm for PIs was borne out by the introduction of a set of indicators to the NHS in 1983, updated two years later, with the police and prison services following suit (Carter, 1988). However, as Pollitt (1985) asserted, PIs could not capture any measurements of the effectiveness of policies except as somewhat contestable proxy measures such as – in health – patients' length of stay, throughput of hospital patients or – in the criminal justice system – recorded crime levels, clear-up rates and the time between committal and trial (Alpsten, 1974).

More recently the UK government has continued to promote and support evaluation as a central device for assessing whether projects, programmes and policies are achieving their stated objectives. In 2003 the Treasury published its Green Book (HM Treasury, 2003) which laid out its guidance for appraisal and evaluation with a particular focus on economic evaluation, and in April 2011 the same arm of government produced a more comprehensive document, the Magenta Book (HM Treasury, 2011), which is aimed at policy makers and senior executives at central and local government level as well as those in the voluntary sector. The current Magenta Book is a revised version of a previous evaluation guide but explains that it has shifted from an 'analyst's manual' to a broader guide aimed at both analysts and policy makers at both central and local government levels.

The Magenta Book is, *par excellence*, rooted in the real world of policy evaluation which, it explains, covers projects, programmes and policies. Its contents cover the whole gamut of why and how to conduct evaluations and makes it clear that, first and foremost, evaluators need to be objective in carrying out their tasks. While it acknowledges the potential for applying a theoretical approach to evaluations, the text of 134 pages devotes just over two pages to this topic, referring to the theory of change, to realist evaluation and to an 'economic model' (p 57). By way of contrast, the document apportions ten pages to the topic of process evaluation and to action research as a possible concomitant.

In the real world of decision making at government level, 'decisions about future policy will not be made on the basis of a single evaluation' (p 125). In this regard, the document argues, there is merit in looking to meta-evaluation and meta-analysis as means of gathering data that could provide more substantive evidence for policy makers. Both these concepts will be examined later in the book.

The development of evaluation

However the term 'evaluation' might be defined – and we shall offer some definitions in Chapter Two – and at whatever period, the process is clearly concerned with improving public services in one aspect or another by applying certain criteria. Quantitatively assessed criteria such as numbers of operations carried out per hospital specialty, pro rata conviction rates for different types of crimes and numbers of council homes built over a specified period can be useful on a number of different levels. For example, they could provide important comparative data on outputs achieved over the past ten years. On a slightly more indicative level as far as policy evaluation is concerned, the figures could compare conviction rates not just across different types of crime but pre- and post-implementation of a new piece of legislation. This latter device introduces what has become the hallmark of project, programme and policy evaluation – that is, an attempt to relate inputs and outputs to outcomes – the attempt to isolate and thus identify attribution or cause-effect.

With this in mind, the somewhat faltering steps in the progress of formal evaluation from mere description to careful analysis appear surprisingly crude in the light of current approaches to and objectives of evaluation practice. However, the movement towards evidence-based medicine, which undoubtedly gave further impetus to evaluation research in the UK and beyond, might well have raised a few eyebrows. The virtually pioneering work of Cochrane (1972) in advocating the randomised controlled trial (RCT) as the primary source of evidence on which to base clinical interventions more than implied that, up to that relatively recent point, medical practice had been based on information gathered from scientifically unproven sources.

Some medical practitioners regarded this inference as an insult to the profession. Fowler (1997) was particularly acerbic in his rejection of the whole notion of evidence-based medicine (EBM) claiming that it was no more than a neologism for informed decision making. 'The presumption is made' wrote Fowler 'that the practice of medicine was previously based on a direct communication with God or by tossing a coin' (p 242). He concluded that EBM was a built-in method for rejecting or delaying medical advances. Equally dismissive and sardonic was the view expressed by Greenhalgh (1997) that EBM is:

> the increasingly fashionable tendency of a group of young, confident and highly numerate medical academics to belittle the performance of experienced clinicians by using a combination of epidemiological jargon and statistical sleight of hand … the argument, usually presented with near evangelistical zeal, that no health-related action should ever be taken by a doctor, a nurse, a purchaser of health services or a politician unless and until the results of several large and expensive research trials have appeared in print and been approved by a committee of experts. (pp 3–4)

One year earlier Smith (1996) had drawn attention to the importance of clinical skills, experience and judgement in decision making and to a wider view of medicine as a human art that is supported by science. Quality, he asserted, cannot always be quantified. However, the establishment on 1 April 1999 of NICE (the National Institute for Clinical Excellence, later re-named the National Institute for Health and Clinical Excellence) accorded official government status to this body which, ever since, has delivered *ex cathedra* judgements on whether a particular treatment has been unequivocally proved to be not only effective but sufficiently cost-effective to be made available to NHS patients. Very soon after it was set up, the pronouncements of NICE proved controversial in some quarters (Smith, 2000; Dent and Sadler, 2002; Gafni and Birch, 2003). The media, too, were keen to carry indictments about the 'postcode lottery' which meant that patients living in some areas of the UK were granted access to certain treatments while those in other, sometimes neighbouring, areas were denied the treatment – usually a specific drug. NICE was set up precisely to prevent such anomalies.

Despite challenges to what appeared to some critics to be a rigidly positivistic model of what constituted cogent evidence, the epithet 'evidence based' has become pervasive in an array of public service literature and practice. Quite early in the 1990s, Raynor et al (1994) were active in developing a 'what works' approach to the various community and custodial sentences available to practitioners in the judicial system while Davies et al (2000) argued that this same approach needed to be applied in the evaluation of a range of public services. Sheldon and Chilvers (2000) reported on the work of the newly established Centre for Evidence-based Social Services which was located in and for local authorities in the south and south-west of England. The Social Care Institute for Excellence was then set up with funding from the Department of Health in England and by the devolved administrations in Wales and Northern Ireland to disseminate knowledge linked to good practice in the field of social work.

In Chapter Five the momentum towards seeking an incontrovertible evidence base for policy will be examined. So widespread has become this quest for convincing and valid data to inform policy making, allied to the question 'What works?', that formal evaluation is likely to continue to play a central role in the analysis of whether the public services are providing value for money. The initial resistance, particularly amongst a few medical practitioners, to what they regarded as a form of bureaucratic meddling, has given way to a commitment by successive governments that public expenditure cannot be allowed to go unbridled, and regarding evaluation research as a means towards ensuring political, managerial and organisational accountability.

Evaluation in the academic context

Evaluation in the academic context will form a substantial element in the chapter dealing with the impact of evaluation on decision making (Chapter Six), and so at this point, the discussion will be confined to drawing attention to the vast opportunities presented to the academic world by politicians' need to be seen to be acting 'rationally', that is, acting on data derived from authentic research. Yet it was not long into the early history of evaluation before academics began doubting whether this recent initiative in policy making was worthy of being labelled a form of research. For example, Suchman (1967) regarded evaluation as an exercise carried out to establish the value of an intervention or programme. Evaluative research, by contrast, had more to do with the scientific methods applied to an evaluation. Similar distinctions – as Clarke (2006) has pointed out – have been proposed by Cordray and Lipsey (1996) and by Patton (1986).

Whatever the nuances suggested by these academics in order to stimulate debate within academic circles, it is obvious that to merit the term 'evaluation' there must be a central research component. Without such an integral feature, the practice of evaluation would not be deemed worthy of any academic interest.

Over the past half century or so hundreds of books and thousands of journal articles have been written by university-based authors on the topic of evaluation. There are currently over a dozen journals worldwide that are dedicated to this topic and several evaluation societies, many of which organise national and international conferences. In Chapter Two we shall be tracing the evolution and development of evaluation as an academic discipline. Voluminous handbooks which deal with the practicalities of carrying out evaluations are available. These tomes – notably those by Rossi et al (1999), Fink (2005) and Shaw et al (2006) – are well over 400 pages in length and cover a wide range of subjects, particularly focusing on research designs, methods of data collection, data analysis and report writing. There are similarly a host of texts setting out how to conduct social research. Since evaluation research is a particular example of social science research using the same procedures, designs and methods it would be difficult to promote evaluation as a unique or even a distinctive academic discipline. Yet the bulk of evaluation-oriented literature implies otherwise. At odds with exponents of evaluation research as a detached, objective exercise involving scientific rigour are those commentators who see it as a political activity. This area of interest will be addressed in Chapter Two.

The fact that we have referred above to 'social science research' and elsewhere in the book to 'social research' highlights what Oakley has characterised as 'the paradigm wars' (Oakley, 2000). This term is a somewhat over-dramatised allusion to two distinct schools of thought among academics with regard to what constitutes *knowledge* and how best to seek it. On the one side are those known as *logical positivists* who view the world as amenable to scientific enquiry in order to reveal facts; on the other side are those known as *social constructionists* who are more inclined to view external phenomena as contingent on the person or persons viewing them. To some, truth is absolute; to others truth is relative. In reality, this is a phoney 'war' because it depends on the type of knowledge that you are seeking. Certainly, many evaluation studies use an experimental and control group design with all extraneous factors or variables being controlled thus leaving only the particular intervention (project, programme or policy) as the defining input. Such a design can be harnessed in order to increase the likelihood of identifying a cause-effect correlation.

Alternatively, where such a design is neither practicable nor, in some cases, ethical, a more qualitative approach would be the more appropriate design. Questions of design and methodology will feature in Chapter Three.

Where the political and academic worlds converge, of course, is in planning and carrying out the evaluation. Since Patton (1988), among others, regards evaluation as an inherently political activity, decisions will have to be made about the extent to which the political agenda influences the research design and this, in turn, raises the question of the integrity of the evaluator. Yet the statement by itself – that evaluation is an inherently political activity – needs to be further explored, and this will be done in Chapter Two. Does it mean that in the 'real world' evaluators must accept that their findings will be used – or not used – in order to further the cause of those who commissioned the research, whether at local, regional or national levels? Does it suggest that any evaluator will bring to the research his or her own ideological perspective and that this will, in turn, determine the way in which the evaluator sets about gathering data? Or could it be suggesting that evaluators *ought to* set out to follow a course of action that will help to further a particular political cause? These are issues that various definitions of 'evaluation' either implicitly or overtly address.

Concluding comment

We have noted that evaluation has become a required attribute of policy making over the past five or more decades. Over this period of time, evaluation studies – commissioned by central governments – have developed from a major focus on economy and efficiency to a concern with effectiveness and to the impact of evaluations on the policy itself. This latter issue, as shall be seen in later chapters, has provoked a continuing debate among academics. Their often plaintive call for the results of evaluations to be seen to be utilised by policy makers prompts the consideration of whether evaluators have been applying their efforts and skills to real-world situations. This, in turn, leads in to the question of what evaluation-commissioners and evaluation-practitioners consider to be the nature and purpose of formal evaluation.

   In the next chapter we move on to a discussion of what evaluation is, and what it is not.

References

Alpsten, B. (1974) 'Methods of evaluation and planning of police work', in *Methods of evaluation and planning in the field of crime*, Reports presented to the First Criminological Colloquium (1973), vol xii Strasbourg: Council of Europe.

Bamberger, M., Rugh, J. and Mabry, L. (2006) *Real world evaluation*, London: Sage.

Campbell, D.T. (1969) 'Reforms as experiments', *American Psychologist*, vol 24, pp 409–29.

Care, F.G. (1977) *Readings in evaluation research*, Beverly Hills, CA: Russell Sage.

Carter, N. (1988) 'Performance indicators in the criminal justice system', in *Crime UK 1988*, Newbury: Policy Journals.

Clarke, A. (2006) *Evaluation research*, London: Sage.

Cochrane, A.L. (1972) *Effectiveness and efficiency*, Nuffield Provincial Hospitals Trust.

Cordray, D. and Lipsey, M.W. (1986) 'Program evaluation and program research', in *Evaluation studies: A review annual*, Beverly Hills, CA: Sage, pp 17-31.

Davies, H.T.O., Nutley, S.M. and Smith, P.C. (eds) (2000) *What works? Evidence-based policy and practice in public services*, Bristol: The Policy Press.

Dent, T.H.S. and Sadler, M. (2002) 'From guidance to practice: why NICE is not enough', *British Medical Journal*, vol 324, pp 842-45.

Department of the Environment (1992) *Policy evaluation: The role of social research*, London: HMSO.

Duke, K. (2001) 'Evidence-based policy making? The interplay between research and the development of prison drugs policy', *Criminal Justice*, vol 1, no 3, pp 277-300.

Fink, A. (2005) *Evaluation fundamentals* (2nd edn), Thousand Oaks, CA: Sage.

Fowler, P.B.S. (1997) 'Evidence-based everything', *Journal of Evaluation in Clinical Practice*, vol 3, no 3, pp 239–43.

Gafni, A. and Birch, S. (2003) 'NICE methodological guidelines and decision-making in the NHS in England and Wales', *Pharmacoeconomics*, vol 21, no 3, pp 149-57.

Goffman, E. (1968) *Asylums*, Harmondsworth: Penguin.

Gray, D.E. (2004) *Doing research in the real world*, London: Sage.

Greenhalgh, T. (1997) *How to read a paper: The basics of evidence-based medicine*, British Medical Journal Publishing.

Henkel, M. (1991) *Government, evaluation and change*, London: Jessica Kingsley.

HM Treasury (1986) *Output performance measurement in central government*, Working Paper No 38 (ed. S. Lewis), London: HM Treasury.

HM Treasury (1987) *Output performance measurement in central government*, Working Paper No 45 (ed. P. Durham), London: HM Treasury.

HM Treasury (2003) *The Green Book: Appraisal and evaluation in central government*, London: TSO.

HM Treasury (2011) *The Magenta Book: Guidance for evaluation*, London: HM Treasury.

Hogwood, J. and Gunn, N. (1984) *Policy analysis for the real world*, Oxford: Oxford University Press.

Hughes, O.E. (1994) *Public management and administration*, Basingstoke: Macmillan.

Oakley, A. (2000) *Experiments in knowing: Gender and method in the social sciences*, Cambridge: Polity Press.

Palfrey, C., Phillips, C., Thomas, P. and Edwards, D. (1992) *Policy evaluation in the public sector,* Aldershot: Avebury.

Patton, M.Q. (1986) *Utilization-focused evaluation*, London: Sage.

Patton, M.Q. (1988) 'Politics and evaluation', *Evaluation Practice*, vol 9, no 1, pp 89-94.

Pollitt, C. (1985) 'Measuring performance: a new system for the NHS', *Policy & Politics*, vol 13, no 1, pp 1-15.

Ranson, S. and Stewart, J. (1994) *Management for the public domain,* London: Macmillan.

Raynor, P., Smith, D. and Vanstone, M. (1994) *Effective probation practice*, Basingstoke: Macmillan.

Robson, C. (1993) *Real world research*, Oxford: Blackwell.

Rossi, P.H. and Freeman, H.E. (1993) *Evaluation: A systematic approach*, Newbury Park, CA: Sage.

Rossi, P.H., Freeman, H. and Lipsey, M.W. (1999) *Evaluation: A systematic approach* (6th edn), Beverly Hills, CA: Sage.

Shaw, I.A, Greene, J.C. and Mark, M. (eds) (2006) *Handbook of evaluation: Policies, programs and practices*, London: Sage.

Sheldon, B. and Chilvers, R. (2000) *Evidence-based social care*, Lyme Regis: Russell House Publishing.

Smith, R.M. (1996) 'What clinical information do doctors need?', *British Medical Journal*, vol 313, pp 3062-68.

Smith, R.M. (2000) 'The failings of NICE', *British Medical Journal*, vol 321, pp 1363-64.

Suchman, E.A. (1967) *Evaluative research: Principles in public service and action programs*, Beverly Hills, CA: Sage.

Walshe, K. (2001) 'Evidence-based policy. Don't be timid', *British Medical Journal*, vol 323, p 187.

Weiss, C. (1972) *Evaluation research*, Eaglewood Cliffs, CA: Prentice Hall.

Weiss, C. (1977) *Using research in public policy making*, Lexington, MA: D.C. Heath.

TWO

What is meant by 'evaluation'?

Later in this chapter we shall be considering various definitions or interpretations of the concept 'evaluation' in order to see how it differs from other forms of assessment in the public sector. 'Interpretation' is probably the more accurate term to apply since this allows for nuances of meaning which are attached to the concept, rather than 'definition' which implies that there is only one meaning. However, 'definition' will be used at appropriate points in the discussion, because writers on this topic usually offer their interpretations as if they are indeed *the* meaning.

As noted in Chapter One, during the 1980s and 1990s in the UK the government needed to ensure that public expenditure was allocated to services on the basis of value for money – in short, where was the evidence that projects, programmes and, in particular, policies had achieved their objectives at the least possible cost? Some of these objectives could be expressed in terms of outcomes but it was also considered essential to concentrate efforts on attaining quantifiable targets which were labelled 'performance indicators' (PIs). Semantically, the term 'indicator' would seem to be well-chosen. An indication of achievement implies that the chosen indicator might not tell the whole story; that there might only be a prima facie connection between some quantifiable index and 'performance'. The temptation has been to use PIs not only as proxy measures of successful policies, but as if they were the only measurements that were necessary. We shall now deal with a number of approaches to and techniques of performance measurement and, later in this chapter, we shall examine whether there is consensus about the nature and purpose of evaluation.

Measurement of performance

How does evaluation differ from other forms of assessment in the realm of public sector performance? Are the criteria for judging merit that are applied in auditing, inspection and accreditation less rigorous or less valid than those used when carrying out formal evaluations? Are the results recorded in audit, inspection and accreditation reports accepted more readily by decision makers than those generated by evaluation research? If they are, is it because the data they set out to gather is more superficial and more easily accessed than the information sought by evaluators? We look first at the extremely quantifiable PIs: those devices that governments assume will provide a clear answer to the question: Are government-prescribed targets – as proxy measures of service quality – being achieved by those organisations responsible for delivering services?

Performance indicators

A relatively early attempt at defining evaluation came from Weiss (1972) who referred to it as 'judging merit against some yardstick' (p 1) while, even earlier, Scriven (1967) identified two kinds of evaluation: formative and summative. Before turning to a whole plethora of evaluation 'types' and 'models' which form the content of numerous academic publications, the succinct definition offered by Weiss prompts the question of how evaluation differs from other attempts to judge merit against some yardstick. It all depends on what is meant by 'merit'. It also depends on the purpose of the formal assessment. Weiss's definition relates only to the *process* of evaluation. It is fairly easy to define the physical process of 'walking' but the decision to walk rather than use another form of transport might have several different purposes such as keeping fit, helping to save the environment or saving money. In the context of public sector services various methods have been implemented in order to assess performance depending on the key purpose of the judgement. The fact that PIs hinge on quantifiable measures of worthiness or value does not detract from their use as a key piece of equipment in the evaluation toolkit.

This is particularly relevant when they feature in sets of comparative data in which performance is displayed alongside similar organisations, departments or in comparison with previous annual statistics. Annual house-building figures, incidence of specific diseases across countries and UK regions, deaths from road accidents, clear-up rates for certain criminal offences – all these statistics can tell policy makers about vital matters relating to efficiency and cost-effectiveness. They rely, of course, on the sources of data being wholly reliable. Yet, to err on the cynical side perhaps, any yardstick can be used in order to judge merit. Exactly what the resulting data shows us could, however, be challenged on economic, ethical and even mathematical grounds.

For example, adapting the methodology applied by NICE, a reduction in instances of football hooliganism over a certain period appears highly commendable but at what cost was this result achieved? This additional yardstick of cost adds another dimension to the slogan 'what works?'

The policy or practice might be worthy but was it worth it? As the economist would suggest: could the resources needed to achieve very commendable figures be used to greater effect elsewhere – what were the 'opportunity costs' involved? In addition, could the same results have been achieved by adopting a different strategy which involved the use of fewer resources? Taking this broader view, it is obvious that PIs are very useful as 'tin openers' (Carter et al, 1992) because they can and, arguably should, be used in order to clarify important questions about what they are *actually* telling us about 'performance' as construed from different perspectives.

This is the value of PIs at their best in the context of service evaluation. They can act as the starting point for closer and deeper analysis that is intended to provide answers to what might be called 'the so-what? question'. Here are some examples of statements that might be encountered:

- Independent schools produce more Oxbridge entrants than state schools.
- The number of students obtaining A grades in exams has been increasing year on year.
- Recently, girls have been out-performing boys at pre-university level examinations.

We can leave readers to draw their own collection of *prima facie* inferences from these bald statements. At worst, those with a particular point to make can interpret such statements according to their own version of 'tub-thumping', thus fulfilling the old adage that 'statistics can be used like a drunken man uses a lamp-post: for support rather than for illumination' (Lang, quoted in the *Wordsworth Dictionary of Quotations*, 1997, p 277). Unfortunately, PIs are frequently used to support a particular standpoint or ideological premise. This abuse of data is at its most malign when it purports to make comparisons between public sector organisations such as hospitals, schools and social communities. The manipulation of unscrutinised numbers can lead to unethical judgements being made about professional competence and human behaviour.

The mathematical fallacy arises when quantitative data are averaged in order to create and promote official government targets that carry sanctions if they are not met. Witness the case of a hospital in Stafford which, in 2010, in slavishly seeking to reach externally-imposed 'performance' targets, failed to provide anything like good quality care to very vulnerable patients (Triggle, 2010). While the culture of target-driven public services is still very much alive, at least in England, within the NHS, there has been a move towards emphasising quality above quantity (Darzi, 2008). In summary, performance indicators can be a legitimate starting point for service evaluation but cannot and should not be the finishing point.

Before offering further definitions of evaluation, it will be helpful to consider whether other approaches to measuring performance in the public sector can be characterised as different forms of evaluation.

Audits

In the public sector all organisations wholly or partly funded by central government are subject to regular auditing. Auditors appointed by the government are tasked with inspecting the organisations' accounts in order to ensure that the proper procedures have been carried out in accounting for income and expenditure on behalf of the public, who in essence foot the bill. In 1983, following the Local Government Act of 1982, and at the behest of a Conservative administration, the Audit Commission was established, The Commission's role was to monitor public sector performance by applying the three 'E's' as the main criteria. These were economy, efficiency and effectiveness. Thus, the remit of the Commission was much wider than that of the auditing of accounts and entered the territory of value for money (VFM) (Simey, 1985; Whynes, 1987).

However, in August 2010 the newly elected Coalition government under a Conservative prime minister announced the dissolution of the Audit Commission, as those in power considered it to be wasting taxpayers' money on what were deemed to be unnecessary projects. This decision was a truly classic example of Juvenal's enquiry: 'Quis custodiet ipsos custodeos?' ('Who will guard the guards themselves?'). The Audit Commission was, one might say, informally audited and found not to be providing value for money. Scotland, Wales and Northern Ireland have retained their Audit Offices with the primary aim of ensuring value for money in the public sector but also having the responsibility to monitor the accounts of private companies if they have received public money.

The increase in auditing by central agencies during the 1980s and 1990s has been described by Power (1997) as an 'audit explosion'. In Power's view, traditional auditing focused on financial regularity and legality of transactions but recently there has been a greater emphasis than previously on efficiency, effectiveness and performance. However, this explosion, Power argues, has had some perverse unintended effects including:

1. a decline in organisational trust
2. defensive strategies and 'blamism'
3. a reduction in organisational innovation
4. lower employee morale
5. the hidden costs of audit compliance as organisations engage in elaborate strategies to make themselves auditable
6. alienation of professionals who see themselves as accountable to their peers as opposed to state-imposed target regimes
7. conflicting interpretations of the meaning of various data
8. an emphasis on what is easily measured as opposed to what might really be important (if it can be measured it probably isn't important)
9. an increase in game-playing (e.g. people attempting to manage expectations of their future performance by keeping their present performance artificially low, thus keeping some 'slack' in the system
10. an increase in 'creative accounting'.

These dysfunctional effects of the audit explosion serve as a reminder that certain monitoring systems put in place by government agencies and others with laudable intentions will often be seen by public sector staff as more trouble than they are worth.

Since the primary aim of audits and other monitoring systems is delivering value for money it is pertinent to ask: 'What amounts to "value for money" and according to what and whose criteria are such assessments made?' The Audit Offices are independent of government, yet one of the criticisms directed at the Audit Commission in England was that it was showing tendencies towards a political stance that was at odds with the incoming Coalition's creed (*Daily Telegraph*, 2010). Judging merit against some yardstick would seem to apply to the mission of devolved government/assembly auditing objectives. It would also appear to correspond with the *raison d'être* of NICE. One undisputed task of audits, whether at local or central government level, is to identify waste: the incurring of expenditure that is deemed to produce very little or no benefit to its intended beneficiaries – members of the public, who indirectly provide the income.

However, it follows that deciding on matters of VFM involves, by definition, value judgements, and values are deep-rooted in individual and collective principles. Indeed, the term 'evaluation' points to judgements being made on the basis of deeply held and not necessarily clearly articulated beliefs about the 'ideal society'. Does this then contradict the view of Carol Weiss that evaluation has the capacity to bring 'greater rationality to social decision-making' (Weiss, 1972, p 128)? The fundamental values inherent in the task of auditing in the public sector are a moral responsibility to ensure public sector organisations are accountable to the public and not just to governments which, naturally in democracies, are themselves accountable to the public. But this statement of underlying values informing the auditing process could be further analysed to reveal not necessarily a benevolent mission to improve the lot of citizens but instead a wholly pragmatic endeavour to secure the survival of a political entity. So, without engaging, hopefully, in too much of a reductionist thesis, the very basic instinct of self-preservation could lie at the root of audit.

Inspections

Whereas audits are a form of inspection, inspections often have a different informing ethos than that which is central to auditing. On the face of it, an inspection seems far removed from what is understood by the term 'evaluation'. It assumes an aura of rather cold, detached judgements being made according to bureaucratically conceived criteria that lay stress on following routinised procedures and regulations. This, of course, is likely to be part of the inspector's expectations but in the fields of health, social care, education, probation and the police service, inspections have developed a more quality-oriented remit – an activity that has increasingly sought to involve service users in the process. In this way, judging merit against some yardstick has become a co-operative venture between officials and lay people. This approach, not only to inspections in the public sector but to the organisation and delivery of public services, seems to have become so embedded in government policy that it might be assumed that this is not a relatively recent development.

  A landmark in central government's policy to involve the public in various examples of monitoring of the quality of services was the Citizens' Charter launched in 1991 (Doem, 1993) which set out a formal policy on the quality of health services. The principles contained within this document emphasised citizens' choice and value for money. This policy was not necessarily embraced or implemented at local government level. As far as the active engagement of citizens in the formal inspection or even informal feedback on services was concerned, two commentators reflected a completely opposite philosophy of public consultation among public servants:

> In our experience managers and professionals in local government still see the public as a nuisance. They are perceived as a nuisance because the demands they make are unrealistic; because one group of citizens want one thing whereas another group wants something else; because they are parochial in their outlook; because they are often prejudiced and because they are never satisfied. (Hambleton and Hoggett, 1990: quoted in Gaster, 1995, p 27)

It was more than ten years later before central government constructed a document that laid down the principles of a more inclusive approach to public services inspection. *The Government's Policy on Inspection of Public Services* was published in 2003. The policy statement applied to all UK government departments responsible for public services and, by extension, 'to any agencies, non-departmental public bodies, (NDPBs), local government bodies, and private or voluntary sector entities commissioned to provide those services' (Office of Public Services Reform, 2003, p 1). The government made it clear that inspection was to be 'user-focused' with an emphasis on outcomes 'which means considering service delivery to the end users of the services rather than concentrating on internal management arrangements' (p 5). The policy document went further in specifying that the inspection process should take into account 'the experience of those for whom the service is provided' (p 5).

Compared with the role and remit of traditional central and local government inspections, this set of principles was little short of revolutionary. The involvement of one of the authors of this book in the early 1990s as the external evaluator of what was called a Quality Action Group was illuminating. Motivated by the need to be conforming with the increasing official emphasis on service user consultation, a social services department set out to establish a group consisting of: the managers of a residential and day centre for disabled adults; voluntary carers; staff and service user representatives. After a brief introduction by the department's middle manager about the purpose of the group, one service user posed the question: "Why, after all these years, are you suddenly asking us what *we* want?" The manager was stumped for a reply. Indeed, as the service users began to stretch the boundaries and started asking for changes such as being part of the staff appointments procedure, the manager of the residential centre resigned. It was more than he could bear.

Inspections, then, of health care institutions, schools, social services and other public service agencies are now seeking to contribute to the improvement of public sector services and involving all key stakeholders – management, front-line staff, service users and, where appropriate, their families – in the inspection process. They have to take into consideration the criteria for assessing the service that are seen as pertinent from different perspectives.

Accreditation

This process of assessing the quality of certain organisations or functions within an organisation often carries with it the prospect or promise of funding. Accreditation involves giving a seal of approval for attaining standards that are nationally and/or professionally recognised. In the public sector a range of services can apply for official recognition that a certain standard of performance has been reached. In some instances, such as in the case of the Healthcare Standards criteria applied in the NHS in Wales, application for approval is obligatory and meeting the required standards can result in funding awards or, if standards are not fully met, sanctions can be applied until the full set of standards has been achieved. However, Finch (2004) has argued that the use of interim or proxy measures of improvement within the NHS has not generated any firm evidence of improvement. She notes that 'there is little or no research or evidence to demonstrate whether the various approaches to evaluating health and social care … actually lead to improved care for service users. The lack of a causal link between compliance with standards and improved clinical results has been raised as a problem in relation to accreditation' (p 184). Finch concludes that there is a need for research into whether evaluation leads to improved health care. In the case of the research carried out by Shaw and Collins (1995) into the outcome of the submission of 47 hospitals in the south west of England to be accredited, the main reasons for non-accreditation related to issues of safety, clinical records and medical organisation – all of which would qualify as 'proxy measures' of actual standards of health care.

As Leeuw and Furibo (2008) point out, accreditation often starts with self-evaluation by the organisation that is seeking accreditation. The outcome of this stage is then reviewed by the evaluator-accreditor in order to check whether the quality of the self-assessment has been carried out to a sufficiently high standard. Increasingly, Leeuw and Furibo assert, particular attention is being paid to risk-assessment and risk management. The lower the likelihood of perceived risks – for example with regard to health care and education – the less often site investigations will take place.

The United Kingdom Accreditation Service (UKAS) is the sole national accreditation body recognised by the UK government to assess, against internationally agreed standards, the calibre of organisations that provide certification, testing and inspection leading to some form of accreditation. There are several such organisations operating in the UK. For example, in the field of higher education, the Higher Education Funding Council in England (HEFCE) delegates to the Quality Assurance Agency responsibility to assess the standard of teaching, learning and the whole student experience. Another organisation, OFSTED, regulates and inspects the care of children and young people and the education and skills development of learners of all ages. One initiative created by the Blair government in 2000 was the creation of City Academies – now known simply as Academies. These are secondary schools which were originally schools with low academic achievement which were subject to 'special measures'. They are free from the control of the local education authority and are funded directly by central government with additional funding from private sponsors who have a say in what is taught in the curriculum. It can be said, therefore, that these Academies were the result of the opposite of accreditation – namely what might be termed a seal of disapproval. More recently, however, many Academies have proved successful and have been attracting a high demand for pupil entry from aspirational parents (Henry, 2008).

The accreditation of hospitals started in the USA in 1917 (Shaw and Collins, 1995). In the UK a pilot scheme was established in the west of England in 1995. Within the NHS in England a form of accreditation has been responsible for the development of Foundation Trusts. These organisations have gained a degree of independence from the Department of Health and from the local Strategic Health Authority. They are organisations that have performed at a high standard in terms of financial competency and in the quality of services provided. In 2010 the government announced that all NHS Trusts should become Foundation Trusts by 2013 – 'should' in the sense of being expected to perform at the required level.

Other accrediting bodies such as Investors in People and the Charities Evaluation Services (CES) offer national recognition for organisations that can convince the awarding body that they place considerable emphasis on staff management and staff development that leads to an overall high performance level particularly in the area of public services, both statutory and voluntary. One such award is PQASSO (Practical Quality Assurance for Small Organisations) which, through the CES, has been taken up by a number of voluntary sector organisations. A much more prominent accreditation is the ISO 9000 and its variants such as ISO 9001 and the official stamp of approval for an organisation's practical commitment to safeguarding the environment, the ISO 14001. During the 1970s the British Standards Institution (BSI) produced ISO 9000, which was the first British standard designed for quality assurance. Originally the standard applied only to industry, but in 1987 it was revised to include service providers as well.

Evaluation

Audits, accreditation bodies, PIs and inspections are all involved with judging merit against some yardstick(s). Can a case be made out for ranking 'evaluation' above these four as a means of assessing performance in the public sector? If the other four methods have evaluation as their central component, it would be rather odd to define 'evaluation' as one form of 'evaluation'. In most texts that deal with aspects of 'evaluation' the word 'research' is added. This attempts to set it apart from the other evaluation approaches. It is depicted as a particular form of social enquiry. 'Research' carries with it the notion of impartial collection of data derived from techniques that prize objectivity and freedom from bias. But those who devise and who apply performance indicators would also claim to proceed impartially and without bias, as would those who conduct audits and inspections.

Is evaluation research, then, different in its purpose? Is the concise definition offered by Weiss (1972) perhaps too limiting?

Green and South (2006) draw attention to the definition promoted by the World Health Organisation in 1998:

> The systematic examination and assessment of features of an initiative and its effects, in order to produce information that can be used by those who have an interest in its improvement or effectiveness. (WHO, 1998, p 3)

In this context, the WHO was not offering a definition of evaluation in its generic sense but referring to evaluation as distinct from any other types of performance or quality assessment. Could it be argued that the definition could equally apply to PIs, audits and inspections? All three forms of judging merit are systematic in their application rather than random, unplanned or haphazard.

However, few exponents of our three examples of evaluation would bless what they do with the cachet 'research'. Therefore, it must be this additional attribute that marks out 'evaluation' as a specialised and more academically acceptable form of fact-finding with a view to service improvement.

A possible complicating factor in seeking a distinctive definition of evaluation is that it can, according to a number of writers, take many forms. Potter (2006), for one, has commented that 'evaluation is an eclectic and diverse field' (p 88). Up to this point in this chapter there would appear to be a common purpose characterising evaluation and the other three methods of judging merit; that is, they are all directed towards a common aim of service improvement. In this respect, they are mainly – but not exclusively – outcome oriented. On the face of it, that shared objective is the hallmark of evaluation:

> (Evaluation is) ... a study designed and conducted to assist some audiences to assess an object's merit and worth. (Stufflebeam, 2001, 448)

This definition, however, does not take us beyond that offered by Weiss (1972). In fact, it suffers from a certain vagueness in referring to 'some audiences' and an 'object' and in implying that 'merit' and 'worth' are conceptually different.

Perhaps a more productive approach in trying to clarify what evaluation is all about is to list various types of evaluation that have appeared in a number of works written by academics. For example, Herman et al (1987) identified seven models of evaluation, as shown in Table 2.1.

Table 2.1: Seven models of evaluation

Model	Focus
1. Goal-oriented	Effectiveness, efficiency and economy of an intervention
2. Decision-orientated	Improve decision making
3. Evaluation research	Providing explanations for outcomes
4. Responsive	Process of evaluation and perspectives of participants
5. Goal-free	Openness to achievements other than those prescribed by the intervention's aims and objectives
6. Alternative explanations	Alternatives to accepted descriptions about what is happening
7. Utilization-orientated	Utility of findings to different stakeholders

Source: J.L. Herman, L.L. Morris and C.T. Fitz-Gibbon (1987) *Evaluation Handbook*, Newbury Park, CA: Sage.

As Green and South (2006) point out, 'in practice it would be unusual to see them as distinct entities' (p 14). In fact, it is easy to imagine a piece of evaluation research (model 3 in the table) which includes elements of the other six 'models'. Interestingly, the clear majority of those who have written on the topic of evaluation have opted for models 1 and 7 as the most distinctive and most desirable forms of evaluation (St Leger et al, 1992; Tones, 1998; Springett, 2001).

Other models of evaluation have been delineated by Hansen (2005) as shown in Table 2.2.

Table 2.2: Models of evaluation

Results	Comparing the results of a program with the goals: a before and after analysis
Process	Perception by client and stakeholders about what is being/has been implemented
System	Analyses input, structure, process and outcome in terms of results
Economic	Cost-efficiency/effectiveness/benefit
Actor	Focuses on the client's and stakeholders' criteria for assessment
Programme theory	Assesses the validity of theory on which the given intervention builds and tries to identify what works, for whom and in which contexts

Source: H.F. Hansen (2005) 'Choosing evaluation models', *Evaluation*, vol 11, no 4, pp 447–61.

Patton (1981) assembled even more different types or models of evaluation but came down strongly in favour of utilisation-focused evaluation. Further discussion of these attempts at categorising evaluation into not necessarily mutually exclusive compartments will be found later in this chapter and in succeeding chapters of this book. At present, we can note that the analysis of what constitutes evaluation has proved to be a fascinating topic for academic professionals. However, without being too disparaging, what about the 'real world' in which evaluators have to operate?

The politics of evaluation

There are many reminders in the literature that evaluation is a political activity, or, at least that it serves a political purpose (Edelman, 1984; Hamilton, 1977; Patton, 1988; House, 1993; Karlsson, 1996; Palfrey and Thomas, 1999; Weiss, 1999). A distinction needs to be made between the two. On the one hand, if we are to adopt Patton's selection of a goal-oriented and utilisation-focused model of evaluation then its contribution to improving services must logically serve the aspirations of decision makers and, as far as the public sector is concerned, those decision makers are politicians, either at a central or local government level.

Some observers, however, have claimed not only that evaluators are often ideologically committed (Hamilton, 1977) but that their political sympathies should influence the design and criteria applied in their evaluations (Guba and Lincoln, 1981). Whichever stance is taken, evaluation has come to be associated for the past few decades as a potent ally of politicians in that it is a means of assessing the 'value' of projects, programmes and policies. In the real world of politics, despite the mass of literature supporting and promoting evaluation as a subject worthy of intense bookish activity, it has to be acknowledged that for all its intellectualising credentials it is a servant and not an equal of politicians.

The link between ideological perspectives and the task of evaluation raises questions about the design and methodology adopted by the evaluator. The argument against leaving evaluation to internal staff derives from a wish to avoid any bias or pre-judgements about the eventual findings. To avoid this possibility, external evaluators are appointed on the assumption that they will carry out a quasi-scientific analysis, hence the attribution of a research model to the process of evaluation. Edelman, for one, advocates this positivist approach:

> Only through inter-personal contacts and by deferring judgement, by sustaining impartiality can the evaluator maintain adequate awareness of the organisation. (Edelman, 1964, p 5)

This is a view supported by Simons (1984) and Hedrick (1988). 'It is extremely important', writes Hedrick, 'that applied researchers maintain the same neutral posture as that of the basic scientific researcher. ... Researchers may be advocates for the responsible use of their results, but not for political objectives' (pp 13–14).

External audit, external inspections and the imposition of performance indicators and targets by central government conform to a policy by those commissioning such assessments of impartial objectivity. However, as far as evaluation research is concerned, this investment in neutrality has been challenged.

For example, quite early in the development of evaluation research Macdonald asserted that 'the political stance of the evaluator has consequences for his (*sic*) choice of techniques of information gathering and analysis' (1977, p 225). A few years later, Sieber (1980) reiterated this view in his discussion of the political and ethical aspects of policy evaluation. The work of Guba and Lincoln will feature in Chapter Three. In essence, these commentators charted the progress from evaluation as initially focused on measurement – for example, determining the status of school pupils – as established by standardised tests - to someone able to adopt a role of collaborator or broker by negotiating with various stakeholders about the whole process of the evaluation.

In attempting to distinguish between evaluation as an activity set firmly within a political context and the unequivocal ideological objectives pursued by the external evaluator, Cronbach (1980) endorses the view that evaluation is a political activity. He contends that goal-based evaluation is politically biased towards those goals considered by dominant groups to be important. Rational decision making, according to Cronbach, is a myth. Yet, we would argue that a departure from some possibly unattainable mission to generate value-free policies and evaluation of those policies does not signal the defeat of rationalism. As we have suggested elsewhere (Palfrey and Thomas, 1999), in the world of politics there are competing rationalities that are all intrinsically valid. This is borne out by those, such as Guba and Lincoln (1987), who advocate the importance of acknowledging and respecting the possibly conflicting criteria held by various stakeholders as crucial to judging the merit or 'success' of certain projects, programmes and policies. Rationality lies in the values of the individual or particular social/political group.

Chapter Six will draw attention to utilisation-focused evaluation espoused in particular by Patton (1988). Here the question – discussed in Palfrey and Thomas (1999) – of whether evaluators should strive to make their work of use to decision makers will be introduced. Patton refers to the early days of evaluation when those who carried out the assessment were supposed to be above politics. Arguing that evaluation is an inherently political activity, Patton distinguishes between internal and external evaluation in the type of political activity in which they might be engaged. The evaluator within an organisation needs to be effective in *bureaucratic politics*. Patton does not elaborate on the distinctive political role of external evaluators other than quoting the diktat of the American Evaluation Association, that external evaluation should set out to make improvements to programs and decisions about programs.

That is an interesting point of view since it could serve to exacerbate the feelings of frustration expressed by some exponents of evaluation as a stimulus to change. House (1993), for example, argues that it is ethically desirable for evaluators to become involved with programmes that offer the opportunity to act as advocates for 'minority groups' and that in so doing political change can be brought about:

> The interests of the poor and the powerless often are neglected or overridden ... whereas those of the powerful are given priority. The views and interests of the poor and powerless should be given at least equal priority in the evaluation. (p 66)

Bryk (1983) too regards evaluation as a vehicle for empowering relatively suppressed stakeholders through appropriate design and methodology while Weiss (1999) affirms that 'The overall aim of evaluation is to assist people and organizations to improve their plans, policies and practices on behalf of citizens' (p 469). To what extent this objective has been realised during or as a result of a piece of evaluation research has not frequently been documented, and this is a defect in much of the literature. In attempting to placate those who detect little evidence of the adoption and implementation of evaluators' findings, Weiss claims that evaluation can lead to 'enlightenment' and 'the slow percolation of new information, ideas and perspectives into the arena in which decisions are made' (p 471). However, the countless books, conference papers and journal articles available provide hardly any evidence that this actually happens in the wide spectrum of policy making.

Such desiderata about the gap between research results and political action call into question the very nature and purpose of evaluation, which will be the topic addressed in the next chapter.

At this point we shall merely express the view that to advocate the function of evaluation as an instigator of change or political action is surely to pre-judge the findings of the research. Despite the thesis propounded by Patton and Weiss, the non-utilisation of the findings might be not only the most rational option but, indeed, the only one.

Project, programme and policy evaluation

Eggers (1999) categorises evaluation into three principal forms of human endeavour: projects, programmes and policies. It is important to attempt a definition of these three evaluation subjects since there might be differing opportunities for the evaluator to contribute to decision making according to the overall or primary aim of the initiative.

Sometimes, however, dictionary definitions are not necessarily very helpful. Some concepts might be amenable to several interpretations depending on individual perceptions or contextual understanding.

For example, the highly authoritative *Shorter Oxford Dictionary* (1933) defines 'policy' as 'a course of action adopted and pursued by a government, party, ruler, statesman, etc; any course of action adopted as advantageous or expedient'. This definition has stood the test of time because *The Chambers Dictionary* (2008) also refers to 'policy' as a 'course of action especially one based on some declared or respected principle'. Immediately, one might think of a policy of inaction: a declared statement of *laissez faire* – a decision not to intervene or to take any action on a particular issue. In recent years, successive governments have adopted a policy of non-interference on the matter of euthanasia. Can this objection to the dictionary definition of 'policy' stand up to scrutiny?

One possible comeback would be the argument that if an organisation or government decides not to intervene – to do nothing – this is more of a 'standpoint' rather than a policy, which surely implies a formulated decision to take action. However, during the General Election of 2010 one political party made it clear in its election manifesto that if elected it would not raise students' university tuition fees. This was certainly a policy statement – a policy of inaction; of maintaining the status quo. However, that same political party, soon after coming into power as part of a Coalition government, announced that fees were going to be substantially increased – an announcement that prompted serious demonstrations by students in protest.

A useful analysis of 'policy' as a concept has been offered by Hogwood (1987). He points out that there are several interpretations of the word. One interpretation sees *policy as aspiration* as, for example, in the slogans: 'Our party's policy is to promote equality of opportunity' or 'to place an emphasis on fairness'. These statements can be regarded as little more than pious rhetoric. They hardly appear to be articulating a clear statement of intent. Refining these declarations down to *policy as proposals* could lead to the publication of government White Papers. Even if these then become enacted in statute they might not be implemented, not solely because of a change of government but perhaps because the resources are not available. In this respect, the phrase 'a course of action' in the dictionary definitions needs to be modified to read 'an *intended* course of action'. We have discussed Hogwood's distinctive categorisations in more detail elsewhere (Palfrey et al, 1992).

One further example of 'policy' described by Hogwood which we wish to acknowledge is *policy as process*, in which proposals are translated into activities. This interpretation also makes the important point that policies do not necessarily remain exactly as announced in a formal, published statement. They might well require amendments in the light of changing external situations such as financial crises or change of party leadership. In certain parts of the UK, local authority policies of 'no redundancies' had to be re-examined and altered in the light of swingeing cutbacks by the central government in the autumn of 2010.

We believe that it is relevant to identify different definitions, or, at least, different aspects or manifestations, of the term 'policy' because the blanket phrase 'policy evaluation' needs to be de-constructed before making any would-be authoritative definitions of the nature and purpose of 'evaluation'.

Throwing caution, perhaps, to the wind, we set out below our own interpretations of 'policy' and of 'project' and 'programme'. Readers may, of course, wish to amend, extend or dismiss these as not consistent with their own understanding of what these concepts convey. Nevertheless, they are intended to provide reasonably acceptable interpretations as reference points to facilitate discussion:

- *Project* – a planned activity aimed at achieving specified goals within a prescribed period.
- *Programme* – a set of separate planned activities unified into a coherent group.
- *Policy* – a statement of how an organisation or government would respond to particular eventualities or situations according to its agreed values and principles.

One instance of the interplay between the three potential subjects of evaluation is the example referred to earlier of the Coalition government's decision to confront the substantial budget deficit in the UK. The policy was announced in May 2010, as soon as the incoming government was in place, namely that there would be cuts in public expenditure that would be implemented immediately. Following this announcement of a general policy, there followed a statement of intention to reduce expenditure across several government departments and in certain areas of public sector spending. This amounted to a programme involving a number of targets forming a coherent whole. Although budget reductions were to take immediate effect, percentage cuts were to be achieved over a specified period, that is, four to five years.

The effect of these decisions about future financing was that public services and voluntary organisations were forced to cut back or abandon various projects such as play schemes and after-hours activities in some schools. It will obviously take time to judge whether policies such as these have achieved their planned targets and whether the overarching aim of economic recovery has been achieved. Yet, within hours of such policy statements being made, the media invites expert economists to comment. Think Tanks, such as the Institute for Fiscal Studies and the Adam Smith Institute are asked to provide a quick assessment of how successful the measures are likely to be, judged against certain yardsticks such as the impact of redundancies on an attempt to revitalise the economy.

Because it sets out to predict possible outcomes, this type of assessment has been labelled 'policy analysis' rather than 'policy evaluation'. House (1993) distinguishes between prospective and retrospective judgements, policy evaluation falling into the latter category. This is helpful since it would defy anyone's definition of 'policy evaluation' to describe it as an *instant* judgement against a certain yardstick.

Formative and summative evaluation

In a relatively early text on evaluation, Scriven (1967) made a distinction between formative and summative evaluation. In the former process, information is fed back during the development of a project or programme to help improve it. Summative evaluation takes place after the project or programme has ended, and provides information primarily on the achievement of goals and on their effectiveness. Thus, 'formative' stands between the prospective or would-be predictive and retrospective assessments referred to above. There would seem to be very little difference, if any, between formative evaluation and *monitoring*, which involves a continuous system of checking to see how a particular project, programme or policy is progressing. For example, the evaluator might ask: 'Are the original objectives still appropriate or achievable?', or 'Does the project need to be drawn to a premature close because of dwindling resources?'.

It could, in fact, be argued that any process of evaluation should always build in a monitoring element even in those instances where the time-scale to complete the evaluation is relatively short. As an extreme example, imagine the situation where the formal evaluation is spread over three years and only at the end is a judgement made about the 'success' of the project, programme or policy. Let us assume that the intended results were not achieved. How easy would it be for those involved in the evaluation to be able to discern where, when, why and how things went wrong? The phrase 'If only ...' comes to mind. As Epstein and Tripodi (1977) pointed out: 'referring to one of our three 'P's':

> Program evaluation … is the process by which program effectiveness and efficiency are assessed. It involves the collection, analysis and interpretation of data bearing on the achievement of program goals, in contrast to monitoring which considers the extent to which program operations follow specifications e.g. of staffing, regulations, procedures, resources etc. (p 111)

Monitoring is essential because: 'Programs are continually changing as are the organizational environments in which they are embedded. Objectives change as the needs of target populations change … Technologies evolve, values change …' (Epstein and Tripodi, 1977, p 7).

While it can be argued that technologies and values are unlikely to change over, say, the lifespan of a six- to twelve-month project, the point is well made that to lose data because of total reliance on a 'Big Bang' summative assessment *ex-post facto* runs the risk of undermining the validity of any concluding judgements. Although the two concepts 'formative evaluation' and 'monitoring' come close to being synonymous, it would not perhaps be too pedantic to classify 'monitoring' as the gathering of information en route to a time-limited subject of summative evaluation, while formative evaluation is the interpretation of that information by the evaluator. For example, during a project aimed at enabling citizens to play a more active role in helping to design and shape methods of service delivery in a public sector organisation, the monitoring function could record the frequency and location of public meetings; the range of different methods of trying to engage with the public; the number of 'hits' on the organisation's website – all being previously agreed indicators of how the project is progressing. The formative evaluation element would analyse the logging of the data, in order to turn it into information about whether the main aim of enhancing citizens' influence over the policy-making process and service design and delivery is 'on target', or whether certain weaknesses are being exposed during the course of the project.

Approaches, models and systems

We are beginning to enter more deeply into the particular vocabulary which has become attached to a very large corpus of academic literature focusing on evaluation. The question which must be posed at this point in our discussion is 'Does it really matter if we use the above three terms interchangeably?'. The same question could reasonably be asked about the possible semantic distinctions between 'aims', 'goals' and 'objectives'. They are all to do with intended outcomes – another concept which shall be considered later in this chapter.

One reason for spending time on analysing various terms used in the literature is to see whether they are used in a way that clarifies what they are meant to convey, or whether they only serve to lend the publication a kind of academic legitimacy.

Once again, dictionary definitions will not necessarily be of help. In seeking to establish whether an 'approach' is conceptually different from a 'model', or 'a model' is distinct from 'a system', it might be more fruitful to depict a scenario in which a commissioner of a piece of evaluation is having to decide who, of a number of applicants, should be granted funding. A relevant question might be: 'What is your approach to carrying out an evaluation?'. There could be a number of responses depending, to some extent, on how the question is interpreted. We would suggest that the most likely interpretation would be to think of the 'approach' as the *modus operandi*. How do you go about deciding on how you will arrive at the key criteria by which to evaluate? What methods of data collection will you use? Who do you consider to be the important stakeholders and how will you come to that decision? Do your answers to these questions bespeak a truly collaborative and participative approach or fundamentally a top-down approach? In the real world, we would contend, that basic question is far more likely to be put to the competing tenderers than 'What particular model (or system) of evaluation will you be following/adopting if you are granted the funding?'.

But perhaps we are on the brink of dismissing 'models' and 'systems' before we examine their usage in the relevant literature.

One rather confusing contribution to this debate comes from an article by Hansen (2005). In identifying a number of models of evaluation: the economic, goal-attainment, and the stakeholder model, Hansen also refers to them as 'approaches'. He is, however, not alone. As noted earlier, Green and South (2006) reproduce Herman et al's (1987) list of 'models of evaluation'. When the accompanying brief accounts of the models' primary focus are considered, it would be hard to imagine (a) that more than one would not need to be combined in order to make the evaluation worthwhile; or (b) that one particular model – evaluation research – is adequately covered by the defining focus, which is providing explanations for outcomes. Surely, all evaluation, other than perhaps the prospective kind – and this might well be based on prior research – is a form of research.

Green and South add another 'model' to Herman et al's categorisation: 'illuminative evaluation'. This term, derived from the work of Tones and Tilford (2001) means focusing on the *process* of the evaluation in order to provide answers relating to how the particular end result was or was not achieved. In our view, Green and South rightly use the terms 'approaches' and 'types' as equivalent to 'models'. Perhaps, then, we need to re-appraise our reference to 'confusing' with regard to Hansen's use of the words 'models' and 'approaches' as interchangeable. The quasi-scientific term 'model' in the context of some examples of evaluation literature can be substituted by the more mundane word 'type'. However, we would argue that there is a difference between 'approach' and 'type'. To re-visit the earlier scenario of the commissioner and the would-be evaluator, the question 'What type of evaluation will you be intending to carry out?', or even more of a real-world question: 'What type of evaluation do you expect us to commission in this particular case?', would probably be implying a focus on outcomes and/or outputs and/or process.

Before returning to an attempt to clarify what is meant by *output, outcome* and *process* and their usual 'friends' *input* and *impact*, our attention will turn to *evaluation systems.*

What are 'evaluation systems'?

Leeuw and Furibo (2008) pose two questions: 'When can a set of evaluative activities be called an evaluation system?' (p 158) and 'Why study evaluation systems?' (p 164). They then set out the four criteria in order to label a set of evaluation activities as a system. These are:

1. *A distinctive epistemological perspective.* The set of activities has to display a certain 'cultural-cognitive perspective'. They explain: 'This means that there should be some agreement among the players involved about what they are actually doing .and why they are doing it' (p 159). This seems a reasonable proposition. Participants need to be aware of the *type of knowledge* that the evaluation is seeking to generate, such as. knowledge of what works; of why it works or doesn't work; knowledge of 'a more procedural nature' (p 159). Again, this sounds eminently sensible. Those who have an interest in the evaluation would no doubt wish to know what it was trying to assess and according to which criteria.

2. *Organisational responsibility.* The essence of this criterion is that there must be more than one active organisation. 'Alongside the producer of evaluative knowledge, there must be at least one *other organization* that requests this information and that strives to use the findings' (p 159; emphasis in original). Hopefully we are not misconstruing what is being said here, but it is difficult to picture a situation in which only one organisation, for example the organisation carrying out the evaluation, is involved in the enterprise. What else would they be evaluating but another organisation's project, programme or policy?

3. *Permanence.* To qualify for the designation of an evaluation system, Leeuw and Furibo state, there should be a high degree of ongoing evaluation activities and not just a few ad hoc activities. In addition, there should be 'a certain volume of activities taking place over time' (p 160).

4. *A focus on the intended use of evaluations.* Evaluative activities are planned in advance taking into account the point at which the information should be submitted to decision makers.

Leeuw and Furibo then go on to mention the possible distinctions between evaluation systems and evaluation *paradigms*, *theories* and *traditions*, although they admit that '… sometimes an evaluation theory or tradition almost equals an "evaluation system"' (p 160). Just what constitutes 'almost an evaluation system' is left unsaid and a possibly heretical comment could be 'Does it really matter?'.

This earnest attempt to distinguish an evaluation system from various other classifications culminates in a list of 'Evaluation Systems in the Western World' (p 161). The list is compiled from the *International Atlas of Evaluation* (Leeuw and Furibo , 2008); from the work of Alkin (2004); and from symposia and workshops. The list is not offered as comprehensive. The systems comprise:

- performance monitoring
- performance audit, inspection and oversight
- (quasi-)experimental evaluation and the evidence-based policy movement
- accreditation and evaluation system
- monitoring and evaluation system.

Leeuw and Furibo provide a detailed analysis of the particular characteristics that set these five systems apart from each other and some answers to the question 'Why study evaluation systems?'. These sections of the article (pp 161–166) will be left for inquisitive readers to pursue.

The policy-making process and evaluation

One of the major claims for the value of evaluation in the public sector is that it helps to create more rational decision making (Weiss, 1972). As noted earlier in this chapter, this assertion does not imply that much, or even any, decision making in the political or organisational sphere is irrational. Although the texts that defined 'rationality' in these contexts pre-dated the political cry for 'evidence-based' policy', the process by which Simon (1957), for example, believed policy making was developed depends heavily on choosing the 'best' option from a menu of possible policy directions. It is acceptable to present Simon's thesis as a 'model' of the policy-making process because it is in effect an idealised version of how decisions are actually made.

Simon's initial demonstration of the policy-making process – which he called 'comprehensive rationality' – involved six stages:

1. faced with a given problem or issue, decide goals
2. search for possible means to achieve those goals
3. evaluate each set of options
4. select the 'best' option
5. implement
6. review.

The idea is that the decision maker(s) will identify all the potential consequences and calculate the costs and benefits of each option before making a decision. However, in constructing his 'ideal' comprehensively rational model, Simon was aware that this was more of a prescriptive rather than a descriptive account of the decision-/policy-making process. In the real world, politicians and senior officials were limited or bounded by often negative prevailing circumstances such as economic exigencies and, therefore, had to take the next best option. He called this model one of 'bounded rationality' where those who took decisions had to compromise. So Simon coined the portmanteau verb to 'satisfice' – the compression of 'satisfy' and 'suffice'.

Some possible problems that could persuade decision makers to take a pragmatic option rather than the one that ideally would have been the first choice have been suggested by Smith (1976). These are:

- *Technical problems* – for example, the inability to forecast future resources and provide reliable financial assumptions for planning purposes. Partly for this reason, governments are reluctant to offer long-term predictions that would, in any case, take them beyond the next set of elections.
- *Politico-administrative problems* – policy planning is difficult enough within a single organisation. When it involves inter-agency co-operation the problems are often multiplied. There have in the past, for instance, been serious points of dissension between central and local government levels of decision making, as when local authorities of a certain political persuasion dragged their feet over implementing the sale of council houses in the 1980s
- *Political problems* – this obstacle is in effect an extension of the previous problem inasmuch as the implementation stage of the policy process can be thwarted by individuals or organised groups such as trade unions; by what Lipsky (1980) defined as 'street-level bureaucrats'. Thus, for example, by exhibiting less than welcoming behaviour, front-line staff could easily subvert an organisation's or government's policy of 'putting the customer/service user first'.

Several other analysts of the policy-making process have put forward their own descriptive and prescriptive models of how decisions are made or how they ought to be made, notably Lindblom (1959),Vickers (1965), Etzioni (1967), Dror (1989) and Parsons (1995).

However, Simon's original model of comprehensive rationality provides a useful if idealised analogy by which to provide a 'model' structure for the process of evaluation in the public sector. His idea of a linear progression was soundly criticised by Lindblom (1959) who contested what he regarded as an unrealistic depiction of how policy is or should be made. His interpretation of the policy process was one more akin to 'muddling through' than a strictly sequential step-by-step phenomenon. According to Lindblom, creating policies depends on 'partisan mutual adjustment' by which key stakeholders concede ground in order tp make progress towards a decision. In the UK, published memoirs of former Cabinet members provide evidence of this 'two steps forward one step backward' approach (Macmillan, 2003; Redwood, 2004).

Much of the evaluation literature assumes a linear model of the evaluation process. An early exponent of this approach was Suchman (1967). His contention, and that of Schulberg and Baker (1968), was that the most important and yet most difficult phase of evaluation is the clarification of objectives or goals. As Luker (1981) noted:

> The emphasis on objectives or goals stems from a conceptualisation of evaluation as measurement of the success or failure of an activity, in so far as it reaches its predetermined objectives. (p 89)

This goal-attainment form of evaluation focuses on the extent to which the 'activities' contribute to the attainment of the stated objectives of the project, programme or policy. This attempt by means of formal evaluation to discern a cause-effect relationship between what are commonly called *inputs* and *outcomes* can be less than straightforward, as shall be noted in later chapters. One effort to construct a framework for carrying out an evaluation was made by Donabedian (1969) in the arena of medical care. His three components of the evaluation enterprise are: *structure*, *process* and *outcome*.

Structure relates to the organisation's facilities and equipment, staffing; levels, styles of management and the characteristics of the care given *Process* involves the appropriateness and quality of care given to patients by nurses and other clinical staff, while *outcome* is concerned with the results of the care given in terms of its effect on the patient. Elsewhere (Phillips et al, 1994) we have classified 'structure' as *inputs*. By this we mean not only the physical resources made available during the course of a programme or project or attached to the implementation of a particular policy, but also the *values* that guide the actions of key participants. An extended linear version of Donabedian's evaluation framework would feature as:

inputs ------$\rightarrow$ process------$\rightarrow$ outputs-------$\rightarrow$ outcomes--------$\rightarrow$ impact

Within the context of health services, the distinction between outcome and impact can clearly be observed. The process of administering a mastectomy on a patient might focus on the outcome of a clinical output – namely the operation itself. The outcome is hopefully a non-recurrence of breast cancer. However, the longer-term impact on the individual could be a diminished self-image.

This example draws on an approach to evaluation research that is essentially linear – a formal sequence of stages similar to that set out in Simon's rational models of the policy-making process. The terms 'formative' and 'summative' serve to reinforce this image of how formal evaluation works and how it ought to work:

- Identify the goal(s) to be achieved.
- Put in place the resources needed in order to achieve the goal(s).

- Decide on how these resources will be used.
- Decide whether the end result has been achieved.

This is a limited linear structure that, on the face of it, pays no attention to the factors that led to the achievement, part-achievement or non-achievement of the desired outcome. But it is also defective in its characterisation – or almost caricature – of how all evaluations proceed. Just as in the policy-making process itself, the original objectives might require adjusting or even abandoning, to be replaced by more realistic and therefore more achievable intended outcomes. Moreover, the notion that the term 'summative evaluation' conjures up is one of closure – of the final assessment having been made. Certainly, as far as policy evaluation is concerned, the evaluation findings should contribute to ongoing monitoring of how the policy is working out in practice; and possibly to a policy review in order to consolidate, amend, revise or, in time, to suspend the policy.

It is also conceivable in the world of project or programme evaluations that objectives might not be clearly and unequivocally identified and agreed prior to any resources being made available. The process might proceed along the lines suggested by Lindblom – that is, an incremental approach is adopted in which limited resources are committed and provisional outputs and outcomes are monitored. Depending on the interim outputs and outcomes, additional resources might or might not then be seen as required for further development of the project.

Reverting to the idea of 'what works' as an impetus for decision making in the public sector, a provisional result of incarcerating an increasing percentage of offenders will obviously prevent further offences being committed by the inmates while they are detained. However, in the longer term, after release from prison those who have served their sentence might not have been deterred from helping to increase the number of crimes recorded in the future. It is, of course, difficult to imagine a project being launched, a programme being devised or a policy being decided upon without some declared purpose.

The point that we are making about the evaluation process not necessarily being progressively linear is that, at any stage, there could be a loop back to a previous stage before moving on. For example, a multi-agency initiative to enable members of the public to have a greater say in the design and delivery of services might have as its desired output an increase in the number of people accessing individual organisations' websites. If successful in achieving this objective, this might lead to a reconsideration of part of the consultation process because as a result of greater recourse to the websites, fewer local residents are attending public forum meetings. A measurement of the output has led to a loop back to and revision of the *process* element in the evaluation.

In summary, just as the policy-making process is likely to depart from a logical sequence of decisions based on objectively derived data, so the evaluation process might also follow a somewhat disjointed pattern of provisional assessments that lead to a reorientation of the initial research design and/or methods of data collection. It must, however, be conceded that – despite claims that external evaluators not only do, but that they should, bring to the evaluation their own set of values (Cronbach et al, 1980) – evaluation, because it is a form of social research, is expected to produce findings based on a fair-minded representation of facts and opinions. On the other hand, policy makers and, in particular, politicians have the right to ignore a so-called 'rational' approach to decision making because of their allegiance to a particular ideological or pragmatic point of view. In any decision-making process there will be 'competing rationalities'. Whether the results of a systematically researched evaluation will be acted upon by those who have the power or authority to do so is discussed in Chapter Six.

A number of different types of/approaches to evaluation have already been mentioned, but there are others that deserve consideration and which shall be attended to in subsequent chapters. Here, we shall briefly outline those that have come to be fairly prominent in the literature. As a reminder, the list below includes those mentioned earlier in the chapter with a brief explanation of their particular characteristics:

- *Formative* – giving feedback through monitoring how the evaluation is proceeding.
- *Summative* – a final assessment after completion of the project programme or implementation of the policy.
- *Economic* – evaluation which focuses on issues such as cost-benefit, cost-effectiveness and value for money.
- *Goal-attainment* – attempts to discover whether the goals/objectives have been achieved.
- *Alternative explanations* – examines whether there might be more than one reason why the objectives have or have not been (fully) achieved.
- *Stakeholder* – adopts an approach that seeks to interpret the process and results from different stakeholders' perspectives.
- *Illuminative* – equivalent to process evaluation.
- *Utilisation-orientated* – concentrates on carrying out evaluations that can be useful to decision-makers.

The final type or approach in this list, utilisation-orientated, will receive further attention in this chapter and in Chapter Six. Gray (2004) identified 22 types of evaluation but defines each in terms of their 'key question or approach' (p 158) and the heading to the list reads 'Focus or type of evaluation' (p 158). In all, 14 out of the 22 types described adopt a particular focus such as *effectiveness focus*, *efficiency focus* or *goal-based focus* and can, therefore, be more appropriately classified as *approaches* rather than *types*. Gray's list, however, is easily surpassed in numbers by that of Patton (1981), who referred to the six evaluation categories defined by the US Evaluation Research Society Standards Committee (p 44). Patton commented that within each of the six categories there were numerous types of specific evaluations. He then lists 33 types and stresses that the list is by no means exhaustive. He points out that in one of his other works – *Creative Evaluation* (1981) – 'I reported an additional one hundred types' (p 47).

Forms of evaluation

Earlier in this chapter, 'evaluation systems' were discussed, and the issue of the relevance of 'systems' to economic evaluation will be highlighted in Chapter Five. We now go on to introduce 'forms' of evaluation that have gained perhaps more currency over the past two decades than those listed above or which are contained in Patton's list (1981), except for the last one which he has selected as an important form of or approach to evaluation elsewhere (Patton, 1986). These forms of evaluation are:

- naturalistic evaluation;
- realistic evaluation;
- theory-driven evaluation; and
- 'utilisation-focused' evaluation.

Naturalistic evaluation

This form of evaluation research was heralded in the United States as something of a radical departure from the traditional 'paradigm' of experimental and quasi-experimental research designs and methods of collecting data. Guba and Lincoln (1987; 1989) were the most influential academics to promote the value of applying qualitative data collection methods such as observation and in-depth interviews to program evaluation. Although the justification for this new approach is now not in dispute, the contestable interpretation of what constitutes 'truth', 'knowledge' and 'reality' has been adopted in those particular efforts to evaluate projects, programmes and policies, which accept that different stakeholders might harbour different expectations of intended outcomes and different perspectives on how well events have worked out.

In a collection of contributions edited by Williams (1986) on various aspects of naturalistic evaluation, Guba and Lincoln tackle the challenge of ensuring that the qualitative approach to data collection produces findings that are reliable and valid. They set out a number of ways in which rigour and trustworthiness can be built into the evaluation process. In his paper Williams (1986) makes the point that naturalistic evaluation might not be appropriate for all occasions. His discussion centres on key questions that need answering before deciding whether the more participative approach is the most appropriate. One of the most important methods advocated by Guba and Lincoln is the triangulation of data; checking to find out whether the data stands up to scrutiny by using more than one means of gathering the data. This advice forms one of the key themes in the work carried out and reported by Smith and Cantley (1985). They classify their approach as *pluralistic evaluation* – a term not included in either of the main lists referred to above. This naturalistic approach will be discussed further in Chapter Four.

Realistic evaluation

In the context of a book on evaluation for the real world this category looks highly compatible with a search for clarity about the function of evaluation research, how it should be conducted and reported on. On closer examination, however, Pawson and Tilley's (1997) thesis is not that previous commentaries on the purpose and methods of evaluation have been largely divorced from 'reality'. Their view is that a good deal of evaluation in practice and in academic discussion has been rather superficial, particularly in the type of evaluation categorised as *outcome evaluation*. They argue that rather than just attempting to come to a conclusion about whether a specified outcome has or has not been achieved, there needs to be a much more detailed analysis of how and in what circumstances, and for whom a particular programme works or fails to work. Pawson and Tilley's framework focuses on a programme's *context,* its intervention *mechanism* and the particular outcomes for various stakeholders.

Recollections from the work of Guba and Lincoln (1981) resonate in the starting point for Pawson and Tilley's main proposition, namely that experimental evaluations depending on randomised controlled trials (RCTs) cannot reveal enough about how and why certain interventions work. As the authors of this book have noted elsewhere (Palfrey et al, 2004), RCTs produce 'black box' evaluations (Bickman, 1987; Clarke, 1999) in which change is measured mainly by taking account of inputs and outputs while controlling for extraneous and intervening variables. Such 'black box' evaluations typical of clinical tests are considered to be 'unable to provide any real insight into the underlying causal mechanisms that produce treatment effects' (Clarke, 1999, p 52).

Projects, programmes and policies rely for their 'success' on interactions between different people and interactions between people and often different environments, including not only physical contexts but value – how they view and interpret the world around them. In this scenario the social construction of 'reality' plays a central role. A scientific world view posits an external reality that is observable and measurable by applying scientific modes of enquiry. Calculating the extent to which outcomes have or have not been reached in the realms of policies and political decision making has to take into account multiple factors that are not amenable to wholly objective instruments of measurement.

Pawson and Tilley (1997) and also Ho (1999) call for more 'theory driven evaluations' – a topic that shall be returned to in this chapter and in Chapters Six and Seven. Summing up their quest for a movement towards realistic evaluation they argue that 'evaluators need to penetrate beneath the surface of observable inputs and outputs of a program' (Pawson and Tilley, 1997, p 216). The work of Pawson and Tilley will be considered when the nature and role of evidence and the extent to which it influences policy making is discussed in Chapters Four and Five.

To an extent it is surprising that the plea for greater precision in analysing the problematic relationship between cause and effect or what White (2010) refers to as 'attribution' should come so late in the day. Do we know whether – after several decades of project, programme and policy evaluations – the 'gold standard' experimental 'model' is still common practice? In addition, how do we know that many if not the majority of evaluation research activities merely arrive at a conclusion about *whether* the hoped-for outcomes have been successfully achieved? We would contend that a good deal of literature on such topics is deficient in putting forward any evidence that what they are trying to change actually exists; or, if it does exist, is there a preponderance of such faulty examples or just a few? With some exceptions, books and peer-reviewed journal articles rarely contain summaries or even references to project, programme or policy evaluations that have been completed 'out there'. The world of meta-evaluation will be dealt with in later chapters. The opportunity to determine whether the call for less superficial evaluations of outcome is justified will rely on the corpus of published accounts of systematic reviews of published papers on actual evaluation research projects, which will feature in Chapters Six and Seven.

Theory-driven evaluation

This phrase can be interpreted in a number of different ways. Donaldson and Lipsey (2006) draw attention to the often closely related and sometimes interchangeable terms such as *theory-based evaluation, theory driven evaluation, program theory, evaluation theory* and *theory of change*. If the views of two eminent evaluation commentators were to be accepted, it would be possible, at this point, to discount all of these theories as redundant to the process of formal evaluation. For example Scriven (2004) and Stufflebeam (2001) are not won over by the insistence from some fellow evaluation experts, such as Alkin (2004), Chen (1990), Fetterman (2003) and Rossi et al (2004), that certain theoretical applications – program theory, evaluation theory and social science theory in particular – have an important role to play in evaluation research.

Of course, the word 'theory' is often misused. In informal interchanges, the assertion that 'I've got a theory' might mean no more than 'I've got a working hypothesis'. In the text by Donaldson and Lipsey it is clear that their concept of 'theory' as applied to *evaluation theory* amounts to little more than an agreed set of principles and methods which should inform evaluation practice.

Social science theory

Among the allegedly useful and important social science theories favoured by Donaldson and Lipsey (2006) are the *theory of mentoring, theories of practical intelligence and leadership, theories of re-employment training* and *the theory of interpersonal expectations and self-fulfilling prophecies*. They claim that these and other such theories can provide existing knowledge about how to confront and reduce social problems and how to design an evaluation that does not recreate mistakes from the past. However, they warn against trying to compare the results of different evaluations in order to provide evidence of broadly generalisable (externally valid) findings. This caveat echoes the advice offered by Pawson and Tilley

(1997) that outcomes are likely to be explicable only with reference to the particular context in which the project or programme takes place.

Program theory

This example of a theory claimed to be relevant to carrying out evaluations focuses on the assumptions that guide the way specific programs, treatments or interventions are implemented and expected to bring about change (Shaw et al, 2006). Since a theory by definition is a research-derived explanation of how, why and under what circumstances certain interventions work, this would appear to be at odds with the criticism by Pawson and Tilley (1997) that such explanations are missing from evaluation in practice.

One of the problems with adopting the terminology of science to the field of evaluation research is the acknowledgement by the adherents of (a) the interchangeability of terms; (b) differences in the definition of, for example, program theory; and (c) the confusion about which term to use to sum up the theory. Here are three definitions of program theory quoted in Shaw et al (2006, p 64):

> The construction of a plausible and sensible model of how a program is supposed to work. (Bickman, 1987)

> A set of propositions regarding what goes on in the black box during the transformation of input to output, that is, how a bad situation is transformed into a better one through treatment inputs. (Lipsey, 1993)

> The process through which program components are presumed to affect outcomes and the conditions under which these processes are believed to operate. (Donaldson, 2001)

Compared with theory-building in physics, chemistry or other scientific domains there is a certain tentative quality to these 'definitions'. The words 'plausible', 'presumed', 'believed', do not – one could argue – inspire much confidence in program theory as a particularly well-developed framework for carrying out evaluations, especially since we are informed by Shaw et al that the origins of this phrase can be traced back to the 1930s. To compound this seeming lack of consensus about the definition of program theory, a considerable number of labels purporting to represent what program theory offers to evaluators can be found in the literature: for example theory-oriented evaluation, theory-based evaluation, theory-driven evaluation, program theory evaluation, intervening mechanism evaluation, theoretically relevant evaluation research, program theory, program logic and logic modelling (Shaw et al, 2006). In order to bring some semblance of order to this *melange* of definitional phrases, Donaldson and Lipsey (2006) coin the term *program theory-driven evaluation science,* thus adding another 'model' along with *comprehensive evaluation* and *tailored evaluation* (Shaw et al, 2006) to the extensive evaluation lexicon.

'Utilization-focused evaluation' (U-FE)

To continue adding to the list of types of evaluation that can be found in the literature would serve little purpose. Instead, attention will be turned to one of Michael Quinn Patton's works which deals with what is a percurrent concern among writers on evaluation: the extent to which evaluation research findings have influenced policy. This is a topic that will inform a good deal of the discussion in Chapter Six. After all, if the main or only purpose of evaluation – as Eggers (1999), Weiss (1999), Feinstein (2002) and many others have asserted – is to provide crucial information about how projects, programmes and policies can better serve their intended beneficiaries, then it would follow that all evaluation should be utilisation-focused. Chelimsky (1999) would dissent from this view, as we shall note in Chapter Six, but the preponderant position is that evaluation needs to contribute to decision making.

Patton's (2002) standpoint is unequivocal. Evaluations should be judged by their utility and actual use and in a statement very much in harmony with the central thesis of this book he writes:

> Use concerns how real people in the real world apply evaluation findings and experience the evaluation process … Utilization-focused evaluation does not advocate any particular evaluation content, model, method, theory, or even use. (p 1)

Instead, the 'primary intended users' are given the opportunity to decide for themselves which methods etc will suit their objectives. Patton makes some distinction between key people who want the evaluation to be carried out (presumably the commissioning agency) and 'various stakeholder constituencies' (p 2) which Patton does not define. Finding appropriate stakeholders remains the task of the evaluator. Because of this onus on the evaluator to select 'constituencies' and to involve them with the primary intended users in the planning and design of the evaluation, U–FE promises a degree of collaboration in clarifying the use to which the findings will be put. Nevertheless, even this approach does not guarantee that the eventual results of the evaluation will inform, influence or change any particular project, programme or policy. In the 'real world' – and for perfectly logical reasons – 'real people' have the right to behave in ways that evaluators might find bewildering and frustrating.

Concluding comment

There is general agreement that evaluation is a form of social research aimed at improving public services. To this end, those who have the authority and the means to commission this type of research initiate, or assist others to initiate, particular projects and programmes often designed to test government policies in the social domain.

Other kinds of assessment, such as audits, inspections and accreditation are more limited in time, methodology and evaluative criteria. A number of writers on the subject of evaluation have described various approaches to and models of evaluation while others have presented a case for evaluations to be informed by theory. These issues will be discussed further in Chapter Six.

The next chapter sets out a range of methods for collecting and analysing evaluation data, and we shall argue that a degree of caution needs to be applied in drawing inferences relating to the issues of reliability and validity.

References

Alkin, M.C. (ed) (2004) *Evaluation roots: Tracing theorists' views and influences*, Thousand Oaks, CA: Sage.

Bickman, L. (1987) 'The functions of program theory', in L. Bickman (ed) *Using program theory in evaluation*, San Francisco, CA: Jossey Bass.

Bryk, A.S. (ed) (1983) *Stakeholder-based evaluation*, New Directions in Program Planning Evaluation No 17, San Francisco, CA: Jossey-Bass.

Carter, N., Klein, R. and Day, P. (1992) *How organizations measure success: the use of performance indicators in government*, London: Routledge.

Chen, H.T. (1990) *Theory-driven evaluations*, Newbury Park, CA: Sage.

Clarke, A. (1999) *Evaluation research: an introduction to principles, methods and practice*, London: Sage.

Cronbach, L.J. and associates (1980) *Towards reform of program evaluation*, San Francisco, CA: Jossey Bass.

Daily Telegraph (2010) 'Audit Commission scrapped as austerity drive intensifies' [by N. Triggle], 24 February.

Darzi, Lord (2008) *High quality care for all, NHS Next Stage Review: Final report* (June) Cmnd 7432.

Doem, G.B. (1993) 'The UK Citizens' Charter: origins and implementation in three agencies', *Policy & Politics*, vol 21, no 1, pp 17-29.

Donabedian, A. (1969) 'Evaluating the quality of medical care', *Milbank Memorial Quarterly*, vol 44, pp 166-206.

Donabedian, A. (1980) *The definition of quality and approaches to its assessment*, Ann Arbor, MI: Health Administration Press.

Donaldson, S.I. (2001) 'Overcoming our negative reputation: evaluation becomes known as a helping profession', *American Journal of Evaluation*, vol 22, pp 35-6.

Donaldson, S.I. and Lipsey, M.W. (2006) *Roles for theory in contemporary evaluation practice: developing practical knowledge*, Ann Arbor MI: Health Administration Press.

Dror, Y. (1989) *Public policy making re-examined* (2nd edn), New Brunswick, NJ: Transaction Publishers.

Edelman, M. (1984) *The symbolic use of politics*, Urbank: Illinois Press.

Eggers, H.W. and Chelimsky, E. (1999) 'Purposes and use: what can we expect?', *Evaluation*, vol 5, no 1, pp 92-6.

Epstein, I. and Tripodi, T. (1977) *Research techniques for program planning*, New York: Columbia University Press.

Etzioni, A. (1967) 'Mixed-scanning: a "third" approach to decision-making', *Public Administration Review*, vol 27, pp 385-92.

Feinstein, O.N. (2002) 'Use of evaluation and the evaluation of use', *Evaluation*, vol 8, no 4, pp 433-39.

Fetterman, D. (2003) 'Empowerment evaluation strikes a responsive chord', in S. Donaldson and M. Scriven (eds) *Evaluating social programs and problems,* Hillsdale, NJ: Erlbaum.

Finch, J. (2004) *Evaluating mental health services for older people*, Oxford: Radcliffe.

Furibo, J.-E., Rist, R.C. and Sandahl, R. (2002) *The international atlas of evaluation*, NJ: Transaction Publishers.

Gaster, L. (1995) *Quality in public services: Managers' choices,* Buckingham: Open University Press.

Gray, D.A. (2004) *Doing research in the real world*, London: Sage.

Green, J. and South, J. (2006) *Evaluation*, Maidenhead: Open University Press.

Guba, E.G. (1981) *Improving the usefulness of evaluation results through responsive and naturalistic approaches*, San Francisco, CA: Jossey Bass.

Guba, E.G. and Lincoln, Y.S (1981) *Effective evaluation: Improving the usefulness of evaluation results through responsive and naturalistic approaches*, San Francisco, CA: Jossey Bass.

Hambleton, R. and Hoggett, P. (1990) *Beyond excellence: Quality local government in the 1990s*, Working Paper No 85, Bristol: School for Advanced Urban Studies, University of Bristol.

Hamilton, D. (ed) (1977) *Beyond the numbers game: A reader in educastional evaluation*, London: Macmillan.

Hansen, H.F. (2005) 'Choosing evaluation models', *Evaluation*, vol 11, no 4, pp 447-461.

Hedrick, T.E. (1988) 'The interaction of politics and evaluation', *Evaluation Practice*, vol 9, no 3, pp 5-14.

Herman, J.L., Morris, L.L. and Fitz-Gibbon, C.T. (1987) *Evaluation handbook*, Newbury Park, CA: Sage.

Ho, S.Y. (1999) 'Evaluating urban regeneration programmes in Britain', *Evaluation*, vol 5, no 4, pp 422-38.

Hogwood, B.W. (1987) *From crisis to complacency*, Oxford: Oxford University Press.

House, E.R. (1993) *Professional evaluation: Social impact and political consequences*, London: Sage.

Karlsson, O. (1996) 'A critical dialogue in evaluation', *Evaluation*, vol 2, no 4, pp 405-16.

Lang, A. (1844–1912) quoted in C. Robertson (ed) (1997) *Wordsworth Dictionary of Quotations*, Ware, Herts: Wordsworth Editions, p 277.

Leeuw, F.L. and Furibo, J-E. (2008) 'Evauation systems: what are they and why study them?', *Evaluation*, vol 14, no 2, pp 151-69.

Lindblom, C. (1959) 'The science of "muddling through"', *Public Administration Review*, vol 19, no 3, pp 517-26.

Lipsey, M.W. (1993) 'Theory as method: small theories of treatments', *New Directions for Program Evaluation*, vol 57, pp 5-38.

Lipsky, M. (1980) *Street-level bureaucracy*, NY: Russell Sage.

Luker, K.A. (1981) 'An overview of evaluation research in nursing', *Journal of Advanced Nursing*, vol 6, pp 87-93.

Macdonald, B. (1977) 'A political classification of evaluation studies', in D. Hamilton (ed) *Beyond the numbers game*, London: Macmillan.

Macmillan, H. (2003) *The Macmillan diaries: The Cabinet years 1950–57* (ed P. Catterall), London: Macmillan.

Office of Public Services Reform (2003) *The government's policy on inspection of public services*, London: Cabinet Office.

Palfrey, C. and Thomas, P. (1999) 'Politics and policy evaluation', *Public Policy and Administration*, vol 14, no 4, pp 58-70.

Palfrey, C., Thomas, P. and Phillips, C. (2004) *Effective health care management: An evaluative approach*, Oxford: Blackwell.

Palfrey, C., Thomas, P., Phillips, C. and Edwards, D. (1992) *Policy evaluation in the public sector*, Aldershot: Avebury.

Parsons, W. (1995) *Public policy: An introduction to the theory and practice of policy analysis*, London: Edward Elgar.

Patton, M.Q. (1981) *Creative evaluation*, Beverly Hills, CA: Sage.

Patton, M.Q. (1988) 'Six honest serving men', *Studies in Educational Evaluation*, vol 14, pp 301–30.

Patton, M.Q. (2002) *Utilization-focused evaluation.* Available at www.wmich.edu/evalctr/checklists/

Pawson, R. and Tilley, N. (1997) *Realistic evaluation*, London: Sage.

Phillips, C., Palfrey, C. and Thomas, P. (1994) *Evaluating health and social care*, London: Macmillan.

Potter, C. (2006) 'Psychology and the art of program evaluation', *South African Journal of Psychology*, vol 36, no 1, pp 82-102.

Power, M. (1997) *The audit society: Rituals of verification*, Oxford: Oxford University Press.

Redwood, J (2006) *I don't like politics but I want to make a difference,* London: Politico's Publishing Ltd.

Robson, C. (1993) *Real world evaluation research*, Oxford: Blackwell.

Rossi, P.H., Lipsey, M.W. and Freeman, H.E. (2004) *Evaluation: A systematic approach*, Thousand Oaks, CA: Sage.

Schulberg, B.C. and Baker, F.B. (1968) 'Program evaluation and the implementation of research findings', *American Journal of Public Health,* vol 58, pp 1238-55.

Scriven, M. (1967) 'The methodology of evaluation', in R.W. Tyler, R.M. Gagne and M. Scriven (eds) *Perspectives of curriculum evaluation*, Chicago, IL: Rand McNally.

Scriven, M. (2004) *Practical program evaluation: A checklist approach*, Claremont Graduate University Annual Professional Development Workshop.

Shaw, C.D. and Collins, C.D. (1995) 'Health service accreditation: report of a pilot programme for community hospitals', *British Medical Journal*, vol 310, pp 781-784l.

Shaw, I.A., Greene, J.C. and Mark, M.M. (eds) (2006) *Handbook of evaluation: Policies, programs and policies*, London: Sage.

Sieber, J. (1980) 'Being ethical: professional and personal decision in program evaluation', in R. Perloff and E. Perloff (eds) *Values, ethics and standards in evaluation*, San Francisco, CA: Jossey Bass.

Simey, M. (1985) *Government by consent*, London: Bedford Square Press.

Simon, H.A. (1957) *Administrative behaviour*, London: Macmillan.

Simons, H. (1984) 'Negotiating conditions for independent evaluation', in M. Simey (1985) *Government by consent*, London: Bedford Square Press.

Smith, B. (1976) *Policy making in British government: An analysis of power and rationality*, Oxford: Martin Robertson.

Smith, G. and Cantley, C. (1985) *Assessing healthcare: A study in organisational evaluation*, Milton Keynes: Open University Press.

Stufflebeam, D. (2001) *Evaluation models*, New Directions for Evaluation No 89, San Francisco, CA: Jossey Bass.

Suchman, E.A. (1967) *Evaluative research*, NY: Russell Sage.

Tones, K. and Tilford, S. (2001) *Health promotion: Effectiveness, efficiency and equity*, Cheltenham: Nelson Thornes.

Vickers, G. (1965) *The art of judgement*, London: Chapman and Hall.

Weiss, C. (1972) *Evaluation research*, New Jersey: Englewood Cliffs.

Weiss, C. (1999) 'The interface between evaluation and public policy', *Evaluation*, vol 5, no 1, pp 468-86.

White, H. (2010) 'A contribution to current debates in impact evaluation', *Evaluation*, vol 16, no 2, pp 153-64.

Whynes, D.K. (1987) 'On assessing efficiency in the provision of local authority services', *Local Government Studies*, vol 13, no 1, pp 53-68.

Williams, D.D. (1986) *Naturalistic evaluation*, San Francisco, CA: Jossey Bass.

World Health Organization (1998) *Health promotion evaluation: recommendations to policy makers*, WHO Copenhagen Regional Office for Europe.

THREE

Designing evaluations

Methodological issues and the nature of evidence

In our view, one of the limitations of much of the literature on evaluation research is that it gives insufficient attention to the problems involved in undertaking evaluations. The problems include a less than sceptical approach to data and to data collection, and a tendency to approach evaluation work from a single perspective, giving inadequate attention to the plurality of interests which are commonly present in public services.

When evaluating a policy or service, data obviously need to be collected and analysed. It is therefore important to be aware of the ontological and epistemological foundations on which the data are being built. Ontology is a branch of metaphysics and is the study of 'being'. It concerns itself with the question of whether things exist and (if they do exist) the nature of those things. Epistemology is a related philosophical field: it is the study of knowledge, and helps us to distinguish between an unsupported assertion (and its more subtle relation the undersupported assertion) or mere opinion on the one hand, and a justified belief on the other hand.

These issues are important because they help us to be sceptical about what might appear at first sight to be valid evaluations, especially when evaluating processes about which there might be significant disagreements. Consider, for example, the evaluation of various ways of assessing and resolving interpersonal conflict between members of a management team trying to work together in the planning and delivery of public services. Different observers of the managers' behaviour patterns might easily make totally different judgements about the sorts of conflict that exist, or about whether there was any conflict at all. One observer might see the raising of voices in a meeting as clear evidence of conflict and hostility. Another might see it as no more than a normal exchange of views and perspectives being expressed assertively by those present. These different perceptions by the observers point to the inevitable subjectivity of such judgements, even where the observers are taking care to be as objective and systematic as possible.

This is an example of a more general point about the objective/ subjective debate. Philosophers generally acknowledge that observers (or evaluators) have no direct access to the things they are observing. If person A is observing something and feels confident about what is there to be seen 'clearly', might it be that A is dreaming? We have no access to the noumena (things in themselves; things as they actually are), only to phenomena – which is what we perceive. Even if we ask for a second opinion, we are still left with the perceptions of those whose opinions and perceptions we are consulting. The present authors are not professional philosophers, but we are tempted to claim that in observing or evaluating things one can never be absolutely objective. While evaluators might seek to be as objective as possible, there will always be an element of subjectivity in trying to find out what is happening. The only tools we have in finding out about things 'out there' are our senses, and empirical evidence will therefore always be uncertain and contestable.

It is generally accepted that some data collection methods are likely to be more subjective than others. For example, the illustration above about observing behaviour patterns is likely to be more subjective than measuring increases in the life expectancy of a defined population. Research methods are often seen as lying on a spectrum with experiments and numerical measurements at one end (the 'objective' positivist paradigm) and ethnography at the other (the interpretivist, constructivist, more subjective paradigm).

There is, of course, no one 'best' method of collecting and analysing data. What is crucial is that the methods used should be appropriate to the aim of the evaluation research being undertaken. This is not a book on research methods but what follows is a consideration of some of the key methodological issues which need to be taken into account when planning and carrying out evaluation research. The data collection methods and research designs that feature here are probably those most likely to be used in evaluation research.

Many evaluations are carried out using more than one data collection method. In the case of each method there are a number of issues that need to be considered when undertaking evaluation projects.

In-depth interviews

In evaluation research this method is usually used for the collection of qualitative, rather than quantitative, data and it is therefore quite difficult to ensure a high degree of reliability. Two interviewers can interview the same interviewee, one after the other on the same day, and arrive at different conclusions about the perceptions and opinions of the interviewee. There are various possible reasons for this, concerned with the different experiences, perceptions and attitudes of the interviewers and with the specific pattern of interactions between interviewer and interviewee.

Nevertheless, interviews represent an important approach to data collection and are often the most appropriate approach for particular evaluations, especially where it is considered important to probe an informant's responses thoroughly. Based on our experiences in evaluation and in supervising evaluations of a wide range of services, we have noted the problem of inexperienced interviewers recording an interviewee's comments and then rushing on to the next question. This often leads to rather superficial data. It is important for interviewers to ask pertinent supplementary questions such as 'Tell me more about that', 'What happened after that?' or 'How did that work in practice?'.

In planning the interviews it is first necessary to decide whether people will be interviewed individually or in groups, as in focus groups. A benefit of doing the interviews on an individual basis is that interviewees might be prepared to be more honest, especially if being asked about their opinions of (possibly senior) colleagues. On the other hand, interviewees in groups might be more forthcoming because their thoughts might be stimulated by the comments of other members of the group, especially if being asked for new ideas about how a policy or service might be improved. Some might argue that this is an 'either/or' question. In practice, of course, it is nothing of the sort. In the real world there is no reason why both kinds of interviews – individual and group – cannot be conducted within the same evaluation project, and the authors have done just this in evaluating a number of local government services.

Secondly, decisions need to be made about how the data (the interviewees' comments) will be captured. Should they be audio-recorded with the recordings being transcribed afterwards? Or should field notes be taken during the interview and be relied on later? Again there are pros and cons to the options. Transcription tends to take a great deal of time, a resource which is rarely plentiful when undertaking evaluations. For practical reasons, transcriptions are usually untenable and note taking is often likely to be the preferred method. This point was brought home to the authors when a face-to-face interview was recorded in an open plan office. Later, when attempting to make notes from the tape, it was found that the 'background' noise in the office had all but obliterated the interview.

Thirdly, what degree of structure should be used in the questioning? Should the interviews be highly structured – with every interviewee being asked exactly the same questions in the same way, with no deviation between one interviewee and another, or completely unstructured, where there is clearly a danger of the interview degenerating into an unfocused and irrelevant chat? Or should the interview be semi-structured so that the same (or similar) interview checklist is used for each interviewee but the interviewer will be allowed to follow up an unexpected lead if an interviewee says something which seems to have the potential to reveal something relevant and important?

Fourthly, it is important to remember that the way in which the questions (choice of words, tone of voice, etc) are asked will have an important influence on the way in which interviewees will respond, including the extent to which they will openly discuss their views. Those doing the interviewing need to have a high degree of interpersonal communication skills.

Fifthly, it will be necessary to consider whether the questions will be open (for example, 'What are your views on the new policy?') or closed/coded (for example, 'Do you approve of the new policy – yes or no?'). Both kinds of questions have their place. Sometimes, a closed question can usefully be followed by an open one so that interviewees are encouraged to enlarge on their answer to the closed question.

Finally, will the interviews be done once, or repeated over a long period of time as the issues being researched unfold and develop?

Observation

There are a number of issues to be clarified when choosing to use observation as a key method of qualitative data collection. Ethnographic research involves the researcher observing for an extended period the behaviour of subjects in their day-to-day surroundings, for example the boardroom, hospital ward, teachers' staff room, operating theatre or administrative offices. It is a method commonly used in combination with interviewing or with the scrutiny of documents. Evaluators could be tempted to observe only those things which they want or expect to observe. And even if evaluators record accurately what happens, bias can still creep in to the interpretations that are made concerning the behaviours observed. An inappropriate degree of subjectivity can easily intrude, and it is therefore a difficult method to use effectively. Key issues for consideration include the following.

- To what extent are the observations systematic? For example, will a prepared chart be used for ticking off examples of specific behaviours or will descriptive field notes be collected with coded analysis to follow? If the former is used, accusations of 'box ticking' can easily arise; if the latter is used, the process can become more time consuming and time is a resource that evaluators often find is scarce.
- Will a grounded theory approach be used (Glaser and Strauss, 1967) in which themes 'emerge' from the data, as opposed to using 'off the shelf' categories to which pieces of data will be slotted? These two approaches – the inductive grounded theory and the deductive model respectively – are often presented as an 'either/or' choice. This is not necessarily so. Evaluation researchers may use a combination of the two approaches. The deductive approach is useful when there are apparently relevant theoretical frameworks which can be used to analyse the data in question; inductive approaches are more useful where an open mind is needed to interpret new data in order to construct new theories.
- Is participant observation to be used (involving complete immersion in the day-to-day life of the group being studied so that empathy can be developed with the group's experiences) or non-participant observation (by a non-involved spectator or 'fly on the wall')? Again there are pros and cons to be considered. For example, in participant observation one can get very 'close to the action' and develop a thorough understanding of what is going on. However, there is then a danger of getting *too* close, so that the researcher becomes too much of a participant and not enough of a detached observer.
- Will the observation be undertaken overtly or covertly? In many cases in evaluating policies and services, observation is carried out in an open or transparent (overt) way; but sometimes there might be something to gain undertaking some observations more covertly, as when using 'mystery shoppers' to assess how good the service seems to be from the perspective of a service user.
- To what extent and in what ways might the act of observation modify the behaviour of those being observed – an example of the Hawthorne effect (Roethlisberger and Dickson, 1939)? This is usually less of a problem in the case of covert observations, but there are ethical issues to be considered relating to deception and confidentiality. Issues of ethics in evaluation will be considered in Chapter Four.

In many projects which utilise observation, it is important to remember that analysis takes place *during* the data collection process. Analysis is not confined to the post data collection stage. For example, during observations decisions need to be made from minute to minute about which observations are relevant or significant and which are not.

In our experience of real-world evaluations we have found that the boundaries between observation and interviewing can be quite blurred. A member of staff in an organisation whose services are being evaluated might be showing the evaluator around a building to demonstrate how things work. At the same time a detailed discussion might be taking place (between staff member and evaluator) about the pros and cons of alternative ways of delivering the service. These 'interview' and observation data might also be supplemented by information in a document from within the organisation (or a related organisation) which provides further details and evidence about the service. Such a combination of data collection methods is not uncommon and the authors of this book have used this approach in evaluations in local government, in the NHS and in higher education institutions. It is a useful version of triangulating data.

An example of the value of cross-checking data collected by one method by applying another was somewhat fortuitously provided while the authors were carrying out an evaluation of the regimes in a local authority's care homes. In one home, the officer-in-charge was explaining that the place was run very democratically, with residents and staff on an equal footing. An elderly gentleman came into the room and engaged in brief conversation with the male member of staff who, at the end of the conversation, patted the resident on the head and said he would see him later. That one patronising gesture managed to yield fairly cogent evidence that the officer-in-charge had been less than truthful in what he had been telling us about the relationship between staff and residents.

Scrutiny of documents

This is often done to supplement data collected in some other way. It can be the primary or even the exclusive method of data collection or a stage used in order to clarify which questions need to be asked or which other data collection methods would be appropriate. The analysis of documents requires a critical eye and evaluators need to ask themselves questions about who prepared the document in question. Was the author writing the document in order to persuade someone of a particular argument? What sources did the author use in compiling the document? To what extent was the author using an appropriate degree of scepticism in selecting and using information?

In addition, questions need to be asked about how the documents became available. It is possible that they were selected by parties with a vested interest and thus present a possible source of bias.

Documents which might be relevant to evaluation research include reports (for example, identifying a problem with a service), minutes of meetings (for example, indicating committee discussions and decisions related to identified problems), government papers and Parliamentary debates (indicating government and Parliamentary intentions in relation to the policy to be evaluated), Select Committee reports and minutes (offering informed opinions about the policy), letters and diaries (indicating personal opinions about aspects of the policy), and newspapers reports (which might offer alternative views about the policy).

Questionnaires

Self-administered questionnaires can be useful for collecting information from a large number of people in a relatively short period of time. But again there are issues to be addressed. For example, should an existing questionnaire be used or should the questionnaire be tailor-made for each evaluation project? Good questionnaires are quite difficult to design but this can often be worth the effort because the questionnaire is then likely to be more relevant to the particular service being evaluated. A questionnaire which has been designed by someone else at another time is likely to be less sharply focused on the particular evaluation project being undertaken, but has the merit of being readily available, possibly with some information about its validity and likely reliability.

Secondly, how will the questionnaire be piloted with a small sample of respondents to see whether the questions are clear and the questionnaire is easy to complete? The questions should all be relevant to the evaluation project and each question needs to be tested against the aim of the evaluation. The questions should be unambiguous and likely to elicit useful and relevant data.

Thirdly, should the questions be precoded or presented in a more open form asking for narrative replies which will need to be analysed later? One of the advantages of precoded questions is that the replies will be easier to analyse. The advantage of using uncoded questions is that respondents are less likely to be led by the evaluator's preconceived ideas about how the questions should be answered: the result will be 'richer' data but it will be more difficult to analyse them to see what patterns are emerging.

One of the difficulties of using questionnaires is that response rates are commonly low, especially with postal questionnaires. The problem can be reduced by ensuring that the questionnaire does not take long to answer; enclosing a stamped addressed envelope for replies; specifying a date for replies; and following up with reminders (and another stamped addressed envelope) and possibly incentives.

As far as the wording of questions in a self-administered questionnaire is concerned, standard guidance needs to be followed. For example, the questions need to be clear to the intended respondents and unambiguous, and 'multiple' questions should be avoided: for example, if a question asks whether a personal service was provided promptly and with dignity, the respondent might be unclear if they want to say that the service was prompt but *not* provided in a way that protected their dignity, especially if the respondent is asked to answer by way of an attitude scale. It is important in such a case to split the question into two questions, one about promptness and one about dignity.

Experiments

Some writers see evaluation evidence in the form of a hierarchy in relation to the rigour they have for establishing causal relationships. In this hierarchy, randomised controlled trials (RCTs) are seen as the gold standard or 'best' method to measure, for example, the effectiveness of drugs where it is often possible randomly to set up an experimental group and a control group and to control the variables under investigation.

In evaluating a public service or policy, however, it is rarely, if ever, possible to control all the variables involved and so RCTs are less likely to be used. Instead, other experimental methods may be utilised. Such quasi-experimental designs will not have the same degree of validity because randomisation is commonly not possible. In policy evaluation 'natural experiments' might be used. Here the assignment of subjects to experimental and control groups will be haphazard but it is still possible cautiously to infer causal links (between a policy or service and what appear to be the outcomes) so that one can plausibly attribute outcomes to the particular policy or service being evaluated.

A useful account of the merits and limitations of natural experiments has been provided by Petticrew et al (2005), who discuss the experiments they conducted concerning the public health outcomes of two separate initiatives. One was to assess the impact (on public health) of a new hypermarket built in a deprived urban neighbourhood. The research entailed a survey of health and diet and the use of focus groups with local people.

The second project was the provision of new social housing: the researchers set out to assess the impact on the health and well-being of the tenants. Information on self-reported health status was to be collected before tenants moved into their new home and at one and two years after.

One of the major problems in evaluating these two initiatives was that many of the major social determinants of health and health inequalities are not amenable to randomisation, and it is likely that 'the control and intervention groups are dissimilar at baseline' (Petticrew et al, 2005, p 753). This kind of difficulty 'does not invalidate such studies, but it means that the results of natural experiments should be treated as indicative rather than conclusive' (p 753).

Another problem in using natural experiments is that often there is no one single intervention to be evaluated or one single health outcome to be measured. 'Multiple overlapping interventions or policies often occur in poorer areas because this is how policies are often intentionally targeted' (p 753).

Natural experiments therefore require careful handling and they are not likely to provide definitive answers when evaluating the effectiveness of a policy. They can, however, provide the best available evidence.

Further details relating to experiments can be found in Phillips et al (1994, pp 28–38).

A practical example

Whichever methods of data collection are used it is important to recognise that it is usually unwise to have preconceived ideas or formulae about the procedures to be used. Careful thought needs to be given about what kinds of data are needed and about the data collection methods to be used in each case. What follows in Table 3.1, for illustrative purposes, is a summary of some of the methods which the authors used in an evaluation of care for elderly people in the community. The purpose of the table is to clarify the kinds of information which needs to be collected for each evaluative criterion (which are examined in Chapter Four) and some data collection methods which would be appropriate for each criterion.

Table 3.1: The kinds of information which may be collected in relation to criteria for evaluating care for elderly people in the community, together with possible data collection methods

Evaluative criteria	Examples of kinds of information sought for each criterion	Main data collection method used
Responsiveness	• How quickly, accurately and reliably did alarm systems work?	Interviews with clients and scrutiny of authority's records.
Equity	• To what extent are services provided impartially on the basis of need and agreed processes and procedures? • To what extent are charges based on the ability to pay?	Interviews with authority staff and scrutiny of documents.
Equality	• To what extent is it appropriate for resources to be allocated equally for various geographic locations? If appropriate, how much equality is being achieved?	• Census data in relation to possible 'underprivileged' indicators. • Financial data on spending as between different areas.
Effectiveness	• Quality of life of people receiving intensive support in their own home compared with those in residential homes (both groups to be 'matched' for valid comparisons to be made). • To what extent were agreed targets being achieved?	Interviews and questionnaires to clients and their representatives concerning dependency measures and other indicators of 'quality of life'. Follow-up data at appropriate intervals.
Efficiency	• Benefits and costs (including opportunity costs) of the services compared with alternative uses of the resources. • To what extent is regard being had to costs incurred by informal carers? • Number of people receiving particular services.	• Scrutiny of authority records. • Questionnaires to, and interviews with, clients and informal carers. • Interviews with authority staff.
Economy	• Perceived opportunities to provide services in cheaper ways without reducing level or quality of the services.	Records of what services cost and interviews with managers and professionals about possible opportunities to provide the services more cheaply.

Table 3.1: continued

Evaluative criteria	Examples of kinds of information sought for each criterion	Main data collection method used
Accountability	• Was there clarity in the location, direction and content of accountability (i.e. did everyone know who was accountable to whom and for what)? • How was control exercised within, and between, relevant agencies? • Were there adequate reporting mechanisms?	• Interviews with managers within the social service authority and within related organisations. • Organisation charts.
Accessibility	• Were specified services available when they were wanted and needed? • To what extent were clients, and their representatives, able to influence the ways in which the services were being planned and delivered? • Who participates in care planning? • Availability of appropriate information and publicity.	Interviews with and questionnaires to clients and their relatives.
Appropriateness	• Are the services, and the ways in which they were delivered, relevant to the needs of the clients, in the opinion of the clients and of their representatives? • Who determines the needs of clients?	Interviews with managers, professionals, clients and their relatives.
Acceptability	• What levels of satisfaction and/or dissatisfaction were being expressed by clients and their representatives for various aspects of the service?	Questionnaires to clients and their relatives.
Choice	• What realistic choices are available to clients if they are dissatisfied with a service?	Interviews with managers, professionals, clients and their relatives.

Validity

In the collection and analysis of data it is necessary to consider the issue of validity. There are different kinds of validity, including internal validity and external validity, and each kind is commonly defined and developed in many standard books on research methods. As far as evaluation is concerned it is important to ensure that what the evaluator claims or thinks is being assessed is actually being assessed. The question is whether something may be legitimately regarded as a valid indicator of the concept under consideration. For example, in identifying people's social class (a concept), their occupation is likely to be a more valid indicator than eye colour. This is a form of *internal validation* – selecting an indicator which is a proper measure of what one wishes to measure. Such validation is not an exact process, but relies on acceptability to questioning readers and on the traditions of a particular social science.

External validity, on the other hand, is concerned with whether the results of the study can be generalised to other groups (population validity) and/or in other contexts/conditions (ecological validity). In quantitative studies there are well-established methods of assessing the extent to which the results from a sample are likely to be representative of a whole population. Ensuring external validity in the case of qualitative studies is more of a problem. Here validation tends to be based on a consideration of the following:

- checking conclusions against further data sets;
- triangulation (of various methods, various data, various sources and various researchers);
- testing consumer responses;
- testing the feasibility of policy recommendations.

It should also be noted, that validation is often carried out by later researchers – looking back critically at people's earlier work. The results of evaluation research are thus rarely, if ever, uncontestable.

Miles and Huberman (1993) suggest a number of tactics for testing or confirming one's research findings in the interests of ensuring validity. They point out that there are no canons or decision rules in qualitative research to indicate whether findings are valid and procedures robust. In many cases qualitative researchers leap from hundreds of pages of field notes to conclusions, and the reader does not know how much confidence can be placed in those conclusions. The suggestions put forward by Miles and Huberman include:

- Checking for representativeness, e.g. beware of moving too readily from the particular to the general.
- Checking for researcher effects, e.g. being co-opted or 'going native' – swallowing the agreed upon or taken-for-granted version of local events.
- Triangulation.
- Weighting the evidence; there are a number of markers the analyst can use in deciding in the interests of validity whether to give more weight to some data than to others, eg:
  (a) data from some informants are 'better' in the sense that they are more knowledgeable, articulate, thoughtful, reflective, etc;
  (b) the circumstances of the data collection may have strengthened (or weakened) the quality of the data; e.g. data collected later or after repeated contact might be better than data collected early, during entry.
- Looking for deviant cases; can one's 'theory' explain these as well as the 'normal' cases; the temptation to sweep the deviant cases under the carpet needs to be avoided.
- Thinking about possible rival explanations to the one emerging.
- Getting feedback from informants.

Judgements as to 'authenticity' are also important. Runciman (1983) warns us to beware of 'misdescriptions' such as:

- incompleteness: neglect of institutions and practices (such as the omission of some local authorities when evaluating the performance of all the local authorities in a particular region);
- oversimplification: a failure to ask informants for a description in their own terms which would have resulted in further elaboration;
- suppression and/or exaggeration: details being excluded or overstated to make a case for the evaluator's own cause;
- ethnocentrism: assumptions of researcher's own milieu being inappropriately imposed onto the experiences of members of another.

Some disciplines are more self-conscious and explicit than others about research methods, but there are no simple answers to the problems of validity. The methods of data collection and analysis need to be appropriate for the particular evaluation task being undertaken. The degree of validity achieved needs to be acceptable to the informed and sceptical recipient or reader of the evaluation results.

Reliability

Evaluation research also needs to achieve an acceptable degree of reliability. This concerns the extent to which results are reproducible. If a large number of evaluators study the same thing and their findings turn out to be identical, or at least consistent, then the findings are regarded as reliable. This raises the issue of the practice of meta-evaluation which will feature in Chapter Seven.

It has been argued that quantitative research is strong on reliability and weak on validity, while the reverse is true of qualitative research (Walker, 1985). Perhaps we should not be surprised that reliability is a difficult issue for qualitative studies given that such studies are largely about people's subjective interpretations of complex situations. Most qualitative research relies on data collection instruments such as observation, structured, unstructured or semi-structured interviews and documentary sources, and the following rules of thumb can help to achieve some degree of reliability in such evaluations:

- Involve other people – as opposed to relying on the interpretation of one individual.
- Record accurately what is observed and how it is observed (that is, be explicit about your data collection methods).
- Where appropriate, make use of established data collection instruments where there is information available as to their degrees of reliability.

But despite efforts to minimise the difficulties, reliability is often seen as a problem for qualitative evaluation research. Nevertheless, qualitative data remains an important, and often essential, part of many evaluation projects.

Reliability is one of the five elements of 'robust' evidence on which policy making needs to be based (Shaxson, 2005). Given that the provision of evidence for future policy making is one of the expectations of evaluation activities, it is important that the evidence produced by evaluations can stand up to close scrutiny. In her discussion of reliability, Shaxson makes the point that although the standard literature on social research methods emphasises the ability to replicate studies, in practical policy making the luxury of having replicated studies is rarely available. Instead, Shaxson points to the need to consider contextual information and to ensure, as far as possible, that an evidence trail can be followed.

The second of Shaxson's elements of robustness (though these are in no particular order) is credibility, which is similar to internal validity. 'Credibility relies on a strong and clear line of argument, tried and tested analytical methods and on clear presentation of the conclusions' (Shaxson, 2005). Questions worth asking to test credibility include (p 106):

- 'How confident are we that the conclusions flow from evidence?'
- 'Are our methods appropriate to the quality of the evidence?'

The third element is generalisability, sometimes called 'transferability', which refers to the way we make inferences (Shaxson, 2005); this is similar to what some people call 'external validity'. It addresses the issue of the extent to which, and the ways in which, the findings of an evaluation may be used in different contexts. It is particularly applicable when pilot studies precede a wider roll-out (Government Chief Social Researcher's Office, 2003). Relevant questions here include (p 107):

- 'Are findings widely applicable or context-specific?'
- 'Which parts of the context matter?'

The fourth element of robustness is objectivity. As pointed out earlier in this chapter, there is a sense in which absolute objectivity is unattainable. But it is a question of doing what one can to minimise bias and to recognise any bias which is present and to take it into account when assessing the worth of the evaluation findings. Key questions include (p 108):

- 'Has everything practicable been done to minimise bias?'
- 'Has any residual bias been acknowledged and accounted for in presenting evidence to policy makers and others?'

The fifth and final element is 'rootedness', by which Shaxson means 'understanding the nuance of the evidence, exploring assumptions with an open mind, encouraging others to question the status quo ... and thinking about who uses what evidence for what purpose' (p 108). Questions which can help us to address this fifth element include (p 108):

- 'Are there aspects of the evaluation which are in danger of being ignored?'

- 'Have assumptions been examined by people with different specialist knowledge?'

Shaxson (2005) argues that all five assumptions are important in judging the robustness of evidence but that they will need to be weighted differently for each different policy question: they will not always be of equal importance. Judgements will need to be made as to which aspects of robustness are important in which situation, and often such judgements will need to be made under pressure of shortage of time and other resources. It is unlikely that all evidence will be completely robust all of the time. In the ideal world evaluators will always produce perfectly robust evidence; in the real world this is unattainable.

In the ideal world, or when designing the research methods for a PhD thesis, a good deal of explicit attention will normally be given to issues of validity and reliability. But in the case of actual evaluations, time constraints often mean that this is more difficult. It is important for evaluators to be aware of (and to disclose readily) the limitations of their work in relation to the 'rigour'. Time constraints usually mean that it is not possible to comply thoroughly with *all* the standard guidance found in research methods textbooks. Real-world evaluations, like politics, concern the art of the possible.

Analysing data

In the case of quantitative data there are relatively well-established statistical techniques, some using a range of tests to establish the degree of significance of apparent trends in the figures. From the results it is possible, for example, to infer the likelihood of there being causal connections between the variables. This can help to develop an understanding of how and why policies are working, or not working, as the case may be.

With qualitative data, however, the task of analysis is more uncertain and controversial. Generally speaking, qualitative research has more to do with developing or building theories than with testing them. Its emphasis is, therefore, often – though by no means always – inductive (generalising from the particular, as in Glaser and Strauss's (1967) so-called 'grounded theory' approach) rather than deductive (particularising from the general, as recommended by Miles and Huberman, 1993).

Qualitative methods tend to produce 'rich' *intensive* data relating to small numbers of people as opposed to *extensive* standardised data relating to large numbers, and tend to provide more contextual data than do quantitative data.

One of the other important differences between qualitative and quantitative data is that in the case of the latter it is more likely that analysis will take place only when the data collection has been completed. In qualitative research, analysis often starts as soon as data collection begins. For example, a problem of writing up field notes (relating, say, to observations and/or interviews) is that in deciding what was significant, filtering has to take place; some analysis/interpretation is therefore already going on, however unintentionally.

> The analysis of qualitative data is a highly personal activity. It involves processes of interpretation and creativity that are difficult and perhaps somewhat threatening to make explicit. ... There are no definitive rules to be followed by rote and by which, for example, two researchers can ensure that they reach identical conclusions about a set of data. (Jones, 1985, p 563)

Following this brief overview of some of the key issues involved in planning and undertaking the collection and analysis of data in evaluation processes, the discussion will now turn to some of the approaches which are available in conducting evaluation research in particular.

Evaluation frameworks

The purpose of this section is to outline and critically assess a number of key approaches to evaluation. The frameworks or approaches chosen are inevitably highly selective. Our selection is largely based on what we see as some of the major contributions to the field and on what we consider to be some of the key issues involved in undertaking evaluations in the public sector. We have omitted from this selection some of the specific tools which have been 'imposed' on public sector organisations in recent years, such as PIs, league tables and accreditation systems, which are referred to in Chapter Two.

Fourth generation evaluation

As mentioned in Chapter Two, a useful starting point is Guba and Lincoln's (1987) analysis of four 'generations' of evaluation. They point to the early part of the 20th century, in which evaluation often meant little more than measurement. Numerical results from tests (for example, of pupils' achievements in tests) were sometimes taken to speak for themselves and there was little or no description or narrative added to give some meaning or context to what was being measured. 'The figures' can *always* be challenged. However, to understand what numbers are signifying it is important sceptically to consider what was being measured, how it was measured and whether the numbers tell us anything useful. Examples of being misled by 'the figures' could include counting responses to leading questions within poorly constructed questionnaires, using graphs with misleading axes and being presented with averages with no accompanying information as to how they were derived.

Later in the 20th century came the second generation of evaluation (Guba and Lincoln, 1987) which was characterised by descriptions which, potentially at least, could shed some much needed light on raw numerical data. Later still, in the 1960s, came the third generation which involved explicit judgements being made about the evaluand. This approach required the objectives themselves to be treated as problematic, as opposed to taking them as given. Goals, no less than performance, were to be subject to evaluation.

The approach which Guba and Lincoln (1987) developed as an improvement on the earlier generations is referred to as *fourth generation evaluation* (FGE). They see this as a responsive approach which takes as its point of focus not objectives, decisions or effects, but the claims, concerns and issues of various *stakeholder* audiences. (See also Thomas and Palfrey, 1996, on stakeholder-focused evaluation.) Such audiences include service funders or commissioners, potential and actual beneficiaries (or 'target groups') of services, and victims (for example, excluded potential beneficiaries). An important element in this generation is *value-pluralism*. Here the evaluator cannot ethically undertake to render judgements; what the evaluator is expected to do is to act as mediator in a negotiation process. The theme of negotiation is the hallmark of FGE. Earlier generations of evaluation tended to assume a consensus on values; by contrast, FGE sees potential conflict in such matters and suggests that all stakeholders should be involved in negotiating how the evaluation should be carried out. In this context the professional evaluator becomes something of a political broker who is expected to ensure, as far as possible, firstly that no stakeholders are given unfair advantages, and secondly that proper weight is given to all identifiable stakeholders.

FGE is also based on a relativist ontology and epistemology. 'Reality' is not seen as something that exists objectively and independently of the stakeholders; reality is instead multiple and constructed. It follows from this that FGE is a continuous and divergent process. Evaluations are never fully 'completed': as some questions are answered, so more questions emerge. Thus FGE becomes an emergent process, instead of the conventional wisdom in which an evaluation design is specified in advance of the evaluation itself, In FGE the design, to some extent, unfolds as one undertakes the collection and analysis of data. As Guba and Lincoln argue (1987), in traditional evaluations it is possible to predict the format of the outcomes of the evaluation; for example, it might be a statement about the extent to which the effects of a policy are in line with the objectives. In FGE, however, not much can be safely said until the stakeholders' perceptions and concerns have been taken into account, and these of course might well change during the evaluation process and are likely to go on changing after the evaluation has 'ended'. The project is therefore a socio-political, collaborative, learning process.

Guba and Lincoln (1987) have pointed out that in FGE the evaluator has a different role from that traditionally held of evaluators in earlier generations in which evaluators were technicians, describers and judges. In FGE, the evaluator needs to:

- appreciate diversity;
- respect the rights of individuals to hold different values;
- welcome the opportunity to air and clarify various differences;
- be honest, courteous and above suspicion (to be trusted);
- be technically competent not only in relation to technical skills but also in social and political skills;
- have a high tolerance for ambiguity and a high frustration threshold;
- be sufficiently aloof to avoid charges of undue influence by particular stakeholders;
- be prepared to be personally changed by the evaluative process: to be willing to change does not imply a loss of objectivity but a gain in fairness.

As with all approaches to evaluation FGE does, of course, have limitations and inherent problems. Guba and Lincoln (1987) acknowledge that among these is a perceived lack of legitimisation. It is an approach that emphasises qualitative research methods and is likely to be treated with considerable scepticism by those who come from a more traditional and positivist background. Furthermore, FGE's collaborative approach requires those with power to share it with others: this is not easy to bring about and to sustain.

Guba and Lincoln do not regard FGE as a competitor of or replacement for earlier forms of evaluation. Instead, they see it as subsuming them while moving to a higher level of sophistication and utility. The approach has been further developed by others. For example, Laughlin and Broadbent (1996) espouse Caulley's 'fifth generation' approach (1993) which gives greater emphasis to encouraging the staff who run the programme being evaluated to have an influence in the evaluation process.

The key concepts embedded in FGE have been explored by Stake (2004) and by Abma (2006), the latter in the context of evaluating policies and services relating to the rehabilitation of psychiatric patients and to injury prevention programmes. She argues that the evaluation process, if it is to be sensitive to the needs of stakeholders, ought to be responsive not only to their needs but also to the commonly unequal power relations between the stakeholders. It is important to recognise the plurality of interests and values involved and to foster genuine dialogue between all interested parties. What often makes this task difficult is the very asymmetry of power relations and the 'subtle mechanisms of exclusion' (Abma, 2006, p 32); for example, 'those who feel vulnerable or superior may not want to join a genuine dialogue' (p 32). The problematic paradox is that dialogue is often most needed in situations in which it is most difficult to achieve. Resolving this dilemma requires a high degree of political skill in the evaluator and a high level of trust between the evaluator on the one hand and both powerful and less powerful stakeholders on the other. This is because 'silenced voices' are 'often hard to find; they want to remain anonymous or they fear sanctions' (Abma, 2006, p 39). However, Palfrey and Thomas (1999) would err on the side of evaluators being alive to the reality of political motives for commissioning evaluations, rather than the evaluators themselves adopting any particular ideological stance in planning and carrying out evaluations.

The job of evaluators is to examine policies that are value laden and that 'have unequal consequences for those whose interests are at stake' (Abma, 2006, p 42). As the present authors have argued elsewhere, 'evaluation is inherently a political activity as well as a technical one' (Thomas and Palfrey, 1996, p 140). Politics is inevitably a part of our work as evaluators. As Abma puts it, rather than hiding behind the claim of being scientifically neutral we need to 'be open and explicit about the politics, values and normative side of our practice' (2006, p 42).

The sharing of power in evaluation processes is not easy. It is much easier for the evaluation 'experts' to take and keep control. But as Guba and Lincoln argue:

> Fourth generation evaluation mandates that the evaluator move from the role of controller to that of collaborator. The evaluator must share control, however much that appears to threaten the 'technical adequacy' of the evaluation. That is, the evaluator must solicit and honour stakeholder inputs not only about the *substance* of constructions but also with respect to the methodology of the evaluation itself. (1989, p 260)

It is unclear how tolerant commissioners of evaluation work are likely to be to FGE with its emphasis on constructed realities, emergent data and tentative conclusions. Commissioners commonly expect clear results and specific recommendations. Thus in the real world, the work of evaluators can be informed by FGE thinking but compromises will probably need to be made unless the evaluators are able to persuade the commissioners that the FGE journey is worthwhile.

Pluralistic evaluation

The need to recognise that stakeholders will usually bring competing perspectives to evaluation processes is also emphasised by Smith and Cantley (1985) who have used a model of '*pluralistic evaluation*' (PE) in assessing a psycho-geriatric hospital. They developed a persuasive argument about the limitations of the more traditional approaches to evaluation – for example an emphasis on positivist/objective perspectives, the rational model and the 'ideal' of experimentalist approaches – and outlined the main features of their preferred approach as follows (pp 172–3):

- The need to have regard to the importance of 'varied group interests' and power bases, for example professionals, planners, administrators, relatives and patients.
- The need to identify the major constituent groups to the policy initiative and, throughout the research, to compare their respective perspectives and strategies.
- The need to collect data on the groups' interpretations and perceptions of 'success' in service provision and assign to that data a central place in the evaluative analysis.
- The need to document the different groups' strategies as they strive to implement their own perspectives in their own interests.

- The need to assess the extent to which success or failure is achieved on each of the several criteria employed within the agency and in terms of the several meanings assigned to those criteria.
- The need to avoid 'method-bound' and 'interest-bound' single evaluation methods. It is necessary to make constant use of as many different kinds of data as possible to ensure, as far as possible, that the research reflects the full range of interests, ideologies, interpretations and achievements abroad within the agency.

PE inherently looks at a policy or service from different points of view: it does not rely on just one data collection method to collect one kind of data from one group of sources or informants. On the face of it, therefore, PE resembles the social science research notion of 'triangulation'. However, conceptually there is an important difference between triangulation and PE. The former assumes that there is a 'correct' answer or measurement which can be discovered by a process of cross-checking, as when surveyors or navigators seek a 'correct' measurement or bearing. In PE no assumption is made about a 'correct' measurement: rather, the task is to find out about a variety of measures from different perspectives: a complicated or 'rich' picture of the policy or service being evaluated then emerges.

As Smith and Cantley (1985) point out, one of the problems with pluralistic evaluation is that it is unlikely that equal weight will be given to the various stakeholders' views. Indeed there is no particular reason to suppose that such equality would in any case be necessarily appropriate. It is unlikely that an evaluator will give equal weight to all the stakeholders. Indeed it is not clear how evaluators would know how to do this. Whatever weighting is given, this is a possible source of bias in an evaluation and some views are likely to prevail over others. Again we are in the field of organisational and community politics. One way to guard against some powerful parties having an undue influence is for the evaluator to be explicit and transparent about how people's views have been taken into account. It will then, at least potentially, reveal the weightings and allow people to contest and challenge the way in which the evaluation has been carried out. This is an important issue and one which needs to be aired with the commissioners of an evaluation prior to the evaluation work itself. The commissioners need to be aware that a stakeholder consensus on the evaluation findings are unlikely to emerge and that conflicting views are to be expected. Evaluators can help by looking for links between the various stakeholder views and the original aims of the service being evaluated. This could help commissioners to decide how to weight the conflicting views.

One of the contexts in which both FGE and PE are particularly useful is when an evaluator is faced with a great amount of data which seems to have been collected from a narrow range of sources, using a narrow range of methods, such as PIs. Bringing ideas from FGE and PE to bear on the data can reveal what the indicators might be concealing. As noted in Chapter Two, PIs are commonly best seen as 'tin openers' (Carter et al, 1992): they raise questions about the meaning and significance of the data. Evaluators need to be responsive to the views and perspectives of a wide range of stakeholders, and they need to unearth these views in order to draw tentative conclusions from the raw PIs. Evaluation work informed by this multi-pronged pluralistic nature was undertaken for many years by the Audit Commission in relation to a wide range of local authority services.

Participatory evaluation

The work of Guba and Lincoln (1987) and of Smith and Cantley (1985) points to the need for the views of all interested parties to be taken into account in evaluations. In order to reduce the chances of undue bias dominating, interested parties should be encouraged to participate in evaluations. As Plottu and Plottu (2009) point out, the notion of *participatory evaluation* entails an awareness of the importance of representing multiple perspectives. The implementation of active participation by major stakeholders is supposed, according to Plottu and Plottu, to offer the following advantages in evaluation:

- a greater validity of the evaluation by taking account of various points of view and increased credibility;
- a greater utilisation of the results of an evaluation; the more that stakeholders are involved in an evaluation the more likely they are to accept and use the results;
- a collaborative public engagement which facilitates the collective identification of conflict and differences of opinion;
- a contribution to participatory and discursive democracy; this can reduce feelings of apathy, isolation and powerlessness in traditionally less powerful groups and helps with public debate; and
- a process of empowerment: a commitment to shifting more power to under-privileged groups.

However, to succeed in securing the necessary participation by stakeholders there are a number of preconditions (Plottu and Plottu, 2009). Among these is the need to inform, motivate and train participants, especially the interest groups with few resources. It is important to recognise that 'informing' is not enough. The professional evaluator needs to engage opinion leaders and to plan, and ensure the delivery of, training related to what evaluation can and cannot achieve.

One of the potential pitfalls of participatory evaluation is that attempts to encourage participation in the interests of greater democracy might make the task of evaluation more difficult to undertake in a relatively detached way. In this way evaluation and advocacy might become too confused. There is also the possibility that as participatory democracy increases (for example giving the parents of school children more of a say in the way in which a school's services are planned and evaluated), the status of representative democracy might be reduced (as when members of a local education authority see their powers diminish). Participatory evaluation can also be uncomfortable for professional evaluators, who may feel that their autonomy is being reduced. In such situations evaluators need to find ways of adapting to the legitimate involvement of those whose interests might be affected by policy evaluation. This can only be done through a process of genuine engagement and respect between the professional evaluators and those who have legitimate claims to participate.

Achieving all this is a serious challenge for evaluators, but success will increase the chances of meaningful involvement of key stakeholders.

Realistic evaluation

Another important contribution is the approach developed by Pawson and Tilley (1997). The emphasis in their *realistic evaluation* is very different from those addressed above. They argue that evaluations should seek to explain how and why public policies work. It is important, they argue, to reveal the details of the policy-making process and establish an understanding of the ways in which aspects of a policy, programme or service work for some people in some situations. This is a more fine-grained question than simply asking 'Does it work?'. They summarise their approach by the following equation:

Context + mechanism = outcome.

By 'context' Pawson and Tilley mean 'the spatial and institutional locations of social situations together ... with the norms, values and interrelationships found in them' (1997, p 216). 'Mechanisms' refer to 'what it is about a programme which makes it work' (p 66) and when they talk about 'outcomes' they wish to include unwanted and unintended, as well as intended, consequences.

Instead of understanding programmes as undifferentiated wholes, Pawson and Tilley want to address the question for whom (for example, which sub-groups, if any) and in what circumstances do aspects of a programme work, how and why? In so doing the evaluator is therefore attempting to generate a *theory* about the 'why' and 'how' of a programme's effectiveness. The importance of theory-driven evaluation was articulated earlier by Chen and Rossi (1983), who argued that such evaluations were likely to be more useful than method-based approaches. The theory-driven approach does not limit itself to the intended consequences (that is, effectiveness). It also addresses *unintended* consequences. From the theory generated as part of the evaluation it is important, as far as possible, to learn about how and why programmes fail. This can help in the subsequent process of policy improvement. Further discussion of theory-based evaluation is offered in Chapter Seven.

The usefulness of realistic evaluation was tested by Ho in her evaluation of regeneration programmes (1999). The problems which the programmes sought to address involved adverse job opportunities and low income levels, low educational attainment and poor access to training, deteriorating housing conditions and physical environment, and poor quality of life. The programmes which were put into place to tackle these problems were evaluated on the basis of value for money and in terms of the programmes' outputs. No theories were developed which explained how and why aspects of the programmes succeeded or failed for particular groups in the local contexts. Ho argues that '(B)ecause of the lack of refined programme theories, the government was perpetuating some of the practices in regeneration without the sure knowledge that they would work' (p 426). Ho sees Pawson and Tilley's approach as a potential way of overcoming these shortcomings in programme evaluation.

Pawson (2006) has taken the realist perspective further by spelling out explicitly how it can be used in developing explanations of 'what works for whom in what circumstances and in what respects' (p 74). He argues that theories need to be built up incrementally from preliminary hypotheses and to be tested by a series of data sets. When there are contradictions between different studies it might be possible 'to reconcile them by unearthing contextual or implementation differences in the original programmes and showing how these led to opposing outcomes' (pp 74–5). Pawson is at pains to emphasise that his approach is 'about sifting and sorting theories and coming to a provisional preference for a particular explanation' (p 182). Evidence and theory are systematically synthesised as a means towards refined and improved theories.

As far as choosing methods of collecting and analysing data are concerned, Pawson and Tilley's approach is consistent with that developed by Smith and Cantley (1985): pluralism. A variety of appropriate methods is what is required.

There are a number of complex issues which the realistic evaluator has to face (Ho, 1999). For example, there might well be different interpretations of the context: mechanisms: outcome (CMO) configurations between different evaluators. There are often multiple objectives and multiple programmes, especially in relation to 'wicked issues' (Clarke and Stewart, 1997), and the outcomes of one programme might affect other programmes. In services delivered by several agencies attempting to work in partnership, the partners will sometimes have different interests and priorities.

Another real-world problem is that those who commission an evaluation (for example politicians and/or public sector managers) are less likely to be interested or 'have time for' the task of 'theory building' even though such an orientation might be sacrosanct to professional evaluators, especially if they are based within a university. Public sector managers might well impose unwelcome time pressures on evaluators, especially if they are building theories and arguments which some managers might see as challenging their authority. The time pressures might be further exacerbated if there are disagreements between stakeholders about the validity of competing explanations and theories about the success or otherwise of the services in question.

Despite the various complexities, we believe that Pawson and Tilley's theory-driven approach is an important contribution to the field.

Evidence-based evaluation

Earlier in this chapter, some of the issues and problems of acquiring and interpreting valid evidence about policies and services were discussed. In recent years there have been increasing expectations that public services should be *'evidence based'*, for example in relation to healthcare professions (Cochrane, 1972). The idea is that if managers and policy makers make effective use of evidence from research and evaluation, then decision making is likely to be better (Walshe, 2006). Decisions are often made apparently without due regard for suitable evidence. For example, 'research suggests that ... mergers rarely achieve their explicit objectives, that there are often as many diseconomies as economies of scale and that after merger it takes years for the new organisation to become properly integrated and begin to realise any of the potential advantages of its scale' (Walshe, 2006, p 480). So why do managers and policy makers continue to opt for mergers? Sometimes, according to Walshe, it is a combination of not knowing about the evidence, not understanding or trusting it, and other factors such as ideology, fashion, and political convenience tending to predominate in the decision-making process.

> Health policy and management have been on the front line of the developing movement. Clinicians challenged to justify the adoption of a new surgical technique or new pharmaceutical have often responded by arguing that the same evidentiary standard should be applied to management decisions – like proposals to change or reconfigure services, to introduce new organisational structures, or to change payment of incentive systems. It is a difficult argument to resist. (Walshe, 2006, p 481)

But the two arenas have very different cultures (for example, science and empiricism vs experiential learning). In medicine the results of decisions are relatively clear, but in management the results of decisions and the causal relationship between decision and subsequent events is often very hard to determine (Walshe, 2006). While a huge investment has been made in organising the clinical evidence base (for example the Cochrane Collaboration) 'the literature on management and policy issues remains fragmented, heterogeneous, distributed and difficult to access' (Walshe, 2006, p 487). It has been suggested that management decisions are sometimes made on the basis of 'fads and fashions' rather than being based on valid and reliable evidence (Walshe and Rundall, 2001, p 437).

To what extent can we safely trust, and make use of, the findings of policy research? Not all research, even when published in high quality journals, produce findings that are clear or unambiguous. There will be considerable variations in context (geographical, political, social, etc); just because something works in one situation does not mean that it will necessarily work in the same way in a different situation. Reliable universal prescriptions about how policy makers should proceed are unlikely to be available. Thus there are a number of obstacles to using the 'evidence-based approaches' to all management and public policy programmes. The approaches cannot be simply transposed from, for example, medical issues to management problems. This problem has been examined by Dobrow et al (2004) and Nutley et al (2003, 2007), who have emphasised the need to take careful account of the context in which evidence-based decisions are made and the ways in which evidence is utilised. But despite the complexities (see also Sanderson, 2004), the pressure to base decisions on 'good evidence' is unlikely to disappear in the foreseeable future.

Power issues

Another framework for considering evaluation issues is that provided by the literature on the politics of evaluation referred to in Chapter Two. A key concept in this is power, and a number of theories concerning power have been usefully summarised and critiqued elsewhere (Hill, 2005).

When policies and/or services are being evaluated, a range of questions arise. For example, who will do the evaluation and how will they do the evaluation? Who decides on such questions? What criteria are to be used and how are they to be weighted? What information will be collected and how, and how will the information be analysed and by whom? Who will control the extent to which (and the ways in which) any suggested improvements will be implemented? With all these questions there are both descriptive and prescriptive dimensions.

To what extent, and in what ways, will each group of stakeholders have a say in addressing all of these questions? What about those who pay for the services and the intended beneficiaries (clients, users, etc), the front line professionals, the managers and the politicians? There are likely to be variations in all these dimensions just as there are significant differences between various evaluative approaches.

As Palumbo argues (1987), evaluations are inherently and unavoidably political, and evaluators need 'to recognize the existence of multiple decision makers and interests and to incorporate them into the evaluation' (p 19). It could be argued that evaluations should be neutral and 'objective', for example by using triangulation to check the 'accuracy' of the findings. On the other hand it could be argued that, while attempts to achieve an appropriate degree of 'objectivity' are to be applauded, as we have argued earlier, absolute objectivity is impossible and evaluators need to be aware of the biases and perspectives on which their efforts are based.

Being politically aware would require the evaluator not only to judge whether a policy's objectives are being achieved, but also to judge the appropriateness of the objectives themselves (Palumbo, 1987, p 30). In this sense evaluations cannot be value-free.

There are at least three main ways in which political considerations intrude into evaluations, 'and the evaluator who fails to recognize their presence is in for a series of shocks and frustrations' (Weiss, 1987, pp 47–8):

- The policies and programs with which evaluation deals are the creatures of political decisions.
- The reports of evaluations are fed into the political arena; the evaluative evidence has to compete for attention with other factors that carry weight in the political process.
- Evaluation itself has a political stance (for example, deciding how the evaluations are to be carried out and in relation to decisions about which services to evaluate).

For several decades there have been calls for helping the public (defined broadly or more narrowly in relation to a particular service) to be more involved in the public policy processes (for example in shaping the services). Knox and McAlister (1995) have also analysed the issues involved in incorporating the views of service users when evaluating the services in question. They point out that 'there is growing recognition that obtaining feedback from users is a fundamental and integral part of measuring effectiveness and, without such a perspective, policy evaluation will have limited legitimacy' (pp 413–14). However, they go on to suggest that 'it should be recognized that users of public services are but one (albeit important) member in a multiple constituency of stakeholders with a legitimate perspective on provision, but not the only one' (p 414).

One of the problems of discovering users' views has been outlined by Rossi and Freeman as follows (1993, p 424): 'In many cases, beneficiaries may have the strongest stake in an evaluation's outcome, yet they are often the least prepared to make their voices heard. Target beneficiaries tend to be unorganized, and scattered in space; often they are reluctant even to identify themselves.'

Who is the user? As well as direct recipients of services, there are both potential and future users with various degrees of interest in the service. Knox and McAlister (1995) argue that 'uncritical, undiscriminating acceptance of users' wishes may ignore the interest of potential or future users' (p 418). There are also relatives, many of whom are carers (for example in relation to services for older people). Another problem about users' views is that they might reflect low expectations because, from experience, they have received a low level of service. Or they might have unreasonable expectations because they are not aware of the costs of services. In addition, what users *want* might be very different from their *needs* as defined by professionals.

At what level should users' views be sought in evaluating a service – at the strategic level (for example in relation to long-term planning) or the operational level? And what level of resources (money, time and methodological expertise) should be devoted to seeking users' views? But despite all these complexities and problems, the views of those who use the service are an important element in service evaluations.

A different aspect of the relationships between power issues and evaluation has been emphasised by Karlsson (1996), who examines the difficulties that groups who claim they have been unfairly treated face and the issue of how decisions should be made concerning what should be evaluated. Karlsson's concerns include the ways in which powerful groups may threaten the independence of evaluators and how they may disseminate or use evaluation reports selectively. His concern is to make evaluations more democratic and more fair. He believes that the use of critical dialogues between stakeholder groups can move us in that direction.

Among others who have analysed the issues of power relationships are Palfrey and Thomas (1999), who, while sympathising with the position of less powerful groups, warn against an 'evaluator' crudely taking sides within a political arena. 'Evaluation takes place within a political context but it would be arrogant of those carrying out the evaluation to plead their own cause as primary amongst a diversity of stakeholders' (p 69). Taylor and Balloch (eds) (2005) have also pointed to the need for a more critical perspective on the politics of evaluation. Easterby-Smith (2004) and Clarke and Dawson (1999) have also contributed to this debate.

The questions of who undertakes, or who commissions, an evaluation are political in the sense that not everyone will have an equal amount of power, and evaluators (or commissioners) might be able to impose their approach to evaluation on less powerful stakeholders. So who should the evaluators be? For example, should they be insiders (for example, front line staff in the agency being evaluated, or their managers) or outsiders (for example, external inspectorates)? Some of the pros and cons of these options may be summarised as shown in Table 3.2.

A fuller account of the balance sheet between internal and external evaluation may be found in Clarke and Dawson (1999) and in Love (1991).

Table 3.2: Advantages and disadvantages of internal and external evaluators

	Advantages	Disadvantages
Insiders	• Detailed knowledge of the service being evaluated. • Familiarity with the agency's culture. • Likely to be committed to implementing any recommendations.	• Might have vested interests. • Unduly influenced by what managers say. • Less convinced of the need for evaluation.
Outsiders	• Introduction of a fresh perspective. • A more independent and critical/sceptical view. • Less likely to be intimidated by the agency's managers.	• Might be less aware of the complexities within the agency. • Less able to implement recommendations. • Insensitivity to agency's norms and relationships.

As Skinner (2004) has noted, issues of power can also create barriers to evaluation, especially the evaluation of change in public sector organisations. These barriers can prevent an evaluation from being undertaken or can act as inhibitors during an evaluation process where, for example, senior managers might have their minds made up about an initiative which they see as 'self-evidently' worthwhile. Senior managers in this situation might view a systematic evaluation as unnecessary, as a time-waster or as inconvenient. Often under pressure to innovate and manage changes their reluctance is understandable.

Those who have the power and authority to commission and have managerial oversight of formal evaluations have to address some key questions such as:

- What is it that will be evaluated, and what will not be?
- How will a service or policy be evaluated and by whom?
- What criteria will be used and how will they be weighted?
- Who will collect and analyse the data and how?
- To what extent and in what ways will the findings of the evaluation be implemented?

Those with most power are likely to have the greatest influence on how the questions are answered and they will therefore have a significant impact on the evaluation process. However, evaluators need to be sensitive to the nature of the political context and to think carefully about who it is that might be disenfranchised from the process.

Evaluative inquiries, action research and reflective practice

The final approach that we shall look at in this selective sample of evaluation frameworks is what some people refer to as *evaluative inquiry* (Preskill and Torres, 1999) or *action research* (Lewin, 1946; Hart and Bond, 1995). Preskill and Torres emphasise the importance of creating and maintaining a culture within work organisations in which organisational members are continually questioning and improving organisational practices. They argue that this needs to embody at least four distinguishing characteristics as follows.

- Evaluative inquiry needs to be 'integrated into the organisation's work processes and is performed by organisational members. It is not something that is handed over to external consultants ...' (Preskill and Torres, 1999, p 55).
- It needs to be ongoing, iterative and continuous; 'it is not episodic or event-driven as are many evaluations' (pp 55–6).
- It relies heavily on the democratic processes of asking questions and exploring individuals' values, beliefs, assumptions and knowledge through dialogue and reflection (p 56).
- It needs to become a part of the organisational culture so that evaluative inquiry 'becomes embedded in organisational practices' (p 56).

An approach closely related to evaluative inquiry is action research. The pioneer is widely regarded as the social psychologist Kurt Lewin (1946), but in recent years there have been many scholars who have further developed the approach. Examples include Carr and Kemmis (1986), Hart and Bond (1995) and Eden and Huxham (1996). Definitions of action research vary but it is commonly viewed as research into the impact of an intervention by staff members within an organisation. These sorts of definition are not particularly helpful because techniques such as randomised controlled trials could be included and this is certainly not the intention of most advocates of action research.

The fundamental aim of most models of action research is that such research should improve practice. It involves a planned intervention by the researcher into naturally occurring events. The intervention is then monitored and evaluated to determine the extent to which, and the ways in which, the action has produced anticipated consequences. The approach tends to emphasise the use of organisational members to evaluate their own practice in a reflexive, critical, democratic and arguably empowering way, and most of the data used is likely to be qualitative in nature. Out of the data should emerge theories about why and how particular interventions 'worked' or did not work. Such evaluation is an essential element of action research (Lewin, 1946, p 206).

Schon (1983) has argued that for the last couple of centuries a hegemony of positivism and technical rationality has dominated the world of research in the professions (for example, in science, technology, engineering and medicine). Problems in these worlds are relatively well defined: they are on the 'high ground'. On the low ground lie many important messy questions. Many of the problems examined through action research are in what Schon (1987) calls the 'swampy lowlands'. Here problems are ambiguous and confusing, and they defy technical solutions. The problems, he argues, are often more amenable to 'reflective practice' than to more traditional forms of evaluation. On the high ground the problems are relatively clear. The problem is that many of our most important problems are in the swamp!

> The problems of real world practice do not present themselves to practitioners as well-formed structures. Indeed they tend not to present themselves as problems at all but as messy, indeterminate situations. Civil engineers, for example, know how to build roads suited to the conditions of particular sites and specifications. They draw on their knowledge of soil conditions, materials, and construction technologies to define grades, surfaces and dimensions. When they must decide *what* road to build, however, or whether to build at all, their problem is not solvable by the application of technical knowledge, not even by the sophisticated techniques of decision theory. They face a complex and ill-defined mélange of topographical, financial, economic, environmental and political factors. (Schon, 1987, p 4)

Such problems are similar to what some (such as Clarke and Stewart, 1997) have called 'wicked issues': problems which are messy, intractable, multifaceted, persistent and not amenable to single solutions; for example, urban regeneration, social exclusion, crime and community safety, sustainable development and environmental issues. These issues tend not to fall into the territory of any one department or organisation – or even one *level* of government. There is an increasing need for integration (or 'joined-upness') both horizontally (for example between various local agencies) and vertically (for example between agencies at different 'levels of government'). Wicked issues require long-term actions, and performance is difficult to evaluate, for example in relation to causal links.

Evaluative inquiries and action research approaches to evaluation are particularly suitable for situations where there is a good deal of organisational complexity and uncertainty. Often the planning and implementation of organisational changes are ill-defined emergent phenomena where the rigours of positivist measurements are unlikely to be helpful.

The above frameworks are, we repeat, a highly selective group of approaches and others could easily have been included. We have not, for example, explicitly included the various academic disciplines which are represented in the evaluation literature. The approaches draw on political science, economics, sociology and psychology, as noted in Chapter Two. There are also many other ways to focus on evaluation: Patton has listed a hundred of them (1987, pp 198–205) and adds that 'I doubt *not* that there are over a thousand ways of thinking about and doing program evaluations' (p 206).

Concluding comment

So what lessons can we draw from this brief survey of evaluation frameworks? Guba and Lincoln (1987) highlight the need to be responsive: responsive to the perceptions and values of stakeholders, to the nature of the changing service being evaluated and to the context within which the service is being delivered.

Smith and Cantley (1985) show that it is unwise to rely on one kind of data, collected from one source, using one data collection method. It is necessary to escape the 'method-bound' and 'interest-bound' approach of some traditional research methods, and use a richer pluralistic (and therefore more complex) framework.

Pawson and Tilley (1997) instruct evaluators to go further than evaluations have normally done ('has the service worked?') and seek to build explanations (theories) about how and why services work, for whom and in what circumstances. However, we need to recognise that when seeking such explanations it is more difficult to establish the causal links when dealing with policy and management issues with the complication of complex and changing contexts than, for example, when looking at the effects of specific drugs, where randomised controlled trials have become the established evaluation tool. Evidence-based policy is a laudable aim but one that is difficult to formulate in a useful and convincing way.

It is important to recognise and remember the inherently political nature of evaluation, as there will commonly be conflicting views as to evaluation methods and evaluation criteria and their weightings. The issue of evaluative criteria will be addressed in Chapter Four.

Finally, from the worlds of action research and Schon's 'swampy lowlands' we learn that policies to be evaluated are often ill defined and they might require non-traditional approaches to evaluate them.

References

Abma, T. (2006) 'The practice and politics of responsive evaluation', *American Journal of Evaluation*, vol 27, no 31, pp 30-43.

Carr, W. and Kemmis, S. (1986) *Becoming critical: Education, knowledge and action research*, Lewes: Falmer Press.

Carter, N., Klein, R. and Day, P. (1992) *How organisations measure success: The use of performance indicators in government*, London: Routledge.

Caulley, D. (1993) 'Overview of approaches to program evaluation: the five generations', in N. Denzin and Y. Lincoln (eds) (1994) *Handbook of qualitative research*, London: Sage.

Chen, H. and Rossi, P. (1983) 'Evaluation with sense: the theory-driven approach', *Evaluation Review*, vol 7, pp 283-302.

Clarke, A. and Dawson, R. (1999) *Evaluation research: An introduction to principles, methods and practice*, London: Sage.

Clarke, M. and Stewart, J. (1997) *Handling the wicked issues: A challenge for government*, Birmingham: INLOGOV.

Cochrane, A. (1972) *Effectiveness and efficiency: Random reflections on health services*, London: Nuffield Provincial Hospitals Trust.

Dobrow, M., Goel, V. and Upshur, R. (2004) 'Evidence-based health policy: context and utilisation', *Social Science and Medicine*, vol 58, pp 207-17.

Easterby-Smith, M. (2004) *Evaluating management development, training and education*, Aldershot: Gower.

Eden, C. and Huxham, C. (1996) 'Action research for the study of organisations', in S. Clegg and W. Nord (eds) *Handbook of organisational studies*, Beverly Hills, CA: Sage.

Glaser, B. and Strauss, A. (1967) *The discovery of grounded theory*, NJ: Aldine.

Government Chief Social Researcher's Office (2003) *Trying it out: The role of 'pilots' in policy making*, London: Cabinet Office.

Guba, E. and Lincoln, Y. (1987) 'The countenances of fourth-generation evaluation: description, judgment and negotiation', in D. Palumbo (ed) *The politics of program evaluation*, IL: Sage.

Guba, E. and Lincoln,Y. (1989) *Fourth generation evaluation*, Newbury Park, CA; Sage.

Hart, E. and Bond, M. (1995) *Action research for health and social care: A guide to practice*, Milton Keynes: Open University.

Hill, M. (2005) *The public policy process*, Harlow: Pearson.

Ho, S. (1999) 'Evaluating urban regeneration programmes in Britain: exploring the potential of the realist approach', *Evaluation*, vol 5, no 4, pp 422-38.

Jones, S. (1985) 'The analysis of depth interviews', in R. Walker (ed) *Applied qualitative research*, London: Gower, pp 56–70.

Karlsson, O. (1996) 'A critical dialogue in evaluation: how can the interaction between evaluation and politics be tackled?', *Evaluation*, vol 2, no 4, pp 405-16.

Knox, C. and McAlister, D. (1995) 'Policy evaluation: Incorporating Users' views', *Public Administration*, vol 73, pp 413-36.

Laughlin, R. and Broadbent, J. (1996) 'Redesigning fourth generation evaluation: an evaluation model for the public sector reforms in the UK?', *Evaluation*, vol 2, no 4, pp 431-51.

Lewin, K. (1946) 'Action research and minority problems', in G.W. Lewin (ed) (1948) *Resolving social conflicts,* NY: Harper.

Love, A. (1991) *Internal evaluation*, London: Sage.

Miles, M. and Huberman, A. (1993) *Qualitative data analysis: A sourcebook of new methods,* London: Sage.

Nutley, S., Walter, I. and Davies, H. (2003) 'From knowing to doing: a framework for understanding the evidence-into-practice agenda', *Evaluation*, vol 9, no 2, pp 125-48.

Nutley, S., Walter, I. and Davies, H. (2007) *Using evidence: How research can inform public services*, Bristol: The Policy Press.

Palfrey, C. and Thomas, P. (1999) 'Politics and policy evaluation', *Public Policy and Administration*, vol 14, no 4, pp 58-70.

Palumbo, D. (1987) 'Politics and evaluation', in D. Palumbo (ed) *The politics of program evaluation*, IL: Sage.

Patton, M. (1987) *Creative evaluation*, London: Sage.

Pawson, R. (2006) *Evidence-based policy: A realist perspective*, London: Sage.

Pawson, R. and Tilley, N. (1997) *Realistic evaluation*, London: Sage.

Petticrew, M., Cummins, S., Ferrell, C., Findlay, A., Higgins, C., Hoy, C., Kearns, A. and Sparks, L. (2005) 'Natural experiments: an underused tool for public health?', *Public Health*, vol 119, pp 751-57.

Phillips, C., Palfrey, C. and Thomas, P. (1994) *Evaluating health and social care*, London: Macmillan.

Plottu, B. and Plottu, E. (2009) 'Approaches to participation in evaluation: some conditions for implementation', *Evaluation*, vol 15, no 3, pp 343-59.

Preskill, H. and Torres, R. (1999) 'Building capacity for organisational inquiry through evaluative inquiry', *Evaluation*, vol 5, no 1, pp 42-60.

Roethlisberger, F. and Dickson, W. (1939) *Management and the worker,* Harvard, MA: Harvard University Press.

Rossi, P. and Freeman, H. (1993) *Evaluation: A systematic approach*, CA: Sage.

Runciman, W. (1983) *A treatise on social theory: The methodology of social theory*, Cambridge: Cambridge University Press.

Sanderson, I. (2004) 'Getting evidence into practice: perspectives on rationality', *Evaluation*, vol 10, no 3, pp 366-79.

Schon, D. (1983) *The reflective practitioner: How professionals think in action*, NY: Basic Books.

Schon, D. (1987) *Educating the reflective practitioner: Towards a new design for teaching and learning in the professions*, San Francisco, CA: Jossey-Bass.

Shaxson, L. (2005) 'Is your evidence robust enough? Questions for policy makers and practitioners', *Evidence and Policy* vol 1, no 1, pp 101-11.

Skinner, D. (2004) 'Primary and secondary barriers to the evaluation of change: evidence from two public sector organisations', *Evaluation*, vol 10, no 2, pp 135-54.

Smith, G. and Cantley, C. (1985) *Assessing health care: A study in organisational evaluation*, Milton Keynes: Open University.

Stake, R. (2004) *Standards-based and responsive evaluation*, CA: Sage.

Taylor, D. and Balloch, S. (eds) (2005) *The politics of evaluation: Participation and implementation*, Bristol: The Policy Press.

Thomas, P. and Palfrey, C. (1996) 'Evaluation: stakeholder-focused criteria', *Social Policy and Administration*, vol 30, no 2, pp 125-42.

Walker, R. (ed) (1985) *Applied qualitative research*, London: Gower.

Walshe, K. (2006) 'Research, evaluation and evidence-based management', in K. Walshe and J. Smith (eds) *Healthcare management*, Milton Keynes: Open University Press.

Walshe, K. and Rundall, T. (2001) 'Evidence-based management: from theory to practice in health care', *The Milbank Quarterly*, vol 79, no 3.

Weiss, C. (1987) 'Where politics and evaluation research meet', in D. Palumbo (ed) *The politics of program evaluation*, IL: Sage. (Originally a paper presented to the American Psychological Association in 1973.)

FOUR

Selecting evaluation criteria

When we say that a policy is working well (or badly) or that a service is getting better (or worse) what do we mean? Do we mean that some or all members of the public think that it is so? Or that managers or politicians think so? Or that 'performance indicators' suggest that it is so? The words 'well', 'badly', 'better' and 'worse' are, to say the least, ambiguous.

For evaluations to be useful we need to reduce such ambiguities as far as possible and to be explicit about what we mean. This is where the notion of a criterion comes in. A criterion is a principle or standard by which something may be judged or decided and derives from the Greek for a 'means for judging' (*New Oxford Dictionary of English*). In evaluating a policy or service it is important to be explicit about the criterion or criteria being used. Otherwise a claim that, for example, a service is 'good' or 'getting better' would be rather meaningless. Would it be getting better in relation to efficiency, effectiveness, equity, reducing costs, or what?

There are a number of criteria which can be used in making such judgements. The criteria are not mutually exclusive, and sometimes the boundaries between them might be blurred; sometimes the criteria might overlap; for example, the 'acceptability' of a service might depend on its 'responsiveness' to users' needs and wishes. We shall examine a range of criteria commonly used in evaluations (in no particular order) and set out what each is usually taken to mean. We also critically comment on the limitations of each criterion, demonstrating that in real-world evaluations judgements will always be problematic and contestable.

It is important to recognise that criteria are not always set or 'pre-ordained'. Sometimes they 'emerge from the specific social contexts of various stakeholders' (Abma, 1997, p 35). For example, the 'acceptability' of a spending programme, as far as the electorate is concerned, is clearly a largely political question.

Common evaluation criteria

Responsiveness

'Responsiveness' often refers to the speed and accuracy with which a service provider reacts to a request for action or for information. It can also refer to the demeanour and social interactive skills of the person delivering the service, and in this sense adds a dimension of 'quality' to the criterion of 'accessibility' (*q.v.*). Speed can, for example, refer to the waiting time before seeing a hospital consultant or the time taken to receive treatment in an Accident and Emergency department, or to the promptness with which a local authority town planning department responds to a request for planning consent.

In the perfectly responsive organisation (which does not exist in the real world), service users are likely to be delighted with the speed, friendliness, empathy and accuracy of all the providers all of the time.

As far as speed is concerned we would add a note of caution. An organisation might require its staff to answer the phone within so many rings to ensure that staff are 'responding' rapidly; but this might be followed by unhelpful, unfriendly or unsympathetic comments from the staff member. A speedy response is not always enough to qualify the response as a 'good' one. For example, in a care home, if a sick elderly resident calls for assistance when feeling distressed and confused but the carer responding to the alarm call does not have a high degree of communications skills or empathy, then the resident is unlikely to feel that the care has been responsive to his or her needs in any meaningful way. Responsiveness thus has many dimensions and the ticking of boxes relating to the *speed* of response is only one, albeit sometimes critical, element.

Equity/justice/fairness

For present purposes, these three concepts (equity, justice and fairness) will be taken to be synonymous. Many people will agree that they are in favour of equity but they are rarely in agreement about what exactly it means. It is commonly defined as meeting equal needs equally (and correspondingly treating unequal needs unequally). So, for example, in a just world people with equal needs would receive equal services. And people with unequal needs would receive unequal services. Thus an individual with a significant disability would, other things being equal, receive more help than someone with no disability.

It can be helpful to distinguish between 'procedural justice' and 'substantive justice'. For example, while our judicial system does not always get things right, it seeks to follow due process (for example, ensuring that those accused of a crime receive a fair trial) with the intention that just verdicts will follow.

Note that although there are many divergent views about what the terms mean, they are in practice commonly used; for example 'it's not fair'; 'unfair dismissal'; 'a fair day's work'. Political parties of all hues claim that their policies will bring about a fairer society (unless party leaders assert that there is no such thing as society). The difficulty is that in practice there will almost always be substantial disagreement about what counts as 'fair'.

Mooney (2009) has argued that it is important to view barriers (to achieving equity) and the height of barriers in terms of citizens' perceptions. Barriers need to be seen through the eyes of potential users of services. Such barriers can include the lack of information presented in an appropriate form, inconvenient geography, financial issues and lack of confidence. In these senses there are close links between problems of equity and problems of access (*q.v.*). In using equity as an evaluative criterion it is therefore necessary to examine the context in which potential service users are living in terms of educational levels, geography and financial constraints. Equity is also relevant to how finances are raised in order to provide public services. Are council taxes fairer than the community charges (poll tax) which they replaced? At central government level, is it fairer to rely more on direct or indirect taxes; income tax or value added taxes? These issues are important ones, but a detailed discussion of them is beyond the scope of this chapter.

We shall return to the closely related issue of ethics towards the end of the chapter.

Equality

Again, 'equality' is a term which is used in different ways; for example, does it mean equal outcomes? Or equality of utilisation? Equal opportunities? Equal access? Some people are better placed than others to take advantage of what might appear to be 'equal opportunities'. Over the years there have been numerous debates relating to inequalities; for example, geographical or social inequalities (or 'variations', 'diversities' or 'inconsistencies') in health states, treatments and outcomes.

The question of whether continuing inequalities should be regarded as a matter for serious concern is largely one of value judgements and politics. Given that complete equality is unattainable, and arguably not desirable, a useful way to think about inequalities is to ask about what *degree* of inequality is acceptable in various circumstances.

In local government boundaries between local authorities commonly run along the middle of a street, especially in large conurbations. It is not unknown for council officials from different authorities to specify requirements in relation, for example, to food hygiene or health and safety at work. Businesses on opposite sides of the boundary road could be forgiven for feeling aggrieved when different standards are being applied on the other side of the road. Or in the case of national (or international) chain stores, surprise may be expressed by business branches in different localities when they are expected to comply with the law in different ways. The businesses might well expect a degree of uniformity or equality to exist across different local authority areas.

Equality rarely comes top of the list of priorities for people when evaluations are being undertaken, but it is often used in conjunction with other criteria. One often hears, for example, of the need for 'equal access' to services. However, in our view equality will normally lose out to equity as a high priority criterion.

Effectiveness

This concerns the extent to which stated objectives have been achieved. To use effectiveness as a criterion, aims and/or objectives need to be made explicit. Without such explicitness it is impossible to say anything convincing about the extent to which they have been achieved. In such a situation no one can know whether the organisation (or any individual member of staff) has been effective.

Explicit objectives also help in the following ways. To begin with they help professionals and their managers to question and abandon inappropriate and/or outdated objectives. The act of making such objectives explicit makes it easier to challenge them. This can make an organisation more flexible than if things are merely taken for granted and where practices are therefore never questioned. Secondly, having explicit objectives can help when decisions about priorities and resource allocation must be made. Thirdly, explicit objectives can help in undertaking staff appraisals or individual performance reviews; staff can be judged on the basis of whether they are achieving objectives, rather than on whether their 'faces fit'. Fourthly, they can help with staff motivation. If staff do not have a clear idea of what it is they are expected to achieve they may become unfocused and demotivated. In addition, it is easier to feel a sense of achievement (and therefore possibly increased motivation) if clear objectives have been achieved. Fifthly, having explicit objectives can help with coordination. It can reduce the chances of an organisation pulling simultaneously in contradictory directions.

As far as possible and practicable, objectives need to be:

- *explicit:* they should be clearly documented;
- *specific:* they should not be general or vague; for example, 'to achieve a reduction in the infant mortality rate of *x*% in a defined locality by a specific date' is a more specific objective than 'to provide improvements in public health';
- *measurable*, if that is appropriate; it might not be possible satisfactorily to measure, in a quantitative way, all aspects of all services (for example, is it possible to measure all aspects of care for dying patients?); but where measurement is possible, then it can be very useful in preparing to evaluate the effectiveness of a service;
- *scheduled*: it should be clear by what date an objective is to be achieved; otherwise managers would never have to answer 'No' to the question 'Have you achieved the agreed objectives?'; they could simply say 'Not yet';
- *prioritised*: if possible, agreement should be arrived at about which are the most/least important objectives; this is particularly important when there are severe resource constraints on a service;
- *'owned'*: objectives should be seen to be attainable and preferably not imposed in a top-down way;
- *related to each other*: this can help an organisation to be clear about the strategic direction it is going in;
- *communicated* to those who need to know.

One of the reasons that effectiveness is an important criterion for evaluating a policy or a service is that it refers to the extent to which a service is achieving what it is intended to achieve. Or to put it another way: is the service in question having the intended 'effects'? The criterion is commonly used to address the issue of goals, objectives or targets. The principal question that is asked when evaluating effectiveness is 'To what extent and in what ways are the goals (or objectives or targets) being achieved?'.

The terms *goals*, *objectives* and *targets* all refer to some intended effect but they are often differentiated in terms of specificity. *Targets* are often seen as very specific and measurable; for example a local authority might ask 'Have we collected 99% of the council tax due by the end of the financial year?'.

Goals, on the other hand, usually refer to more general intentions; for example, 'to improve the health of a local population'. This is a laudable thing for which to aim but it is fairly vague. It is unclear what would count as improved health: perhaps a reduction in death rates, or better quality of health? And how would this be measured?

Objectives are commonly seen as a half-way house between goals and targets, more specific than goals but less specific than targets.

There are no rigid agreed definitions of goals, objectives and targets, and the three are sometimes used with a degree of interchangeability. One person's 'goals' are another person's 'targets'. There are also aims, purposes, mission statements and so on, again with little agreement on specific definitions. Sometimes the terms are used in a hierarchical relationship to each other. For example, at the highest level a *goal* might refer to improving the health of a local population and within this there might be some *objectives* such as providing hip replacements for everyone who needs them within six months of referral to a consultant. This objective might further be broken down into a number of *targets*, such as reducing waiting times to six months (by a particular date).

The more specific a goal (or objective or target) the easier it is to see what kind of data will need to be collected in order to evaluate the effectiveness of a service. But in evaluating the effectiveness of a service there might also be informal or unofficial goals to be considered. It is not uncommon for staff to have personal objectives or 'hidden agendas' which they hope will serve their own self-interests, and these 'political realities' need to be taken into account if effectiveness is to be evaluated thoroughly. If individual managers are achieving their individual goals relating to departmental growth but the organisation as a whole is failing to achieve its overall goals, one might conclude that the managers are effective at one level (that is, in relation to their informal goals) but ineffective at the organisation-wide level. This kind of conclusion should not be seen as a contradiction. It merely illustrates that multiple, and often conflicting, goals co-exist within organisations. Evaluators need to be clear about which goals they intend to use when evaluating effectiveness.

There can, of course, be 'goal-free' evaluations. This might occur when there are no explicit goals/objectives/targets. Here the evaluator seeks information about what is being achieved by the organisation in terms of benefits delivered for the organisation's clients and about the costs of doing so. Strictly speaking, such an evaluation is not assessing effectiveness but is using some other criterion such as efficiency.

One of the other problems about evaluating the effectiveness of a policy or service is that different stakeholders will often have different objectives and priorities (Karlsson, 1996; Thomas and Palfrey, 1996). The 'clients' (the intended beneficiaries of a service), the clients' families, the front-line staff or professionals, the managers, the politicians, the public at large, pressure groups and the mass media might all have different perspectives. Indeed even within each of these groups of stakeholders there will rarely be identical expectations. Against this background of multiple objectives, which objectives should be used in the evaluation of effectiveness?

One starting point is to look at the 'official' goals and objectives published in a corporate plan or service plan, but it is unlikely that all the stakeholders will agree that these are the most important objectives. Should we just accept the official line or should we also (or instead) look at the objectives of the other stakeholders? If the objectives of various stakeholders are to be taken into account, whose objectives should carry most weight?

There is no simple answer to such political questions. One approach is to be explicit about the objectives and priorities to be used in the evaluation so that people can see what position is being adopted. This might result in an evaluation that concludes something along the lines of 'If we evaluate against the clients' objectives then the service seems to fail in relation to at least some of the expectations, but in relation to the managers' priorities then we have to arrive at a different conclusion …'. One might therefore end up with apparently contradictory conclusions, but this is not necessarily a bad thing. It is often better to provide an evaluation that takes account of multiple perspectives rather than to restrict the evaluation to the objectives of one group with the vested interests that that might entail.

In the often uncomfortable real world, there are some serious limitations and difficulties in using effectiveness as an evaluative criterion. For example, goals and objectives are commonly stated in vague and ambiguous terms. To some extent this is a problem of terminology. When people talk about goals, aims, or mission statements there is often no expectation that these will be specific or measurable. The intention is rather to give the organisation strategic direction. When people talk about objectives or targets, these are usually more specific and, in a managerial sense at least, they are likely to be more useful for evaluating the performance of the organisations or their departments and individual members of staff.

The second problem with the use of effectiveness is that it is easy to fall into the trap of assuming that effective performance is the same as 'good' performance. If the goals and/or objectives being used to evaluate effectiveness are rather unchallenging, or if they are judged to be morally repugnant (as when health care professionals murder their patients – of which there have been several cases), then there has been 'effectiveness' in that the staff member achieved what he or she set out to achieve, but most people would take some convincing that this amounts to 'good' performance.

A third problem is that if, as is often recommended, objectives are focused on outputs or outcomes, then the use of 'effectiveness' as a criterion will mean that the costs of achieving the objectives are likely to be ignored. It is widely accepted that in evaluating a policy or service the question of resources should be taken into account. Those concerned with the public sector are expected to make good use of the public resources made available, and ignoring cost is not a realistic option. One of local government's 'successes' in some parts of the country, London being a good example, has been the significant reduction of smoke pollution. The Clean Air Act 1956 empowered local authorities to declare 'smoke control areas' in which, with specific exemptions, it has become a criminal offence to burn coal. The work entailed a great deal of time spent by environmental health department officials in visiting huge numbers of premises to arrange the replacement of coal burning appliances with those that burned smokeless fuels (certain authorised solid fuels, gas or oil) or that used electricity. The policy outcomes were successfully achieved (significant reduction in smoke pollution and resultant decrease in the incidence of respiratory diseases). However, this evaluation does not take account of the resources used in implementing the policy. Could the similar outcomes have been achieved by a simpler and cheaper policy option, for example the taxation of coal? Policy options are not that simple but the point serves to illustrate the problem of evaluating outputs and outcomes without regard for the inputs (resources).

Another problem is that work undertaken to achieve goals and objectives might well have unfortunate side-effects. For example the reduction of the time that patients spend in hospital is likely to transfer a cost from the hospital budget but may impose an unacceptable strain on others – such as community services or the patient's family or friends. Evaluators, we would argue, need to take the blinkers off and examine the system-wide effects of changes in policies and services, so that account can be taken of the side-effects.

The fifth problem is that of questionable causal links. Effectiveness is largely a question of identifying and assessing the extent to which a policy or service has had (or is leading to) intended effects. But often it is difficult to be sure that a particular policy has been the cause of what appears to be an 'outcome'. This is particularly the case with something which is influenced by a wide variety of factors. Health is a good example. Levels of morbidity and mortality are determined by genetic factors, environmental and economic factors, human behaviour patterns, diet and health care interventions. If an objective is to improve standards of health, and resources are put in place to employ more health care professionals, there could be a temptation a few years later to attribute any improved health to the increase in the number of medical and other staff. But the contribution of these increases could well be marginal in bringing about the apparent outcomes. Caution therefore needs to be exercised in concluding that policies have been 'effective'.

It is also worth noting that outcomes can be intended or unintended, and positive or negative. This is illustrated in Table 4.1.

Table 4.1: Possible outcomes of action

	Intended	Unintended
Positive	Freedom from pain following a hip replacement.	Reduced stress in the family of a patient whose life has been saved.
Negative	Patients murdered by a health care professional.	Iatrogenesis (for example, use of harmful drugs).

One way of classifying outcomes has been outlined by Helen Roberts (1991):

- Clinical studies (e.g. unplanned re-admissions, incidence and results of cases of MRSA infections)
- Health indices
  - Functional status (e.g. physical, mental, social)
  - Health perceptions (e.g. well-being, pain)
- Measures of disability and distress (e.g. Quality Adjusted Life Years; QALYs)
- Patient satisfaction
- Death (e.g. various kinds of mortality rates and ratios).

Another way of thinking about outcomes is that they can relate to individuals or groups in the populations. It might often be easier to attribute causality in the former (for example, the case of a hip replacement) than in the latter.

The task of evaluating organisational structures and processes can be particularly difficult in establishing causal links. Several attempts have been made to do this in relation to the NHS. For example, Sheaff (Department of Health, 2006) has analysed data collected from senior stakeholders in the NHS by interviews, telephone interviews and focus group work relating to the apparent impact and influence of organisational arrangements. The key messages from this work were as follows:

- Highly centralised organisations are not associated with optimal performance.
- Organisational change needs to be developed from within, not imposed from outside, since professional engagement and leadership are crucial.
- Frequent reforms have made the NHS unstable.
- Mergers often miss the point (they should not take place merely to achieve a particular organisational size).
- Occupational 'silos' hamper change and innovation.
- Publishing clinical performance information does not influence consumer choice.
- The government should be cautious about promoting for-profit hospitals.
- There is no 'one right size' for each kind of NHS body.

These conclusions are inevitably contestable but they represent a laudable attempt to tackle the intractable problem of interpreting causality in a complex area.

So it can be seen that although effectiveness is commonly judged to be an important criterion – a judgement with which we concur – there are a number of difficulties and limitations inherent in evaluating effectiveness in practice. Nevertheless, it remains a key criterion. Without it people cannot know whether what they are trying to achieve is in fact being achieved.

Efficiency

Efficiency is the ratio between benefits (outputs or outcomes) and costs/resources (inputs). Efficiency can be increased, for example, by:

- increasing the benefits while holding costs constant;
- reducing the costs while holding benefits constant;
- increasing both benefits and costs, but increasing the former more than the latter;

- reducing both benefits and costs, but reducing the former less than the latter;
- reducing costs while increasing benefits.

It is also important to examine the *distribution* of the costs and benefits; for example a reduction in state provision might require an increase in costs/effort/resources by others (such as informal carers). Thus what might appear to be an increase in efficiency might actually be a mere redistribution of the costs (from the state to families).

Well-known examples of efficiency studies are 'cost benefit analysis' and 'cost utility analysis', for example the use of QALYs in the context of health policy and services. But these approaches are not without their critics and one of the difficulties about using efficiency as a criterion in evaluation is the problem of quantification – of costs, and especially of benefits.

Another difficulty is that because efficiency is essentially a ratio (of benefits to costs), how can one decide when a particular ratio represents an acceptable level of efficiency? In the real world the ratio will need to be compared with something to make the ratio mean something useful. One possibility is to compare it with the corresponding ratio in previous years so that trends can be assessed over time: is the efficiency of the service increasing or decreasing? An alternative is to compare the ratio with that being achieved in comparable organisations.

In the world of politics the notion of efficiency is often misused. When people argue that a change in the way a service is delivered will make it more efficient, it seems they mean that the amount of money that the service will cost will be reduced. This is often asserted without any reference to the changes that might come about in the level or quality of service, and so people are talking about efficiency when they really mean economy. Aspects of economic evaluation will be discussed in greater detail in Chapter Five.

Economy

We have noted that efficiency refers to the ratio between outputs (goods and services provided) and inputs (resources used to produce and deliver the outputs), and that effectiveness commonly refers to outputs and/or outcomes. The third 'E' in this triumvirate of 'value for money' elements is economy, which focuses mainly on the input (resources) side. We find this the least useful criterion of the three if it is used alone. It is of course helpful to know what resources are being used but if it is not used in conjunction with its partner Es then it is of limited value in evaluation work.

It seems that when some politicians call for greater 'efficiency' in public services, they are actually calling for greater 'economy', that is, they wish to see a reduction in expenditure. As we have seen, efficiency is a ratio and it would be perfectly possible to have an improvement in economy with a simultaneous reduction in efficiency. If expenditure is reduced by x% and outputs or outcomes are reduced by more than x%, then efficiency will have worsened, not improved. Thus 'improvements' in economy do not necessarily lead to improvements in efficiency.

And if local authority (LA) A employs one environmental health officer (EHO) per 4,000 population and LA B employs one per 6,000 population, does it necessarily mean that B is performing more efficiently than A? It might mean that B has decided as a matter of policy to provide a lower level of service than A. In the case of social services, it might be that LA A employs one social worker per 1,000 population and LA B employs one per 1,500 population. Again, this does not necessarily mean that LA B is the more efficient; it might simply be that LA B has decided to behave more economically and offer a lower level of service than LA A.

We do not wish to suggest that economy is an unimportant criterion. A consideration of it can help public bodies in relation to good housekeeping, to identify and reduce unnecessary and wasteful expenditure. However, the examples illustrate the point that it is important for commissioners and evaluators to be clear about the distinction between efficiency, economy and policy decisions when considering level of service.

Accountability

At first sight, 'accountability' might seem a strange concept to include in a list of evaluation criteria. It is a criterion which focuses on organisational structure and processes rather than on inputs, outputs or outcomes but it can have a significant impact on these variables. If there are no clear lines and processes of accountability within an organisation, it is unlikely that the service it is providing will maintain effective and efficient services in the longer term. It is therefore a legitimate and useful issue to examine when evaluating a public sector organisation. Accountability is a particularly important issue in public sector management for, as Hudson points out (in Hill (ed), 1997, p 398), 'accountability is the link between bureaucracy and democracy'.

Elcock and Haywood (1980) have set out what they see as the four dimensions of accountability. They are:

- the location of accountability;
- the direction of accountability;
- the content of accountability; and
- the mechanisms of control.

In other words, *who* is accountable *to whom, for what* and *how*?

Location of accountability

Traditionally government ministers were held accountable for everything done by their departments. If things went seriously awry the minister was expected to resign. But in the 1970s this expectation was modified because it was thought unreasonable to expect ministers to be responsible for *all* errors made by civil servants. Furthermore, select committees have established the right to cross-examine civil servants as well as ministers. Accountability has thus become more 'shared'. It is therefore more difficult than it used to be to identify who is responsible or accountable for a particular decision or action.

Direction of accountability

The simplest answer to the question 'to whom are we accountable?' is commonly 'our line manager' or 'the body who has commissioned us'. But the question has become more complex over the years. For example, there is the question of professional status. One of the traits of a 'profession' is that its members expect a relatively high degree of autonomy in the way they plan and implement (and indeed evaluate) their work. Hospital consultants will often prefer to see themselves as being accountable to their peer group or to their patients (a form of 'consumerism'?) rather than to their 'line manager' or hospital chief executive.

A second complexity is the role of trades unions. Members of a profession (for example medics, nurses, social workers, environmental health officers) will sometimes find themselves in a situation where they are receiving conflicting instructions from their employer and their trades union, particularly in a situation where industrial action is being planned. Staff members are likely to feel a conflict of loyalty – to work or not to work. To whom is one mainly accountable?

And to whom is a local authority mainly accountable? To the local electorate? Or the council tax payers? The community at large? Central government? The courts? Service users? The local ombudsman? The mass media? Intended beneficiaries of services? Auditors and inspectorates? Or some combination of these depending on circumstances?

Sometimes, staff believe that they have a wider responsibility than to their direct 'managers'; for example, to what extent do civil servants have a wider responsibility to Parliament and the public if they suspect that a minister is misleading Parliament?

Content of accountability

Traditionally public sector managers were mainly held accountable for probity – which concerns uprightness, integrity and incorruptibility – and for not doing things which were *ultra vires* (that is, outside their legal powers). But as from the 1980s they have been increasingly held accountable for performance in terms of value for money; this is the world of efficiency, effectiveness, economy, centrally imposed targets, performance indicators, league tables and individual performance reviews. These changes have been seen as a part of the 'new public management' (NPM) (Ferlie et al, 1996; McLaughlin et al (eds), 2002) and have not always been welcomed by public sector managers. The measures have had the effect of concentrating the minds of managers, but not always on helpful targets.

Mechanisms of control

Control is the other side of the accountability coin (Peckham et al, 2005). If A is accountable to B, then it is supposed that B has some control over A. The control may be exercised through various mechanisms. An obvious mechanism is money. If B has control over a budget on which A is dependent, then A is likely to be cautious about ignoring guidance, requests or instructions from B.

A second kind of mechanism is democratic accountability. For example, it is one of the principles of democracy that, in theory at least, public sector managers are – directly or indirectly – controlled by voters. This kind of control may sometimes be assisted by reports from inspectorates and the mass media which can draw the electorate's attention to what the managers have been doing and not doing. There is also managerial accountability and control by way of performance review, fixed-term contracts and performance-related pay.

The law can also be an effective control mechanism. Professional staff are accountable to the public through the criminal law as in cases where professionals have been found guilty of assaulting their clients, through the civil law as when patients sue them for negligence, through contracts of employment and through professional conduct committees which can strike members of the profession off statutory registers.

Structures and processes of accountability are not commonly seen as criteria for evaluating public policies and services but we believe they are legitimate and useful yardsticks in evaluation work.

Accessibility

Accessibility is a commonly used criterion for evaluating public services, sometimes in conjunction with another criterion such as equality – equality of access often being seen as a desirable objective in relation to geography, so that some aspects of postcode lottery may be reduced. Examples of this kind of accessibility include distances that people live from the service in question, and these are sometimes measured in terms of journey times.

Another example is that of waiting times – the length of time that people have to wait for a service to be delivered, or for information to be given or for decisions to be made. In this sense the criterion comes close to being the same as 'responsiveness', which we referred to earlier. Other examples include physical access to buildings in relation to wheelchair access and signage in appropriate languages.

Some scholars measure 'use' of services as an indicator of degree of access (Mooney, 2009; Gulliford, 2009). It could be argued that if the potential to use a service exists, then access is present even when an individual makes the choice *not* to use a service (Gulliford, 2009). If one interprets the notion of access as 'freedom (or opportunity) to use' (Mooney, 2009, p 218) a service, then access can be further analysed into the elements of availability, affordability and acceptability (Mooney, 2009). But it is important to recognise that 'freedom to use' is different from use *per se*. For example, some citizens might not see themselves as suitable 'candidates' for a particular service; and services that require people to keep appointments may be more difficult for those with limited resources. Some people will have the resources to address their problems through private means, such as buying a house and moving to the catchment area of a 'good school'; others might struggle to access services because of poor public transport facilities, especially in rural areas.

Policies aimed at increasing access/permeability (Goddard, 2009) include:

- having waiting list targets; but research suggests that disadvantaged groups, such as the elderly, lower income groups and those from ethnic minorities, tend to be given lower priority by professionals when they are trying to improve waiting times; thus policies aimed at improving access might not reduce inequities;
- organisational re-design; for example NHS walk-in centres, NHS Direct, out-of hours primary care provision; but awareness of NHS Direct tends to be lower among lower income groups, and out-of-hours services often require travel at times when public transport is not available;
- targeting 'under-supply'; for example more resources to tackle the shortage of GPs in some parts of the country; but families who fail to benefit from the extra resources may have not defined themselves as in need despite the efforts of professionals; lower-income families tend to view their health in terms of events/crises as opposed to a process requiring maintenance/attention.

Despite the difficulties of defining and achieving accessibility, it remains an important declared aim in public services and it is therefore a useful criterion in evaluations.

Appropriateness

If a service is to be judged as 'appropriate' it should be relevant to the needs of intended beneficiaries. An important issue here is the way in which 'need' is defined because the way in which needs are assessed will often influence, or even determine, the shape of services to be provided. For example if the main need within the NHS is defined to be 'more hospital beds' and if that judgement is widely accepted, then the policy response might well be to plan the provision of more hospital beds. If however the need is defined as 'better health services' then the policy response is likely to be very different. Thus those with the ability – possibly because of their professional status and autonomy – to have their assessment of need 'accepted' in relation to a particular service are likely to be powerful players.

However, 'need' is a slippery concept. A useful taxonomy of need was developed by Bradshaw (1972) as follows.

Normative need is need as determined by a third party, normally a professional or 'expert'. It is the academic who tells students what they *need* to read, the social worker who assesses the *needs* of a family who have a variety of complex problems or the medical practitioner who advises patients on changes they need to make to their life styles.

Felt need is, in effect, the same as 'want'. It is a need that is perceived or felt by the potential beneficiary of a service. When this is then turned into a request for help it becomes *expressed need*. This does not always follow from a felt need because for one reason or another a 'needy' person will not necessarily ask for help.

Comparative need is the situation where one person (A) sees another (B) in similar circumstances (for example in relation to a specific disability) and sees that B is receiving help to cope with the disability. A might compare his or her plight with that of B and conclude that as help is being given to B it should also be given to himself/herself (A).

The four categories of need are not, of course, mutually exclusive and it will often be the case that two or more kinds of need are present at any one time for a particular individual or group. The difficulty is that if appropriateness (or relevance to need) is seen as a useful criterion for evaluating a service, who is to assess the degree and kind of need in the case of the individual or group? In the public sector normative need is commonly to the fore. It is an essential part of the training of many public sector professionals that they should assess people's needs before planning how to provide any service that might be required. This is very different from private sector market-driven goods and services, where the consumer is more likely to be seen as all powerful or sovereign. Here, if consumers are able and willing to pay the price charged, they are likely to be given the service demanded. The degree to which this model of 'choice' is appropriate in the public sector remains a contentious issue and we shall return to the notion of choice later in the chapter.

It is not uncommon for there to be divergence between what is *needed* (normatively), what a client feels he or she needs (what is *wanted*) and the service that is *supplied*. Some examples, taken from Phillips et al (1994, p 160), are given in Table 4.2.

In evaluating services it can be useful to examine the relationship between these three variables (need, want and supply) to assess the extent to which, for example, there are services which are needed but not supplied, or services which are supplied but not needed.

Acceptability

A public policy or service needs to have a degree of acceptability in the eyes of those who are, directly or indirectly, affected by it; otherwise the

Table 4.2: Relationships between need, want and supply

Needed	Wanted	Supplied	Example
No	Yes	Yes	Giving neurotic hypochondriacs what they want to make them go away.
No	Yes	No	Unmet demands of neurotic hypochondriacs.
No	No	Yes	'Trigger-happy' surgeons or inappropriate interventions by social workers.
Yes	No	No	Undiagnosed high blood pressure.
Yes	Yes	No	Waiting lists.
Yes	No	Yes	Pressures to give up smoking or to reduce alcohol consumption.
Yes	Yes	Yes	Palliative care or caring for elderly dependent people in their own homes.

Source: Phillips et al (1994)

policy's sustainability is questionable, as in the case of the community charge (the so-called 'poll tax') introduced by the Thatcher government in the early 1990s. Positive 'approval' by all members of the public might be too much to hope for, and in many cases 'acceptability' might be the best that can be achieved in the real world.

There are a number of mechanisms that are available to assess acceptability. In a crude way, elections could be seen as one such mechanism so that if the electorate strongly rejects what a government is doing they can send a message through the ballot box. But voters make their preferences known at the ballot box on the basis of a wide range of considerations. What an election result indicates regarding the issue of the acceptability of a particular policy would be difficult to judge, though it might be easier in the case of a local election fought largely on a single issue, which is sometimes the case.

Even if more focused mechanisms were to be used to ascertain the degree of acceptability of a policy or service there are a number of issues that require consideration. For example:

- Should everyone's opinion carry equal weight? Or should some views be given greater emphasis if their advocates have some relevant expertise?
- How should the criterion operate when opinions are inconsistent? At one time a majority of a service's intended beneficiaries might approve of the service being evaluated; at a later date the approval or acceptance rating might be reduced, only to rise again later still. The present authors have often encountered situations where a group of students express an opinion about the most and least useful

parts of a syllabus. The following year, following what seem to be appropriate adjustments, the next group of students may think the opposite. This can make it difficult to know how the service should be changed, if at all.

- There might be occasions when the people whose opinions might be relevant are not available. This is a particular problem in the case of policies involving major capital expenditure which are likely to have long-term effects. Judgements often have to be made on behalf of future generations. The opinions of some groups may be difficult to ascertain: evaluators need to think carefully about how to consult any 'hard to reach' groups.

- Are people the best judges of what is in their best interests? If so, why is it that so many people still smoke? Public opinion is an important factor in evaluating public policies but perhaps it needs to be supplemented by the opinion of people who have particular expertise in the specific field. Members of the public are not always well informed, though there is always a danger here of adopting an inappropriately paternalistic or patronising attitude.

- Should we define 'public' widely (for example, the electorate, taxpayers, local community, etc) or narrowly (for example, the users of the service in question)? A decision might be made to define the term narrowly in order to focus attention on the opinion of those who have regular and firsthand experience of the service to be evaluated. For example, in the case of a leisure centre opinions might be sought from those who have used the centre in the last 12 months. The difficulty here is that there might be people who went to the centre more than a year ago and were put off by some aspect of the service (such as loud music) and who have, as a result, decided to stop using the centre. A narrowly defined 'public' (such as current users of the centre) would mean that the opinions of those who have stopped going will not be uncovered.

There are a number of mechanisms available for ascertaining the views of members of the public or service users; they include elections which, as we have seen, are a rather blunt instrument in the context of service evaluation – referenda, letters to state institutions, petitions, opinion polls, user surveys, focus groups, citizen juries and exercises in public participation.

An interesting and potentially useful account of the variables which customers are likely to regard as important determinants of the quality of a service has been provided in the form of a checklist by Morgan and Murgatroyd (1994):

- reliability: e.g. is the service performed at the designated time?
- responsiveness: e.g. willingness to provide the service;
- competence: e.g. possession of the required skills and knowledge to perform the service;
- access: approachability and ease of contact with the providing institutions;
- courtesy: e.g. politeness, respect, and friendliness of contact;
- communication: e.g. keeping people informed in language they understand; also listening to them; explaining the service, options and cost; assuring people that their problems will be handled;
- credibility: e.g. belief that the providers have the person's best interests at heart; trustworthiness and honesty;
- security; e.g. freedom from danger, risk or doubt;
- understanding/knowing the individual; e.g. making the effort to understand one's needs by providing individualised attention;
- appearance/presentation; e.g. the physical facilities, appearance of personnel, equipment used, etc.

Choice

Political parties commonly say that they are in favour of increasing the choice which the public have. It is therefore a legitimate criterion to use in evaluating public services. Evaluators might ask 'To what extent and in what ways has choice improved for members of the public?'. Creating markets in which providers compete with each other for 'customers' on grounds of price and quality will, it is often asserted, improve standards.

Conceptually choice is located at the 'exit' end of the 'voice–exit' continuum developed by Hirschman (1971). At the 'voice' end of the scale services are seen to be improved by the public or service users voicing their opinions and wishes and holding providers to account through the ballot box or other mechanisms for voicing their approval or not as the case may be. As competition and market forces increase their role in public services 'exit' becomes the key. What this means is that as 'customers' become dissatisfied with a service, instead of relying on their 'voice' they can 'exit' from the contract or relationship with a particular provider and 'choose' an alternative. The idea is that as providers become more aware that 'customers' can easily go elsewhere, they are likely to make greater efforts to reduce the costs of their services and to improve the quality of the service.

The notion of choice is closely related to other criteria. For example, how much choice do people have in the ways they can *access* services? And to what extent would increasing choice lead to greater *equity*?

However, how realistic is it for people to have real choice in relation to public services? In some cases the intended beneficiary of the service is not, for most practical purposes, the person given the choice. Patients are likely to be influenced by their GPs when deciding which consultant or hospital to 'choose'. And how much choice is there likely to be for services like fire fighting, police forces and sewage disposal?

In addition, there is no evidence that everyone always wants choice. And in some circumstances, for example in relation to choices of surgery or other health interventions, being given choices could even increase people's levels of anxiety. There is also the argument that not all citizens are likely to be equally able to take advantage of 'choice' (Dixon and Le Grand, 2006).

It thus remains an open question as to how important it is to have choice in public services, especially when it is unclear how we should deal with choice when it conflicts with other public policies. For example, to what extent should parents be encouraged (or allowed) to choose not to have their children vaccinated when the experts and politicians claim that it is in the public interest for all parents to cooperate with the vaccination programme (Gulliford, 2009)?

Nevertheless, given that politicians of several hues argue for increased choice, whether or not it improves services, choice has become an important criterion for evaluating public services.

The story becomes further complicated

Different stakeholders are likely to have different opinions about which evaluative criteria should be given most weight. Whose will prevails about this will depend on the amount and types of power that different stakeholders have, and this in turn might depend on the particular context at any particular time (Thomas and Palfrey, 1996). Possible relationships between stakeholders and the evaluative criteria that they are most interested in are summarised in Table 4.3. These relationships are certainly contestable and we offer the table simply to illustrate the point that not all stakeholders will agree on which criteria should be emphasised during an evaluation.

Those who are commissioning an evaluation might also have different priorities and might be in a position to insist that evaluators take their prioritised list of criteria as given. Evaluators might be able to negotiate

Table 4.3: Possible relationships between evaluative criteria and stakeholders

CRITERIA	STAKEHOLDERS				
	Those who pay for the service being evaluated	Intended beneficiaries	Professionals	Managers	Politicians
Effectiveness		*	*	*	*
Efficiency	*	*	*	*	*
Economy	*			*	*
Equity		*		*	*
Acceptability	*		*		*
Accessibility	*		*	*	
Appropriateness	*	*		*	
Responsiveness	*	*	*	*	*
Accountability		*	*	*	*
Ethical considerations		*	*		
Choice	*	*		*	

Source: Thomas and Palfrey (1996)

at the margins but it may be unlikely that they will be able to persuade the commissioners to make wholesale changes to the criteria to be used. Decisions about the use of criteria become further complicated when, as is commonly the case, several criteria are used at the same time. There is no 'correct' balance between the criteria. How much weight is placed on which criteria is largely a value-laden and political question. There is likely to be a good deal of 'trade-off'. An improvement in efficiency, for example, might be achieved by a reduction in the extent to which the organisation can be held accountable for its actions and inactions. Whether this would count as an improvement in performance or a deterioration depends on the point of view of particular stakeholders and their relative weightings on the criteria in question.

Ethical considerations

Politicians, professionals and managers do not generally like to be thought of as acting unethically. There is therefore a widespread feeling that services should be seen as ethical in the ways they are planned, delivered and evaluated. Ethics, a branch of moral philosophy, can be regarded as an evaluation criterion like those addressed earlier in the chapter or can be regarded as an overarching consideration which can underpin the other criteria. For example, as we have seen, an evaluation of a service's effectiveness might reveal that people delivering the service are effective in achieving explicit aims and objectives, but this is not very comforting if the aims are not very challenging or if they are morally repugnant. In the case of efficiency, one can argue that policy makers and managers have a moral (that is, ethical) responsibility to increase the ratio between benefits and costs as much as possible. So no matter which criteria are being used to evaluate policies and services, the expectation that people should behave ethically is rarely far away.

Ethical theories tend to be more normative than explanatory; they say something about how things 'ought' to be rather than about how and why things happen in the way they do. The theories fall into three main categories.

Teleological theories

These are commonly referred to as consequentialist theories, for example, utilitarianism. In the view of utilitarians (the most famous of whom was Jeremy Bentham) a policy is formulated and implemented (or a service is delivered) ethically to the extent that the consequences produce the greatest good for the greatest number. Evaluation of a policy or service here focuses on the results or outcomes. 'Does the policy produce utility?' is the key question, and by 'utility' Bentham meant 'that property in any object, whereby it tends to produce benefit, advantage, pleasure, good, or happiness … or … to prevent the happening of mischief, pain, evil, or unhappiness' (Honderich (ed), 1995, p 85).

Utilitarianism underpins the way that the National Institute for Health and Clinical Excellence (NICE) evaluates health interventions (particularly drugs) on the basis of the expected outcomes or consequences that will follow their use. NICE investigates the likely outcomes of each intervention in terms of the extra quantity and quality of life and their costs in attempting to ensure that taxpayers' money is spent in a cost-effective way. Underpinning this is the notion that the state has an ethical duty to ensure that scarce public money is spent on goods and services which will produce the 'greatest good'.

A number of ethical objections have been raised to the use of Quality Adjusted Life Years (QALYs), which have become an established method of evaluating the expected cost-effectiveness of health interventions (Edgar et al, 1998). The criticisms 'may all be construed as the accusation that QALYs are inherently unjust' (Edgar et al, 1998, p 74) and the way in which QALYs are used by NICE is evolving over time in an attempt to respond to the objections, but the idea based, as it is, on notions of utilitarianism remains an influential approach in formulating resource allocations decisions within health care systems.

According to utilitarianism, if there were four patients in urgent need of organ transplants (for example, two might need a kidney, one a heart and one a liver) then one could argue *prima facie* that a healthy person should be forced to give up their four organs for the greatest good: one patient dies in order to save the lives of four people. However, it is unlikely that most people would agree that this was the right thing to do as it seems to ignore the 'rights' of the healthy individual who has all his or her organs currently intact. It could be argued therefore that a theory which gives more emphasis to rights and duties would be more appropriate.

Deontological theories

This is where the second ethical school of thought comes in. The argument in this case is that certain acts are right or wrong in themselves irrespective of the consequences. Thus it could be argued that the rights of the healthy individual in the case above should be protected even if it means that the four needy patients will die. The emphasis is on the rights of individuals to enjoy autonomy and the moral duty that we have to respect those rights.

However, there are problems here too. For example, one of the acts which people are obliged to carry out (according to deontologists like Kant) is always to tell the truth. So if someone had the opportunity to save lives by telling a lie or by breaking a promise, then they should not do it. This seems counter-intuitive and many people would probably see it as ethically misguided.

A common example of the use of these theories is the code of conduct with which members of various professions are required to comply. These normally set out duties and the standards of behaviour expected of members of the profession in question, and serious contravention can lead to an individual being struck off the register of professional members and a resultant legal inability to practise the profession in question.

Virtue ethics

Whereas utilitarianism and deontological theories focus on actions (the first from the point of view of the results of the actions and the second based on duties and right motives) virtue ethics emphasise the need to develop in individuals the right characteristics. Based on the early work of Aristotle, Foot (2003) has argued that there are a number of virtues, including courage, temperance, wisdom and justice, which are likely to benefit both the individual with the virtues and other people. Foot sees the virtues as 'dispositions', that is to say the characteristic or trait (such as courage or compassion) will become active in circumstances which require it. The virtuous person is thought or expected to act courageously, compassionately, etc, when the situation calls for it. The virtues are closely related to some of the criteria which were examined earlier in the chapter; see, for example, the notion of justice – the second evaluative criterion in the list set out earlier in this chapter. Generally speaking, the notion of virtue ethics places a responsibility on evaluators and others to fulfill their civic duties and to work for the public good. Evaluation practitioners are expected to act honestly, justly and courageously.

The above theories, in varying ways and degrees, underpin the guidance given to those engaged in the planning, delivery and evaluation of public policies. Gillon (1994) for example has argued that the following 'ethical factors' are relevant to the practice of medicine: honesty; equity; impartiality; respect; and adherence to high levels of competence.

Honesty

It is generally unwise for evaluators to issue promises to service users that an evaluation will lead to improvements in services. Although service improvement is an important aim, it commonly turns out not to be possible for various reasons. For example, there could be a change of personnel within senior management with incoming managers having very different ideas from those of their predecessors about the future shape of services, or there might be increased scarcity of resources compared with the date on which the evaluation was commissioned. Evaluations, and those who commission evaluations, therefore need to be honest with service users about the prospects for service improvements.

However, there are likely to be problems in being honest. Elsewhere we have drawn attention to:

> The possibility of legal action against the authors of evaluation reports when, for example, they have made statements which could be construed as defamatory, or

if they have expressed doubts about the truthfulness of a statement but proceeded without verifying its validity. Conversely, evaluators may feel the need to suppress information or opinions if, by revealing them, they run the risk of exposing the informants to some form of reprisal (Palfrey and Thomas, 1996, pp 282–3).

Honesty and openness are also required about the criteria to be used in an evaluation and about how these came to be selected.

Equity

This principle involves the concepts of impartiality and natural justice. As seen earlier when considering equity as an evaluative criterion, it suggests that special consideration needs to be given to the position of disadvantaged groups. What should evaluators do if they disagree with the aims of a programme? For example, a public policy might be designed with the aim of reducing expenditure on a service which is of particular benefit to low income groups suffering social and economic disadvantage. As we have enquired elsewhere: 'Would (the evaluators) pass the portfolio to someone who did not suffer from such moral scruples or who held views similar to those of the commissioning agents?' (Palfrey and Thomas, 1996, p 283). There is no simple answer to this question but, as a minimum, evaluators need to ensure that the views of all principal stakeholders and interest groups are included in evaluation projects in which they are engaged, and that the contributions of all such groups are considered to be of potentially equal validity and relevance (Palfrey et al, 2004).

Impartiality

Partiality and inappropriate discrimination can take various forms. An important example as far as evaluators are concerned is to exclude the views of people whose opinions might be inconvenient to those in authority. As we have pointed out elsewhere:

> Evaluating a staff appraisal system wholly from the management criterion of its impact on productivity would wrongly exclude relevant and equally valid criteria constructed by staff who have undergone appraisal. (Palfrey and Thomas, 1996, p 283)

In a sense impartiality is a means towards achieving equity and 'although the evaluator can never be a completely neutral observer and interpreter, there has to be an attempt to keep an open mind about the evidence to be gathered and about its meaning' (Palfrey et al, 2004, p 162).

Respect

People's opinions about the policy or service being evaluated should, according to this principle, carry equal weight unless there are convincing reasons for not doing so. It could be argued that evaluators should pay more attention to the opinions of those who seem to be better informed about the issues involved, but this is not what happens in parliamentary elections. The notion of respect is taken seriously by evaluation approaches such as that espoused by Smith and Cantley (1985) in their requirement that a range of data collection methods should be used to collect various kinds of data from a variety of sources. This approach does not address the question of whether it is justified to give more weight to some views than others, but at least it recognises that potentially divergent views should be listened to seriously.

Adherence to high levels of competence

If evaluation projects were to be undertaken in nursing homes in order to make judgements about the quality of care, the commissioners of the evaluation might require a questionnaire to be used as the principal – or even the sole – means of data collection. But evaluators might feel that in order to get a full picture they would also need to spend time in the home observing practices and listening and talking to people (patients and carers) in informal settings at meal times, recreation times, and in sitting rooms etc. The response from the commissioners might be that the evaluation budget will not stretch to this. Evaluators would therefore need to decide whether to design a questionnaire which meets all the expectations for a competently designed questionnaire, or whether to withdraw on the grounds that the questionnaire alone will be an inadequate means of collecting the necessary data. To what extent should evaluators compromise their expectations and standards in this kind of situation? Should evaluators be satisfied if they do all that commissioners require of them? There is no simple answer to these dilemmas. In each case evaluators should at least try their best to persuade the commissioners to find extra resources to ensure that a high degree of competence can be achieved.

The ethical factors discussed above are espoused by Gillon (1994) in relation to medical practice. But there are also a number of ethical principles which have been advocated more broadly across professional life generally (Newman and Brown, 1996, Palfrey and Thomas, 1996). They include:

- respect for people's *autonomy* (including keeping people fully informed so that they can make informed choices);
- *non-maleficence* (attempting to ensure that one's actions cause no harm and to inform people if there are any unavoidable risks);
- *beneficence* (for example, using resources as beneficially as possible);
- treating people *fairly* (for example, providing everyone with the service to which they are entitled and not allowing any personal views about people's lifestyle to affect the quality of service given to them);
- acting with *integrity* (for example, genuinely striving to achieve the stated objectives of our activities).

Sometimes, the following are also included:

- *impartiality*;
- *confidentiality*.

Dilemmas can arise when these various ethical concerns conflict. If this occurs one can either aim for a compromise or give priority to one principle over the others. For example, the principle of autonomy might lead a medical practitioner to spend a lot of time with a patient to ensure that the patient can make an informed choice about treatment; but this might conflict with the principle of fairness/justice because every minute spent with the first patient means one minute less for other patients. There is unlikely to be an 'ethically correct' course of action. We must make a judgement which is 'appropriate' having taken into account the various principles.

Another difficulty relates to the debate between absolutism versus relativism. It can be argued that there are 'moral absolutes'; that is, some rules are universally 'right' in all circumstances. One of the difficulties with this view is that sometimes there might be a conflict between such rules. For example, if you believe that one must always tell the truth and one must always try to preserve human life, would it be right to lie to save a life? Which universal right should you violate? This is the problem to which we referred earlier when we summarised the position of those, like Kant, who espouse deontogical theories. In such circumstances it is necessary to weigh and prioritise various 'absolute' obligations. The alternative is to take the view of cultural 'relativism'. Some relativists see absolutism as smacking of attempts to impose morally superior ideas on other people. Instead it could be argued that 'when in Rome one should do as the Romans do' and that what is 'right' varies from one culture, context or set of circumstances to another.

What is the role of the state in all this? Under the auspices of the Commissioner for Public Appointments in the UK, the Committee on Standards in Public Life has set out a number of principles – known as the Nolan Principles – which holders of public office are expected to follow. These seven principles are often seen as the elements of probity and are as follows (Nolan Committee, 1995):

- **Selflessness** – Holders of public office should act solely in terms of the public interest. They should not do so in order to gain financial or other benefits for themselves, their family, or their friends.
- **Integrity** – Holders of public office should not place themselves under any financial or other obligation to outside individuals or organisations that might seek to influence them in the performance of their official duties.
- **Objectivity** – In carrying out public business, including making public appointments, awarding contracts, or recommending individuals for rewards and benefits, holders of public office should make choices on merit.
- **Accountability** – Holders of public office are accountable for their decisions and actions to the public and must submit themselves to whatever scrutiny is appropriate to their office.
- **Openness** – Holders of public office should be as open as possible about all the decisions and actions they take. They should give reasons for their decisions and restrict information only when the wider public interest clearly demands.
- **Honesty** – Holders of public office have a duty to declare any private interests relating to their public duties and to take steps to resolve any conflicts arising in a way that protects the public interest.
- **Leadership** – Holders of public office should promote and support these principles by leadership and example.

Public officials and their managers and political leaders cannot reasonably be expected to base all their decisions and actions directly on the ethical theories which we examined earlier as this would lead to the paralysis of analysis, but the Nolan Principles provide a useful framework. But again, in the real world there are problems. For example, much of what is contained in the Principles is open to interpretation. In the case of openness, they state that public officials should be as 'open as possible about all the decisions and actions they take'. There is likely to be considerable disagreement about what is possible and what is not in this context. The Principles, therefore, are useful but they certainly do not put an end to debate, nor should they. Nor can public officials, in our view, justifiably wash their hands of their responsibility for behaving ethically by simply 'delegating' such matters to an 'ethics committee'.

Concluding comment

A key issue associated with ethical theories is that of 'values' – the things that people view as important. Values are at the root of decisions about which evaluative criteria are to be regarded as the most important; people's value stances need to be made explicit if opinions about what constitute 'success' is to be as transparent as possible. One of the problems here is that values cannot be arrived at rationally (MacIntyre, 1985). If managers have goals (based on the values of those who set the goals) they can seek to be rational in assessing and selecting the 'best' means to those goals. As we have pointed out elsewhere:

> MacIntyre's view of managers is that they treat ends as given and as outside their scope. In their role as manager, they are unable to engage in moral debate. Their task is to restrict themselves as to the realms in which rational agreement is possible – that is, from their point of view, to the realms of fact, of means and of measurable effectiveness. (Palfrey et al, 2004, pp 166–7)

However, managers need to be aware of the dangers of disadvantaging key stakeholders, especially when an evaluation remit seems to compromise professional standards.

We can conclude that what happens in any evaluation process depends on the value judgements of those with most of the power in the system – be they politicians, professionals, managers, the mass media, pressure groups, a ruling elite, the electorate, or whoever. What evaluators need to do is to make the values which are dominant as explicit as possible so that they become visible and therefore contestable by all interested parties, particularly those whose services are being evaluated. This is one way in which we can ensure that evaluations are ethically informed.

We also need to remember that each of the criteria examined in this chapter can be useful in evaluation work but, as has been seen, each also has its limitations. This is not a reason to eschew the criteria, but these limitations should be recognised in our evaluation work.

References

Abma, T. (1997) 'Playing with/in plurality', *Evaluation*, vol 3, no 1, pp 25-48.

Bradshaw, J. (1972) 'A taxonomy of human need', *New Society*, March, pp 640-3.

Department of Health (2006) *Achieving high performance in health care systems: The impact and influence of organisational arrangements*, NHS Service Delivery and Organisation R&D programme.

Dixon, A. and Le Grand, J. (2006) 'Is greater patient choice consistent with equity? The case of the English NHS', *Journal of Health Services Research and Policy,* vol 11, no 3, pp 162-6.

Edgar, A., Salek, S., Shickle, D. and Cohen, D. (1998) *The ethical QALY: Ethical issues in healthcare resource allocations,* Haslemere: Euromed Communications.

Elcock, H. and Haywood, S. (1980) *The buck stops where? Accountability and control in the NHS*, Hull: University of Hull.

Ferlie, E., Ashburner, L., Fitzgerald, L. and Pettigrew, A. (1996) *The new public management in action,* Oxford: Oxford University Press.

Foot, P. (2003) *Virtues and vices and other essays in moral philosophy*, Oxford: Oxford University Press.

Gillon, R. (1994) *Philosophical medical ethics*, NY: John Wiley.

Goddard, M. (2009) 'Access to health care services – an English policy perspective', *Health Economics, Policy and Law*, vol 4, pp 195-208.

Gulliford, M. (2009) 'Modernizing concepts of access and equity', *Health Economics, Policy and Law*, vol 4, pp 223-30.

Hill, M. (ed) (1997) *The policy process: A reader*, London: Wheatsheaf.

Hirschman, A. (1971) *Exit, voice and loyalty: Responses to decline of firms, organisations and states*, Harvard, MA: Harvard University Press.

Honderich, T. (ed)(1995) *The Oxford companion to philosophy*, Oxford: Oxford University Press.

Karlsson, O. (1996) 'A critical dialogue in evaluation; how can the interaction between evaluation and politics be tackled', *Evaluation*, vol 2, no 4, pp 405-16.

MacIntyre, A. (1985) *After virtue: A study in moral theory*, London: Duckworth.

McLaughlin, K., Osbourne, S. and Ferlie, E. (eds.) (2002) *New public management: Current trends and future prospects*, London: Routledge.

Mooney, G. (2009) 'Is it not time for health economists to rethink equity and access?', *Health Economics, Policy and Law*, vol 4, pp 209-21.

Morgan, C. and Murgatroyd, S. (1994) *Total quality management in the public sector*, Milton Keynes: Open University.

Newman, D. and Brown, R. (1996) *Applied ethics for program evaluation*, London: Sage.

Nolan Committee (1995) *Standards in public life*, London: HMSO.

Palfrey, C. and Thomas, P. (1996) 'Ethical issues in policy evaluation', *Policy & Politics*, vol 24, no 3, pp 277-85.

Palfrey, C., Thomas, P. and Phillips, C. (2004) *Effective health care management: An evaluative approach*, Oxford: Blackwell.

Peckham, S., Exworthy, M. and Greener, I. and Powell, M. (2005) 'Decentralising health services: more accountability or just more central control', *Public Money and Management*, vol 25, no 4, pp 221-30.

Phillips, C., Palfrey, C. and Thomas, P. (1994) *Evaluating health and social care*, London: Macmillan.

Roberts, H. (1991) 'Outcome and performance in health care: survey of current activities', in Public Finance Foundation, *Outcome and performance in health care*, Discussion Paper 40, London: PFF.

Smith, G. and Cantley, C. (1985) *Assessing health care: A study in organisational evaluation*, Milton Keynes: Open University Press.

Thomas, P. and Palfrey, C. (1996) 'Evaluation: stakeholder-focused criteria', *Social Policy and Administration*, vol 30, no 2, pp 125-42.

FIVE

Developments in economic evaluation

Introduction

It is a curious fact that economic evaluation does not feature at all prominently in the evaluation literature although it has to be a major consideration in any official financing of internally or externally commissioned evaluation research. This chapter will develop the discussion introduced in Chapter Four relating to some of the criteria available to evaluators of public programmes and policies, in particular economy, efficiency and equity. These criteria are of particular significance given that this book has been written at a time when virtually all developed economies are grappling with the aftermath of the crisis in the financial sector that has led to one of the most severe economic recessions of recent times. The bailout of economies by international financial agencies and governments has been a common feature of news bulletins and media reports, and in many countries has led to already stretched public service budgets being faced with unparalleled reductions in financial allocations. As a result, public service professionals have become increasingly vociferous in their claims that levels of service provision are unsustainable in the prevailing economic climate.

However, the need to ensure that services are provided as efficiently as possible, for example, is not something confined to times of fierce economic conditions. Demands that scarce resources are used to the best possible effect have become commonplace.

This comes against a background of increasing expectations and demands from their resident populations, which has resulted in a situation in which the provision and funding of public services are clearly one of the most contentious political issues of the day. This has been captured within the context of health care in terms of the health care dilemma (Phillips and Prowle, 1992), but this concept, of ever increasing demand for services against a background of restrictive supply of resources, can be applied across many areas of public service provision. However, this is but a partial view of the broader economic problem – and referred to as *scarcity* in economics-speak (Phillips, 2005) – that affects every area of society and can be considered from a range of perspectives, from that of the individual to a global view. It is based on the fact that while we have unlimited wants and desires, we only have limited resources at our disposal to satisfy them. The discipline of economics – the dismal science, as originally coined by Thomas Carlyle (1849) – emerged because of the existence of infinite demand for goods and services chasing a finite supply of resources.

Economics is founded on the premise that there never have been and never will be enough resources to completely satisfy human desires and therefore, their use in one area or activity inevitably involves a sacrifice in another. Therefore questions as to how society's scarce resources should be allocated amongst the infinite variety of competing activities provide the rationale for an economic perspective in setting priorities and evaluating policies and programmes. The extent of the gap which exists between the demands for commodities and the level of resource available to meet such demands continues to frustrate politicians, professionals and policy makers, and the array of economic systems which have existed and evolved over time bear testimony to the attempts to grapple with the basic economic problem of allocating resources in such a way as to maximise the benefits for society.

The need for economic evaluation

An economic appraisal is thus an essential component within most evaluation processes to ensure that resources committed to the programme being evaluated deliver what has conventionally been termed 'value for money' and would not have been better used elsewhere. The theoretical underpinning for economic evaluation is to be found in welfare economics, which seeks to assess the social welfare of societies, viewed as an aggregation of individuals' well-being and welfare. The underlying premise is that adjusting the allocation of resources will generate changes, hopefully improvements, in welfare for individuals and communities – *efficiency considerations* – and in the distribution of the resources between individuals and communities within society – *equity considerations*. The measurement of efficiency in its purest form is depicted by the notion of utility, which is difficult to conceptualise in practice, but tends to reflect benefit, well-being, satisfaction and value. In applied welfare economics, efficiency gains have generally been measured in monetary terms, as in cost-benefit analysis (CBA). However, a recognition of the limited and restrictive nature of utility (and indeed monetary approaches) has led to other innovative developments in relation, for example, to the capabilities approach (Sen, 1985) and the extra–welfarist approach (Culyer, 1989). The capabilities approach emphasises the multivariate nature of activities that give rise to well-being (and welfare) and has a focus on the capability of a person to function and the ability to take advantage of opportunities. The extra–welfarist approach supplements the utility individuals receive from consumption of goods and services with other sources of utility, such as being out of pain, having freedom to make choices, being able to have relationships and other components of what would be regarded as well-being.

Efficiency, as discussed initially in Chapter Four, therefore seeks to compare the extent to which a programme delivers additional benefits, however expressed, relative to the additional costs used to provide the programme. In its simplest sense, efficiency is synonymous with economy (also discussed in Chapter Four), where output is expected to be maintained, while at the same time making cost reductions, or where additional output is generated with the same level of inputs. This type of efficiency is known as *technical efficiency* and is applied where a choice needs to be made between alternatives which seek to achieve the same goal and exists when output is maximised for a given cost or where the costs of producing a given output are minimised. However, technical efficiency is not sufficient for establishing priorities within and between publicly funded services. In order to determine whether and how much of certain services should be provided, *allocative efficiency* must be used. This type of efficiency has been defined as *economic efficiency* (HM Treasury, 2003) and exists when nobody can be made better off without someone else being made worse off. It is often referred to as *Pareto-efficiency*, but is essentially a theoretical construct, since in reality, there may well be situations where a re-allocation of resources would result in some people being made better off and others would be worse off, but there could be a net gain if the beneficiaries were to compensate the losers and still be better off – a situation known as *social efficiency* (McGuire and Henderson, 1987; Phillips, 2005).

The purpose and goals of evaluation have been addressed in Chapter Two, where terms such as worth and value have been used to assess the quality and merit of the evaluand. These are, in many senses, synonymous with the notion of efficiency, and how these can be measured and specified is where economic evaluation fits into the evaluation logic. This has been succinctly and usefully depicted by Haynes (1999), who suggests three questions that serve to guide the evaluation process, namely:

- Can it work?
- Does it work?
- Is it worth it?

The purpose of economic evaluation is therefore to shed light on the third of these questions 'Is it worth it?'. Is it relatively efficient? What benefit is gained relative to the additional cost? While the precise specification of the question may vary, the answer requires that the evaluator has to identify, measure and value the resources used in providing the service or implementing the policy along with the identification, measurement and valuation of the benefits generated. These are the requisite processes within any economic evaluation and enable the evaluator to gauge whether the evaluand represents a good use of limited resources in terms of society's welfare and well-being or whether their deployment elsewhere would be a better option. However, it is not possible for the evaluator to capture all aspects of resources used and benefits generated, yet alone quantify and value them. It therefore has to be stressed that while economic evaluation should be regarded as a necessary component of an evaluation framework, it cannot be viewed as a sufficient condition. It is a tool that serves to inform the decision maker of the relative worth of the project, but this needs to be viewed and weighed in the light of other benchmarks and criteria.

For instance, the dangers of sole reliance on economic evaluation are portrayed in a cost-benefit analysis of smoking, undertaken by the tobacco giant Philip Morris for the Treasury of the Czech Republic in 1999. The costs of increased medical care for smokers and time lost through tobacco-related health problems were compared with the income gained from taxes on tobacco and the money saved to pension funds and housing costs resulting from premature mortality resulting from smoking. This study concluded that smoking resulted in a net gain of US$224 million (Mallenson, 2002)! This alleged 'net gain,' in this case, thus provides an indication of the relative efficiency of the programme – although one would seriously question the underlying assumptions of this particular example. The one positive aspect of this study is that the cost-benefit ratio does portray an assessment of the relative efficiency – from the perspective of allocative efficiency – whereas many of the findings from cost-effectiveness studies present a ratio (for example, cost per job seeker assisted; cost per quality adjusted life-year (QALY) gained) that only serves to provide an indication of efficiency from the narrower, technical efficiency perspective. That said, it is probably true to say that health economics has seen more methodological developments and progression than other branches of applied welfare economics (Blaug, 1998), with the techniques and methods being gradually imported into social care, criminal justice and other areas of economic evaluation where the extent of full economic evaluations is limited (Byford et al, 2010; Marsh, 2010). The use of applications and illustrations from the health field, in this chapter, reflect the extent to which economic evaluation has featured within health relative to other areas. The next section considers the processes involved in the economic evaluation in turn, commencing with the notion of cost.

The notion of cost

It is essential to emphasise at the outset that cost, in economic terms, is not only concerned with the financial imperatives of saving money and reducing expenditure. If that were the case, economists would only be concerned with spending less and focusing on programmes and policies that contributed to achieving an improvement in financial budgets rather than an improvement in the welfare and well-being of society.

The cost of using a resource in a particular service, therefore, is not necessarily the money cost or the price that is paid for that particular resource, but rather it is the sacrifice incurred – the benefits forgone (the opportunity lost) by not choosing the alternative course of action. In a powerful newspaper article the *real* cost of a bag of salad was demonstrated, with the headline:

> You pay: 99p
> Africa pays: 50 litres of fresh water

Producing a small 50g salad bag consumes 50 litres of water, while a mixed salad containing tomatoes, celery and cucumber requires 300 litres of water from countries where water is in extremely limited supply (Laurance, 2006). In other words, while we pay less than £1 for the privilege of accessing our salad directly from the fridge without need for washing, the opportunity cost of the bag of salad is the benefits that would have resulted from the use of 50 litres of fresh water in communities that have to struggle to access adequate water supplies.

A similar example, was also found on the front page of *The Times* newspaper on the day that the allied forces invaded Iraq. An estimate of the costs of the campaign was presented along with what other uses could have been made of such resources in terms of hospitals and schools that could have been constructed, for example. The costs of an intervention or service are therefore not only the staff inputs, materials and equipment contributed by providers, but also include the costs to other agencies that are affected or contribute to the service provision, costs to service recipients from having to travel to receive the services or other expenses that need to be incurred. There are, in addition, the indirect costs or productivity costs associated with the programme or intervention or with the particular issues that the policy seeks to address. For example, the costs of crime are not merely the direct material losses that occur but, in addition, the victims of crime may suffer to the extent that they are absent from work due to the trauma or they may not operate at full productivity if they are able to continue working. Another example of indirect costs would be those incurred through the informal care process – for example as a result of a carer giving up paid employment or sacrificing leisure time to provide care for a relative, which would otherwise have been provided by formal care agencies. There are also intangible costs, which in the context of health relate to the impact of health problems on the quality of life of patients, their families and communities. These aspects of cost provide the biggest headache in determining the real cost associated with health, and cannot be adequately captured within any financial statement but nevertheless are essential components of the balance sheet connected with health care services. An illustration of this was provided in an editorial which highlighted the 'real' costs associated with pain management (Phillips, 2001) as:

- costs of interventions and therapies for treating pain and securing pain relief (e.g. drug costs and staff costs);
- costs which are incurred as a result of ineffective interventions being provided (e.g. costs of additional GP consultations);
- costs to health service and patients and their families due to lack of appropriate facilities within locality (e.g. costs of accessing alternative therapies);
- costs resulting from inappropriate self-medication and treatment by patients (e.g. costs of treating overdoses);
- costs of treating and preventing adverse events which arise as a result of prescribing decisions (e.g. costs of gastrointestinal bleeds);
- costs of disability claims resulting from people's inability to work;
- costs to economy of reductions in productivity and absenteeism;
- costs of providing social care and support to people suffering with pain (e.g. costs of home care and respite care);

- costs of informal care provided by families (e.g loss of earnings);
- costs of intangibles associated with deterioration in the quality of life of patients and their families.

The intricacies involved with the costing of programmes are not discussed further here, since there are many relevant texts that are readily available for more in-depth consideration of the processes and issues (for example, Brouwer et al, 2001; Drummond et al, 2005; Phillips, 2005). However, in moving towards another component of the economic evaluation process, that of measuring and valuing effect, it is worth concluding this section by quoting from a recent editorial in the *British Medical Journal*:

> Money is tight, so getting value for money has to be a top priority for us all in healthcare. As Jim Easton, the man in charge of improvement and efficiency for the NHS, says whenever he speaks, cost is an ethical issue. (Godlee, 2010, p c7377)

Measuring and valuing effects: outcomes and impacts

The aim of policy initiatives and public service programmes is ostensibly to improve the welfare and well-being of citizens. It is this principle which underlies the notion of welfare economics and the drive for efficiency. While there are major issues in specifying and measuring the notion of utility, the intention of these policy initiatives and programmes is not simply to generate a financial return as would be the case in conventional commercial transactions. However, in order to make the necessary comparisons required to determine allocative efficiency a common currency is required, and monetary measures fit this particular bill, albeit with a number of caveats and limitations.

Nevertheless, it is unrealistic to assume that educational attainment, health gain, lives saved, improved housing conditions, environmental enhancement can be accurately and precisely specified in monetary terms. Within health care for example, measurement of health outcomes using QALYs and undertaking cost-utility analysis (CUA) has become the accepted approach in many countries. QALYs reflect the additional life years generated by health care interventions and the quality of the additional years. The quality dimension is derived by the use of health-related quality of life instruments or by employing stated preference techniques, such as standard gamble or time trade-off approaches (Phillips, 2005; Drummond et al, 2005; Dolan, 2001).

However, the challenge with employing CUA or cost-effectiveness analysis is that the economic evaluations will be dependent on the use of a single metric and will, in all probability, fail to capture all the effects resulting from the intervention. For example, interventions to tackle substance misuse will improve health outcomes, but can also be expected to reduce offending and improve employment chances, neither of which can be captured using QALYs. The obvious limitations associated with these approaches have led to calls for alternative approaches to be employed, such as cost consequences analysis (CCA) or cost benefit analysis (CBA). However, these are not without their problems. While CCA provides a 'balance sheet' of outcomes that policy makers can weigh up against the costs of an intervention, the drawback is that it provides no guidance as to how the different outcomes included in the 'balance sheet' should be weighed against each other. This is especially problematic when outcomes move in different directions.

There are other aspects that require consideration when seeking to measure and value effect, given the complexity of many public service interventions. Firstly, assuming that effect can be measured and appropriately valued, there are several reasons which make it difficult to attribute change to any one particular intervention or scheme. Public services interventions are not always immediately suitable to experimental evaluations, seen by some authors as the gold standard of evaluation. Moreover, the effectiveness of interventions depends on a multiplicity of factors, thus making outcomes difficult to attribute and generalise (NICE, 2007). A potential solution lies in the use of 'threshold analysis', which estimates the 'extent' of benefits necessary for the intervention to be regarded as being good value (Phillips and Prowle, 1993).

Another difficulty in measuring the extent of the effect of interventions is the potential lag between the implementation of the intervention and the realisation of benefits, especially where the benefits generated are only evident in the distant future. The technique of discounting is employed to allow for the impact of time on benefit realisation since benefits in the future are not valued as highly as those that occur now. For example, the important societal benefits generated by enhancing early years' education are unlikely to emerge for over 20 years, and so will have relatively limited current value when compared with schemes designed to reduce crime where benefits emerge within a relatively short time, especially when political expediency is the order of the day.

In addition to the timing of effects, their extent and duration also require consideration. For example, in schemes that seek to address drug abuse, the effects are likely to be variable and fluctuate over time. As noted by Zarkin et al (2005), 'drug abuse is a chronic condition that typically includes periods of use and non-use, interspersed with periods of drug treatment, over an individual user's lifetime' (p 1133). A model structure was therefore employed to 'represent the reality that drug abuse treatment is not always effective in the short or long term and that episodes of drug use and/or treatment may recur throughout an individual user's lifetime. To ignore these recurring episodes of drug use and treatment may provide a misleading picture of both the costs and benefits of treatment' (p 1134). In general terms it is therefore important that appropriate model structures are adopted within economic evaluations to capture the dynamic nature of many behavioural and social outcomes.

The third point relates to the challenge of identifying, measuring and valuing *all* of the effects of interventions, which will impact on different agencies and groups within society. For example, a building regeneration scheme will obviously enhance the housing conditions and quality of life of those directly affected but there will undoubtedly be spin-off benefits for the community and surrounding areas, in that social problems resulting from poor housing are likely to be affected by default, with consequential efficiency gains at virtually zero cost for the respective agencies. Another example emerges from local authorities' attempts to keep major roads free from the effects of ice and snow during severe winter conditions. The benefit stream from such endeavours would impact on the local authority itself from avoidance of potential congestion and keeping the local economy on the move, but there also would be efficiency gains for local citizens from lower repair costs for road surfaces leading to lower council tax bills, and lower car insurance premiums plus fewer road traffic accidents, which would also impact on the health care system and police and other emergency services. The failure to accurately specify all benefit flows would therefore potentially lead to sub-optimal findings and inappropriate recommendations from evaluations.

Addressing the challenges

The limitations of cost-effectiveness analysis and cost-utility analysis in determining allocative efficiency can be overcome by valuing outcomes monetarily and undertaking a cost-benefit analysis (CBA). CBA is recommended by the HM Treasury's Green Book (HM

Treasury, 2003) due to its ability to 'to take account of the wider social costs and benefits' (HM Treasury, 2003, p 4) and provide outcome measures that are directly comparable with intervention costs. In the absence of market prices for outcomes, which is often the case when evaluating public policy, the Green Book recommends that either revealed preference or stated preference methods are used to value outcomes. Revealed preference studies are used to value outcomes using the preference information revealed through existing markets. For example, the value of preventing a fatality (VPF) has been calculated by estimating the compensating differentials for on-the-job risk exposure in labour markets, or the price–risk trade-offs in product markets, such as for automobiles and fire alarms (Dolan, Metcalfe et al, 2008). However, the validity of the estimates produced by revealed preference techniques depend on the ability to isolate the impact of VPF from the other factors that determine wages and prices. Furthermore, the revealed preference approach is based on the assumption that markets work well. The difficulty in fulfilling these requirements is thought to explain the large variation in estimates produced by revealed preference studies, with, for example, VPF estimates ranging from £0.5 million to £64.0 million (Dolan and Metcalfe, 2008).

Putting a value on human life is clearly contentious, although it has a history dating back to the notion of the 'wergild' in Anglo-Saxon England – the monetary compensation that a killer had to pay the family of a murder victim (Ackerman and Heinzerling, 2004). The ethical and philosophical questions that surround attempts to place a monetary value on a life resound, while rescue attempts following natural disasters are not dependent on a cost-benefit analysis being undertaken before the decision is made to proceed (Ackerman and Heinzerling, 2004). Given the difficulties posed to the revealed preference approach by imperfect markets and a lack of data, economists have turned to stated preference approaches to value non-market commodities and services. Since the 1990s, the stated preference literature has grown rapidly, especially within environmental economics. Stated preference studies construct a hypothetical contingent market where the individual is asked to state their willingness to pay (WTP) for the non-market commodity or service. The beauty of contingent valuation questions is their ability to elicit exactly the information that is required. However, stated preference techniques are not without issues. For example, the assumption that individuals have a coherent set of preferences is at best dubious (Dolan and Metcalfe, 2008).

Concerns about the challenge facing the revealed and stated preference-based approaches to valuing policy outcomes have caused economists to turn their attention to measuring people's experiences rather than their preferences. In particular, given data on how satisfied people are with their life overall, their health, income, and other relevant background characteristics, statistical techniques can be employed to estimate the amount of income that is required to hold life satisfaction constant following a change in health (Dolan and Metcalfe, 2008). In other words, measures of subjective well-being (SWB) can be used to value policy outcomes as an input to public policy making (Dolan, Peasgood and White, 2008). Furthermore, the possibilities of SWB measures are also being recognised by policy makers themselves. For example, the OECD convened a conference of academics and policy makers to discuss the use of such measures in policy making (OECD, 2007), and a recent HM Treasury position paper stated that SWB methods had the potential to support policy analysis and that the approach accorded with the strategic objectives of the Treasury (HM Treasury, 2009). It is important, however, to note that the approach is still in its infancy and that a number of methodological questions need to be answered before this approach can be used to generate evidence to inform policy making (Newman et al, 2010).

Methods employed in environmental economics also provide insight into how the challenge of multiple outcomes can be dealt with. The principal frameworks developed for the appraisal of environmental and transport interventions revolve around the notions of CBA and multiple criteria decision making (Romero, 1997). Within the CBA framework a variety of approaches have been advocated and applied – travel cost method (based on time and travel costs incurred in accessing amenities and services); hedonic price method (used to assess economic value of environmental qualities and amenities; contingent valuation (CV) approaches, based on willingness to pay or accept (HM Treasury, 2003; Johansson, 1987; Pearce and Turner, 1990; Bateman et al, 2002; Bateman and Willis, 1999; Jones-Lee, 1990) – all of which are beset by limitations to varying degrees.

Multiple criteria decision analysis (MCDA) provides a framework for evaluating interventions with multiple outcomes, while at the same time formally engaging decision makers in the research process (Hajkowicz and Higgins, 2008). MCDA approaches vary according to the source and nature of information used to inform decision making. However, a key characteristic of MCDA is what is referred to as 'the socio-technical system', or the balance between decision maker input and researcher measurement. The different components of the MCDA can each be classified as either deliberative or data-driven, depending on the source of data drawn on. Deliberation refers to the process of negotiation between various stakeholders, based on factors such as their own knowledge of the field, existing policy commitments, ethical values and so on. Data-driven components are those which are primarily based on research evidence, such as assessments of the clinical effectiveness or cost-effectiveness of particular interventions.

There is disagreement in the literature as to exactly what balance should be struck between decision maker and researcher input into a MCDA. Consequently, a mix of approaches to combining deliberative and data-driven components is adopted in the literature (Heller et al, 2006; Maciosek et al, 2006a; Maciosek et al, 2006b; Wilson et al, 2006; Wilson et al, 2007). However, MCDA's ability to evaluate interventions across multiple outcomes, while formally incorporating decision makers into the evaluation process, provides the potential to overcome a number of the challenges facing economic evaluations of public sector schemes, with examples of MCDA having been successfully applied to the prioritisation of public health interventions (Maciosek et al, 2006a; Maciosek et al, 2006b), which in and of themselves are faced with differing stakeholder agendas, perspectives and preferences.

What is evident is that there is no clear consensus as to which is the preferred method for measuring and valuing the benefits resulting from public service interventions and programmes. Evaluators, therefore, need to be explicit regarding the design and method employed and the limitations associated with the approach, so that policy makers are fully informed of the cautions that should be applied to the findings produced.

Further, it emphasises the need for sensitivity analysis to be used in conjunction with the findings, so as to consider the impact of methodological limitations, variation in parameter estimates and general uncertainties surrounding the extent of benefits captured within the evaluation – and also incidentally around the estimates of costs incurred.

Sensitivity analysis involves re-running the analysis with different parameter values and asking 'what if' type questions. 'One way' sensitivity analyses show the effects of amending each of the cost and effect components separately. There are no rules regarding by how much the original estimates and values should be varied and a simple $\pm 50\%$ is often used. This allows evaluators to generate caveats around the baseline findings conclusion, for example, the conclusion that A is more cost effective than B is highly sensitive to fluctuations in parameter X but not to fluctuations in parameters Y and Z. It is also possible to amend parameters simultaneously – for example to put a new intervention in the worst possible light. If on the basis of these collective 'worst case' assumptions the new intervention is still more cost effective than the old, then a change in policy is clearly indicated. Another approach is to use *threshold analysis* where the parameter values are adjusted until the findings alter and the decision as to which programme to adopt or reject is reversed. For example, to what extent do the costs of programme X need to be increased to make it more efficient than programme Y? In recent years more sophisticated approaches have been employed to estimate the effect of uncertainty. For instance, NICE require a probabilistic sensitivity analysis to be conducted to establish the probability that cost/QALY ratios lie within willingness-to-pay thresholds, as shown in Figure 5.1.

Figure 5.1: Cost-effectiveness acceptability curve

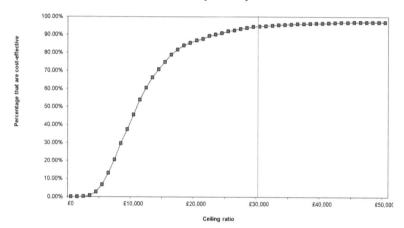

The cost-effectiveness acceptability curve highlights the probability that the cost-effectiveness ratio – in this case the cost/QALY – will be at least equal to the ceiling ratio, designed to reflect society's willingness to pay for that outcome.

Importance and significance of whole systems frameworks

There is, however, an inherent danger that economic evaluation – and evaluation per se – employs a relatively narrow perspective and fails to appreciate and consider the broader picture as reflected in the whole systems perspective. The whole systems perspective is a powerful, and could be argued necessary, device for understanding how the various elements in a system interact and 'depend' on each other, thus enabling the 'big picture' to be seen (Senge, 1990) which is otherwise unlikely to be 'visible' to a single individual or agency. These dependencies, interactions and their associated complexities have led to a number of attempts to encapsulate a 'whole systems' perspective. For example, a Canadian ethnographic study which aimed to gain insight into stakeholder perspectives on the barriers and facilitators for return-to-work initiatives categorised the emerging themes into three levels of systems – micro system, meso system and macro system, which are depicted in Figure 5.2.

Figure 5.2: Micro, meso and macro systems

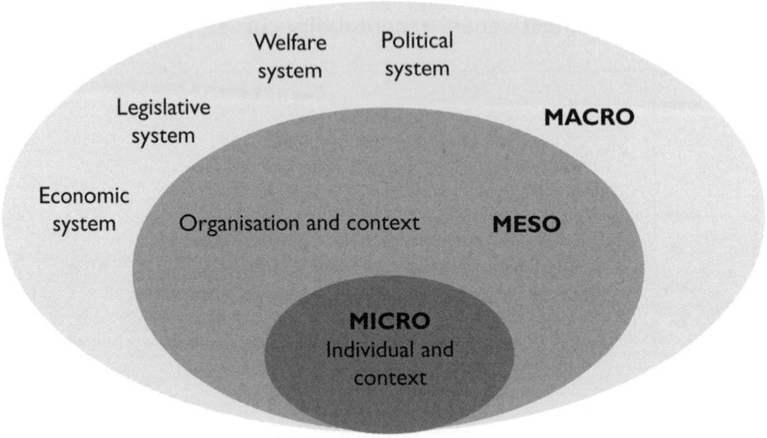

However, the authors acknowledged the complexities that underlie return-to-work initiatives and their evaluations and, as with other studies (for example Frank et al, 1996, 1998), highlighted the interplay and interactions between various system components. It is therefore far too simplistic to suggest that a simple, linear, static and predictable approach to systems thinking is adequate to explain the complexities surrounding work retention and return to work issues, for example, while systems are generally too complex to permit good predictions of their behaviour based on simple reductionist scientific studies.

The development of *network research* (Barabasi and Bonabeau, 2003; Bell and Koithan, 2006) and *complex systems* (Waldorp, 1992; Plesk and Greenhalgh, 2001) represent moves towards a whole systems approach and provides additional, and ostensibly a more appropriate, set of frameworks for evaluations of what might be termed complex programmes or interventions. Network research is concerned with the inter-relationships and interactions between the component parts of a system or whole system, while in complex systems, the guiding principle is that the whole is greater than the sum of the parts and that comprehension of the individual aspects does not guarantee an understanding of the operation of the whole system.

In relation to virtually all public and human services projects, schemes and programmes there are highly important interactions between the various systems, but the boundaries between the systems are often 'fuzzy', with systems embedded within each other, and where different organisations are responsible for different components or having to work collaboratively in partnerships, with considerable potential for conflict and uncertainty. In such situations, system inter-relationships and interdependencies are particularly important, when organisations work in 'joined-up' collaborative partnerships, where individual, organisational and societal needs are rarely compartmentalised according to convenient boundaries, and the extent of complexity and potential for conflict and uncertainty increases as one moves from micro systems through to macro systems. Small changes in one system can lead to large changes if they occur at critical points in the dynamics of the whole systems or where problems at the interfaces between systems can lead to progressively more difficulties and issues as complex systems evolve over time (Bell and Koithan, 2006). For example, it is evident that in relation to work retention and return-to-work initiatives, the turbulence and uncertainties require the engagement and active involvement of all relevant stakeholders if systems are to function effectively and efficiently (White, 2000; Bunker and Alban, 1994).

In the next section, the nature of system deficiencies as potential constraints and obstacles to 'successful' evaluations being undertaken will be explored.

System deficiencies within complex systems and their effect on the evaluation process

In August 2006, the Commonwealth Fund Commission published a framework for a high performance health care system for the United States. The introduction to the report is damning:

> The United States has some of the best-equipped hospitals and best-trained physicians in the world. With much dedication to helping patients, they often provide extraordinary care. Nevertheless, the evidence clearly shows that, overall, the performance of the US health care system falls far below the level it can and should achieve. On

many dimensions of performance—from timely access to needed services to the deployment of health information technology—we lag behind other industrialised nations. Within our own borders, there are wide disparities from region to region and from state to state. We spend more on health care than any other country. But we allocate our resources inefficiently and wastefully, failing to provide universal access to care and failing to achieve value commensurate with the money spent. In the US, many patients receive treatments and procedures known to be ineffective, while other effective treatments are vastly underused. Tens of thousands die annually from preventable errors. Nearly half of all adults worry they will not be able to pay their medical bills if they become seriously ill, will not get high quality care, or will experience a medical error. (Commonwealth Fund Commission on a High Performance Health System, 2006, p 1)

The diagnosis of the problem basically revolved around what was referred to as a 'lack of systemness', with numerous system failures evident and which led to some important considerations when designing and undertaking evaluations. As highlighted earlier, no system (or sub-system) is isolated and an action on the part of one individual or organisation, or a policy or initiative developed within one system, has an impact which often influences the responses of others within the whole system, irrespective of the evaluation approach employed. The lack of joined-up thinking at organisational and governmental level can result in the situations emerging where a change in one arena can generate large, and potentially unintended, consequences elsewhere. For example, *The Economist*, contrary to virtually every other media outlet, argued after the Hatfield railway crash in October 2000 that 'Britain spends too much money, not too little, making its railways safe' (*The Economist*, 2000a) and 'that overreaction to last month's rail crash has increased the risks to rail passengers, not reduced them' by making it more difficult to travel by rail resulting in people increasing their reliance on car travel – which is much more risky than rail travel (*The Economist*, 2000b). It concluded that:

From society's point of view it is far from rational to spend 150 times as much on saving a life on the railways as on saving a life on the roads. A bereaved mother cares little how her child was killed. Many more lives could be saved if the money currently being poured into avoiding spectacular but rare railway crashes were spent instead on avoiding the tragedies that happen ten times every day on the roads. (*The Economist*, 2000a)

Communication issues represent major obstacles at all stages in the evaluation process. For example, in terms of work retention and rehabilitation schemes, James et al (2006) argued for the co-ordination of the rehabilitation process by the creation of systems that facilitate sufficient communication, discussion and 'joined-up' action between all potentially relevant stakeholders. Further, Friesen et al (2001) argued that there was general agreement, across a wide range of stakeholders, that delays of all types and ineffective communication were important barriers to successful and effective rehabilitation. Similarly, the implications of a lack of a joined-up approach were evident in a Dutch study, which concluded that the lack of communication and agreement by general practitioners and occupational physicians in medical diagnosis and management of employees on long-term sickness absence due to mental health problems were indicators of sub-optimal medical treatment and inadequate return-to-work strategies (Anema et al, 2006).

Seddon (2008) argues forcibly that 'bureaucracy and red tape' have driven public services in the wrong direction and at great cost – not merely the cost of bureaucracy itself, but an additional cost:

> because the changes being mandated by that bureaucracy are the wrong things to do. The bureaucracy has made services worse; and public sector morale has been sapped … We invest in the wrong things believing them to be the right things … These plausible but wrong ideas have been promulgated through a massive specifications and inspection industry … [with] thousands of people engaged in telling others what to do and inspecting them for compliance. Public services have requirements placed on them by a plethora of bodies, the biggest single weakness of which, common to them all, is that they are based on opinion rather than knowledge. (Seddon, 2008, p iv)

Fragmented policy-making processes that fail to encompass a whole-system perspective therefore tend to focus on the system components that are easily observed and the outputs and outcomes that are easily quantified and assessed. The problem of these approaches is that the 'iceberg effect' is often ignored. Decisions are often made on the basis of costs and benefits that are visible, above the water, while those which lie below the water, and are often of considerable magnitude, are ignored (Phillips, 2005). The fragmentation of public service provision – in the UK at least – has also brought with it what has been termed 'budgetary myopia' (Phillips, 2005). For example, a narrow budgetary-focused approach fails to grasp the consequences that decisions made in one area to contain costs can have on other budgets and the adverse events and iatrogenic costs that can result from the interventions and services provided. For example, in a study carried out in Hong Kong to assess the cost-effectiveness of strategies for managing pain after limb injury, the per-unit cost of ketorolac was nearly three times as much as that of morphine – $HK7.53 compared to $HK2.81. However, the mean overall cost per person amounted to $HK43.60 for those in the ketorolac group and over five times more, $HK228.80, in the morphine group ($P < 0.0001$), with much of the difference between the two groups accounted for by the management of adverse events (Rainer et al, 2000).

Similarly, narrow emphases on budgets often fail to grasp the nature and extent of wider iatrogenic costs resulting from interventions and services in other parts of the system or indeed in other systems. For example, it has been estimated that one in every eight patients admitted to hospitals in England and Wales each year experience preventable adverse events, leading to an additional three million bed days at a cost to the National Health Service (NHS) of £1,000 million a year (Vincent et al, 2001). Other examples of iatrogenic costs are to be found in the area of medicines management, with the prevalence of adverse drug events reported by a retrospective record review of nearly 19,000 patients in two acute care hospitals being 6.5% of all hospital admissions; and in 80% of these 1,225 cases these adverse events were the direct cause of admission. The cost of such admissions was estimated to be £466 million per year (Pirmohamed et al, 2004). Another study reported that adverse drug events in UK hospitals cost the NHS £380 million a year – which in health currency units represented 15 to 20 400-bed hospitals (Wiffen et al, 2002). It is the representation of real cost that indicates the extent to which resources are being used efficiently to maximise the benefits for society.

It is also apparent that a fragmented approach to service provision and the lack of a whole system perspective has resulted in 'target overload' and 'conflicting targets'. The multiplicity of targets, which in some cases clash with each other, and certainly conflict with targets set for other organisations, represents a major obstacle in the drive for economic efficiency. For example, a scathing account of targets in education has been offered by Mansell (2007). In the foreword to that book, Seldon argues:

> the pressure on teachers to deliver the improving test statistics by which the outside world judges them is proving counter-productive. Schools have been turning increasingly into exam factories … Intellectual curiosity is stifled. And young people's deeper cultural, moral, sporting, social and spiritual faculties are marginalised by a system in which all must come second to delivering improving test and exam numbers. (Seldon, 2007, foreword)

In the UK, the media has utilised many 'column inches' highlighting the queues of ambulances waiting to discharge their patients into hospital emergency departments, but unable to do so due to the reluctance of the emergency department to take responsibility and put undue pressure on meeting their target of time to triage! One target in one part of the system would therefore be met but another part of the system – the ambulance service – would be unable to meet its response times.

In advocating a move to whole-system perspective, an element of caution needs to be introduced when trying to generalise from evaluations that are highly context and time specific. Differences in public policies and practices, structures and funding mechanisms make it extremely difficult to assess the likely effectiveness and efficiency in one context of policies and interventions that have been implemented and assessed in different countries and jurisdictions. However, while recognising such a caveat, developing appropriate policy (and evaluation) frameworks is not beyond the realm of possibility and there are examples of relevant approaches in the field of chronic disease management, where, for example, the WHO has adapted the US chronic disease model (Wagner, 1998) to encompass a wider constituency of health care systems and generated the Innovative Care for Chronic Conditions framework, which reflects 'whole systems' thinking and includes components at the micro, meso and macro levels (Epping-Jordan et al, 2004).

Economics and evidence-based policy

This chapter began with a description of the underlying premise of economics. The very existence of the economic problem itself represents another obstacle in moving towards evidence-based policy. The ever-increasing demands placed on public services against constraints on the resources available to meet them continue to be a major headache for those at all levels of policy making, decision making, commissioning and the provision and delivery of services. In such an environment the ratio of costs and benefits in applying evidence is a crucial factor in determining whether the efforts are worthwhile. The costs of acquiring, accessing, processing and assessing relevant evidence, relative to other factors in developing policy, have to be carefully weighed in relation to their likely impact on the policy and the degree to which it is successfully implemented. For example, the translation of evidence from research into everyday situations and the importation of evidence generated from other cultures and contexts may require a significant amount of further analysis and scrutiny, and it has been shown in applied trial-based cost-effectiveness studies that few of them provide sufficient evidence for decision makers to establish the relevance or to adjust the results of the study to their location of interest (Sculpher et al, 2004). Further, the value added of additional information or evidence relative to cost in terms of its impact on decision making is a bourgeoning field of enquiry in its own right (Jansen and Koffijberg, 2009; Runge et al, 2011; Yokota and Thompson, 2004) and has to be an important determinant in the design and structuring of evaluations in the future.

Similarly, the weight attached to different criteria and the outcomes used to assess policies against criteria is something that should be pre-specified in the evaluation design. For example, health technology assessments have conventionally relied on the assumption that each QALY gained has the same value to society. The idea that the value of a QALY may vary between contexts and across sub-groups of patients has, however, recently been acknowledged in NICE's supplementary advice on the treatment of QALYs gained by patients at the end of life (Rawlins et al, 2010). To date, however, the empirical evidence to support such value judgements is limited. For example, most of the few studies that do exist explore ordinal preferences and thus do not enable the derivation of quantitative weights (Dolan and Tsuchiya, 2006). Further, the development of equity weights raises a number of questions that have yet to be answered. For instance, how should the distinction be drawn between advantaged and disadvantaged groups – for example, on grounds of gender, race or socio-economic considerations? Some work has been initiated in this area through the development of a checklist for equity considerations within the Cochrane and Campbell collaborations (Evans and Brown, 2003; Ueffing et al, 2010) but much work remains before equity can be fully integrated into such decisions.

Another issue relates to the perspective that the evaluation embraces and which costs and benefits should be included in an evaluation. The dangers of a restrictive and narrow perspective were alluded to earlier in the chapter. NICE's reference case for health technology appraisals (NICE, 2008) suggests that only costs to the UK National Health Service (NHS) and Personal Social Services (PSS) should be considered. However, this approach fails to recognise the interdependence of policies, programmes and schemes whose delivery involves expenditure being incurred by a range of government and non-government organisations and individuals while the effects may impinge on an entirely different set of stakeholders. For instance, interventions targeted at people with mental health problems alleviate the costs faced by the families of those with mental health problems, as well as impacting on employers' costs associated with the productivity and absenteeism of those with mental health problems (Knapp, 1999). Similarly, a study that was designed to assess the effectiveness and cost-effectiveness of a policy to introduce thermostatic bath valves in social housing to reduce the risk associated with bath scalds encompassed a range of stakeholders – health service, social services, housing associations, local government (building regulations), voluntary sector and individuals and their communities (Phillips et al, 2011).

In response to the multi-sector nature of such interventions, it is advocated that a broad perspective should be adopted (HM Treasury, 2003). However, there is still some debate about what form this broader perspective should take. NICE guidance on the evaluation of public health interventions suggests that the reference case should include all public costs when public health, rather than health technologies, are being evaluated (CPHE, 2006). Byford et al (2003) recommend that a societal perspective should be adopted when evaluating social welfare interventions, where an intervention would be recommended if the benefits to society were greater than the costs to society, but they also recognise that such a perspective would rarely be the perspective of choice to specific interest groups. A societal perspective is only justified where decision makers both set and allocate within budgets (Claxton et al, 2007) and where the objective of the decision maker is to maximise the welfare of society. However, from the perspective of the individual decision maker, budgets are usually fixed at departmental level and objectives are generally narrower than societal well-being (Byford et al, 2003; Claxton et al, 2007). In a situation of department-specific budget constraints and objective functions, a multi-sector perspective is more appropriate, and an intervention should be recommended if the overall benefits exceed the costs from the perspective of all stakeholders involved in delivering the programme and in receipt of the benefits, which might involve net beneficiaries 'compensating' those who are net contributors (Claxton et al, 2007). However, such a decision rule would only be optimal and lead to economic efficiency if the allocation of budgets between departments was also considered optimal, which itself is a major assumption and would involve considerable effort and data to determine whether it was the case (Claxton et al, 2007).

Further, a multi-sector perspective requires that each sector has a well-understood generic measure of outcome and acceptable valuation of it – referred to as the shadow price of the budget constraint (Drummond et al, 2007). However, this is seriously lacking in many sectors and requires further development (Byford et al, 2010) if a multi-sector societal perspective is to become the norm. A number of other barriers and obstacles to the use of economic evaluations have been identified and these in turn suggest ways in which this situation can be improved, including (Williams and Bryan, 2007; Williams et al, 2008; Byford et al, 2010):

- lack of understanding of the philosophy behind such evaluations on behalf of policy makers; for example, economic evaluation is often misinterpreted by non-economists as a cost-containment exercise rather than as a framework to facilitate maximisation of the benefits obtained from limited resources;
- lack of consistency in design of economic evaluations and methods employed, which undermines comparability of findings;
- lack of consideration in relation to equity considerations and wider benefit streams;
- lack of precision and specification in relation to issues that require evaluation;
- lack of centralised strategy at the policy level obstructs the development and acceptance of a consistent and systematic approach to economic analysis; and
- lack of independent research capacity in many sectors limits the delivery of economic evidence; the delivery of such analysis requires the development of infrastructure, expertise, knowledge and understanding, training, and adequate access to existing literature.

Further, it is probably the case that the discipline of health economics (and other branches of applied welfare economics) 'has been distorted with too much effort being put into the broad advocacy of the techniques of economics evaluation and too little emphasis being placed both on methodological quality and development and on the broader application of the economics techniques to health policy' (Maynard and Sheldon, 1997, p 157). The propensity to bolt economic evaluations with narrow perspectives onto randomised controlled clinical trials and to model the economic impact of interventions over a longer time period, without giving sufficient consideration to the broader issues that affect the overall impact of treatments and therapies, has been very noticeable in the last few years, as the focus has switched more to the assessment and appraisal of health care technologies. While valiant efforts are being made to deal with the effect of uncertainty so as to aid the decision-making process, the fact remains that the everyday world of health care is very different from the quasi-laboratory conditions under which clinical studies are undertaken and, irrespective of the number of simulations of the available data, it is impossible to capture all possible scenarios and situations that might arise in the real world of clinical practice. The catastrophic adverse event, the unforeseen circumstances which result in litigation and claims for compensation, changes in patients' preferences and perceptions and other unintended consequences can all conspire to transform the costs associated with a health care intervention assessed as being cost-effective at initial assessment. Similarly, the actual outcomes resulting from such interventions over a period of time, way in excess of the duration of any clinical study programme, cannot be adequately confined to a single measure which encapsulates the effect on a single patient (Phillips, 2005).

What has been advocated in health economics and has validity elsewhere, is that a broader perspective and set of approaches be employed (Coast, 2004) whereby the economic framework would enable decision makers (on behalf of society) to impute their own values to the profile of costs and consequences, which could differ according to local context, and where decision makers would be able to clearly identify what is included and what is omitted.

Developing a research agenda

There is no doubt that the evidence base for informing decisions and policy development is most developed in relation to health care. However, it has been argued that even in this area of investigation and evidence collection, the reliance on systematic reviews and narrow cost-effectiveness studies fails to embrace the broader societal and distributional issues, which are possibly even more applicable in other areas. A new research agenda to address the complexities inherent in whole systems perspectives is therefore clearly needed.

The limitations of conventional 'reductionist' approaches (Plsek and Greenhalgh, 2001; Lessard and Birch, 2010) have been highlighted and alternatives suggested (White, 2000; Plsek and Greenhalgh, 2001; Bell and Koithan, 2006; Lessard and Birch, 2010) to grapple with the complexities associated with the different system perspectives and structural interactions associated with public services programmes, but also with the design and methodological challenges that such situations pose. What is required are broadly-based, explicit and accepted inclusion and exclusion criteria, which seek to encompass the widest set of stakeholders, to allow 'disturbances' to be created in order to enable 'emergence' (White, 2000), recognising of course the difference between individual and system level perspectives. In adopting such a view reliance will be on accessing opportunistic and observational evidence rather than the 'high quality evidence' (and yet inappropriate in this context) as advocated in relation to evidence-based policy and decision making. Further, using economic evaluation as an indicator:

> the theory and practice of economic evaluation must expand to include different types of knowledge and methodologies, so that it can better adapt to practical realities and the needs of patients, decision makers, health care and social systems and ultimately society. New paradigms that incorporate a dynamic and emergent view of the world must replace reductionist approaches to health care. Complexity thinking offers an alternative model ... and would thus expand the scope of economic evaluation and increase its real-world applicability. (Lessard and Birch, 2010, p 169)

Further, it would be remiss if the issue of equity was not further considered within this chapter. The early words of this chapter made reference to the notion of social welfare and its two components, efficiency and equity. While the objective of endeavouring to maximise the benefits to society given the level of resources available appears, at first sight, to be perfectly valid and commendable, there are consequences associated with rigid adherence to the pursuit of such an objective. For example, it has been stated that 'as efficient as markets may be, they do not ensure that individuals have enough food, clothes to wear, or shelter' (Stiglitz, 2002, p 224). The eminent economist J. K. Galbraith had alluded to a similar picture some 30 years earlier when he outlined the theory of social balance and the problems caused by excessive reliance on market mechanisms, such as 'an opulent supply of some things and a niggardly yield of others' which leads to 'social discomfort and social unhealth'

(Galbraith, 1958, p 251). This thesis has been recently documented in what is termed the Spirit Level (Wilkinson and Pickett, 2010), where the evidence is presented for the relationship between an array of social and economic indicators and the extent of inequalities within countries and communities; the case being made that the narrower the differentials the more positive the social and economic benefits that are likely to emerge. As alluded to above, much more work needs to be undertaken in relation to equity weights and their incorporation into the array of measures currently purporting to reflect economic efficiency.

Concluding note

This chapter has sought to emphasise the need for and purpose of economic evaluations within evaluation frameworks and processes. The permanent existence of the economic problem, that of limited resources with which to address infinite demands on public provision, makes it imperative that the 'Is it worth it?' question is addressed so as to ensure – within obvious constraints and limitations – that the available resources could not have been better used to generate more benefits.

The discipline of economic evaluation is continuing to evolve – and at different rates in different areas of policy – but has come a long way since the earliest cost benefit studies were undertaken (Eckstein, 1958; Krutilla and Eckstein, 1958; McKean, 1958). Nevertheless, much work remains to be done to establish a clear consensus as to what are the most appropriate approaches to employ and techniques to utilise. It is often tempting to attribute a negative recommendation to the 'bottom line of money' but efficiency, as we have attempted to demonstrate, is much more than a mere financial assessment (economy) and involves the relationship between all costs and what is generated by the use of limited resources, with the specific aim of maximising the benefit to societies. It therefore has to be an integral component of all evaluations, and whilst not being a sufficient condition for 'successful evaluations' is nonetheless a necessary condition, but also dependent on the array of other criteria and circumstances surrounding the policy evaluation.

References

Ackerman, F. and Heinzerling, L. (2004) *Priceless: On knowing the price of everything and the value of nothing*, NY: The New Press.

Anema, J.R., Jettinghoff, K., Houtman, I. et al (2006) 'Medical care of employees long-term sick listed due to mental health problems: a cohort study to describe and compare the care of the occupational physician and the general practitioner', *Journal of Occupational Rehabilitation*, vol 16, no 1, pp 41-52.

Barabasi, A.L. and Bonabeau, E. (2003). 'Scale-free networks', *Scientific American*, vol 288, pp 50-9.

Bateman I.J, Carson, R.T., Day, B., Haneman, M., Hanleys, N., Hett, T., Jones-Lee, M., Loomes, G., Mourato, E., Ozdemiroglu, E., Pearce, D,. Sugden. R. and Swanson, J. (2002) *Economic valuation with stated preferences*, Cheltenham: Edward Elgar.

Bateman, I.J. and Willis, K.G. (1999) *Valuing normal preferences: Theory and practice of the contingent valuation method in US, EU and developing countries*, Oxford: OUP.

Bell, I.R. and Koithan, M. (2006). 'Models for the study of whole systems', *Integrative Cancer Therapies*, vol 5, no 4, pp 293-307.

Blaug, M. (1998) 'Where are we now in British health economics?', *Health Economics*, vol 7, no 1, pp 63-78.

Brouwer, W., Rutten, F. and Koopmanschap, M. (2001) 'Costing in economic evaluation', in M.F. Drummond and A. McGuire (eds) *Economic evaluation in health care: Merging theory with practice*, Oxford: Oxford University Press.

Bunker, B. and Alban, B. (1994) *Large group intervention*, San Francisco, CA: Barret Koehler.

Byford, S., McDaid, D. and Sefton, T.A.J. (2003) *Because it's worth it: A practical guide to conducting economic evaluations in the social welfare field*, York: Joseph Rowntree Foundation.

Byford, S., Barrett, B., Dubourg, R., Francis, J. and Sisk, J. (2010) 'The role of economic evidence in formulation of public policy and practice', in I. Shemilt, M. Mugford, L. Vale, K. Marsh and C. Donaldson (eds) *Evidence-based decisions and economics: Health care, social welfare, education and criminal justice*, Oxford: Wiley-Blackwell.

Carlyle, T. (1849) 'Occasional discourse on the negro question', in *Frazer's Magazine for Town and Country*, Vol XL, London. Available at: http://www.efm.bris.ac.uk/het/carlyle/occasion.htm. (accessed 02/01/2012)

Claxton, K.P., Sculpher, M.J. and Culyer, A.J. (2007) *Mark versus Luke? Appropriate methods for the evaluation of public health interventions*, University of York, Centre for Health Economics Research Paper 31.

Coast, J. (2004) 'Is economic evaluation in touch with society's health values?', *British Medical Journal*, vol 329, pp 1233-36.

Commonwealth Fund Commission on a High Performance Health System (2006) *Framework for a high performance health system for the United States*. New York: The Commonwealth Fund. Available at: www.cmwf. org/usr_doc/Commission_framework_high_performance_943.pdf.

CPHE (2006) *Methods for the development of NICE public health guidance*, London: NICE.

Culyer, A.J. (1989) 'The normative economics of health care finance and provision', *Oxford Review of Economic Policy*, vol 5, no 1, pp 34-58.

Dolan, P. (2001) 'Output measures and valuation in health', in M.F. Drummond and A. McGuire (eds) *Economic evaluation in health care: merging theory with practice*, Oxford: Oxford University Press.

Dolan, P. and Metcalfe, R. (2008) 'Valuing non-market goods: A comparison of preference-based and experience-based approaches'. Available at http://cep.lse.ac.uk/seminarpapers/25-02-08-DOL.pdf.

Dolan, P. and Tsuchiya, A. (2006) 'The elicitation of distributional judgements in the context of economic evaluation', in A. Jones (ed) *Companion to health economics*, Cheltenham: Elgar, Chapter 36.

Dolan, P., Peasgood, T. and White, M. (2008) 'Do we really know what makes us happy? A review of the economic literature on the factors associated with subjective wellbeing', *Journal of Economic Psychology*, vol 29, pp 94-122.

Dolan, P., Metcalfe, R., Munro, V. and Christensen, M.C. (2008) 'Valuing lives and life years: anomalies, implications and an alternative', *Health Economics, Policy, and Law*, vol 3, pp 277-300.

Drummond, M.F., Sculpher, M.J. and Torrance, G.W. (2005) *Methods for the economic evaluation of health care programmes*, Oxford: Oxford University Press.

Drummond, M., Weatherly. H., Claxton, K. et al. (2007) *Assessing the challenges of applying standard methods of economic evaluation to public health interventions*, Public Health Research Consortium, York. Available at http://www.york.ac.uk/phrc/D1-05%20RFR.pdf.

Eckstein, O. (1958) *Water resource development*, Cambridge, MA: Harvard University Press.

Epping-Jordan, J.E., Pruitt, S.D., Bengoa, R., Wagner, E.H. (2004) 'Improving the quality of health care for chronic conditions', *Quality and Safety in Health Care*, vol 13, pp 299-305.

Evans, T. and Brown, H. (2003) 'Road traffic crashes: operationalizing equity in the context of health sector reform', *Injury Control and Safety Promotion*, vol 10, no 1-2, pp 11-12.

Frank, J., Sinclair, S., Hogg-Johnson, S., Shannon, H. et al. (1998) 'Preventing disability from work-related low-back pain. New evidence gives new hope – if we can just get all the players onside', *Canadian Medical Association Journal*, vol 158, pp 1625-31.

Frank, J.W, Brooker, A.S., DeMaio S.E., Kerr, M.S., et al. (1996) 'Disability resulting from occupational low back pain: Part II: what do we know about secondary prevention? A review of the scientific evidence on prevention after disability begins', *Spine*, vol 21, pp 2918-29.

Friesen, M.N., Yassi, A., Cooper, J. (2001) 'Return-to-work: The importance of human interactions and organizational structures', *Work*, vol 17, pp 11-22.

Galbraith, J.K. (1958) *The affluent society*, Cambridge. MA: The Riverside Press.

Godlee, F. (2010) 'Wishing you a rational new year', *British Medical Journal*, vol 341, c7377.

Hajkowicz, S. and Higgins, A. (2008) 'A comparison of multiple criteria analysis techniques for water resource management', *European Journal of Operational Research*, vol 184, pp 255-65.

Haynes, B. (1999) 'Can it work? Does it work? Is it worth it?', *British Medical Journal*, vol 319, pp 652-653.

Heller, R.F., Gemmell, I., Wilson, E., Fordham, R. and Smith, R.D. (2006) 'Using economic analysis for local priority setting: The population cost-impact approach', *Applied Health Economics and Health Policy*, vol 5, no 1, pp 45-54.

HM Treasury (2003) *Green Book*, London: HM Treasury. Available at http://www.hm-treasury.gov.uk/d/green_book_complete.pdf.

HM Treasury (2009) *Developments in the economics of well-being*, Treasury Economic Working Paper No. 4. Available at http://webarchive.nationalarchives.gov.uk/20100407010852/http://www.hm-treasury.gov.uk/d/workingpager4_031108.pdf.

James, P., Cunningham, I. and Dibbren, P. (2006) 'Job retention and return to work of ill and injured workers: towards an understanding of organisational dynamics', *Employee Relations*, vol 28, no 3, pp 290-303.

Jansen, M.P. and Koffijberg, H. (2009) 'Enhancing value of information analyses', *Value in Health*, vol 12, pp 935-41.

Johansson, P.-O. (1987) *The economic theory and measurement of environmental benefits*, Cambridge: Cambridge University Press.

Jones-Lee, M.W. (1990) 'The value of transport safety', *Oxford Review of Economic Policy*, vol 6, pp 39-60.

Knapp, M. (1999) 'Economic evaluation and mental health: Sparse past . . . fertile future?', *Journal of Mental Health Policy and Economics*, vol 2, pp 163–67.

Krutilla, J.V. and Eckstein, O. (1958) *Multiple purpose river development*, Baltimore, MD: John Hopkins University Press.

Laurance, J. (2006) 'The real cost of a bag of salad', *The Independent*, 29 April.

Lessard, C. and Birch, S. (2010) 'Complex problems or simple solutions? Enhancing evidence-based economics to reflect reality', in I. Schemit et al (eds) *Evidence-based decisions and economics: health care, social welfare, education and criminal justice*, Oxford: Wiley-Blackwell, BMJ Books.

Maciosek, M.V., Coffield, A.B., Edwards, N.M., Flottemesch, T.J., Goodman, M.J. and Solberg, L.I. (2006) 'Priorities among effective clinical preventive services: results of a systematic review and analysis', *American Journal of Preventive Medicine*, vol 31, no 1, pp 52-61.

Maciosek, M.V., Edwards, N.M., Coffield, A.B., Flottemesch, T.J., Nelson, W.W., Goodman, M.J. and Solberg, L.I. (2006) 'Priorities among effective clinical preventive services: methods', *American Journal of Preventive Medicine*, vol 31, no 1, pp 90-6.

Mallenson, A. (2002) *Whiplash and other useful illnesses*, Montreal: McGill-Queen's University Press.

Mansell, W. (2007) *Education by numbers: The tyranny of testing*, London: Politico Publishing.

Marsh, K. (2010) 'The role of review and synthesis methods in decision models', in I. Schemit et al (eds) (2010) *Evidence-based decisions and economics: Health care, social welfare, education and criminal justice*, Oxford: Wiley-Blackwell, BMJ Books.

Maynard, A. and Sheldon, T.A. (1997). 'Health economics: has it fulfilled its potential?', in A. Maynard and I. Chalmers *Non-random reflections on health services research: on the 25th anniversary of Archie Cochrane's Effectiveness and Efficiency*, London: BMJ Books.

McGuire, A. and Henderson, J. (1987). *The economics of health care: An introductory text*, London: Routledge and Kegan Paul.

McKean, R. (1958) *Efficiency in government through systems analysis*, New York: Wiley.

Newman, M., Bird, K., Tripney, J. et al (2010) *Understanding the drivers, impact and value of engagement in culture and sport*. CASE, London. Available at http://www.culture.gov.uk/images/research/CASE-supersummaryFINAL-19-July2010.pdf

NICE (2007) 'Behaviour change at population, community and individual levels', *Public Health Guidance* 6, London: NICE.

NICE (2008) *Guide to the methods of technology appraisal*, London: NICE.

OECD (2007) 'Is happiness measurable and what do those measures mean for policy?', Available at www.oecd.org/document/12/0,334, en_21571361_31938349_37720396_1_1_1_1,00.html

Pearce, D.W. and Turner, R.K. (1990), *Economics of natural resources and the environment*, Hemel Hempstead: Harvester Wheatsheaf.

Phillips C.J. (2001) 'The real cost of pain management', *Anaesthesia*, vol 56, pp 1031-3.

Phillips, C.J. (2005) *Health economics: An introduction for health professionals*, Oxford: Blackwells BMJ Books.

Phillips, C.J. and Prowle, M.J. (1992) 'Evaluating a health campaign: the Heartbeat Wales no-smoking initiative', *Contemporary Wales*, vol 5, pp 187-212.

Phillips, C.J. and Prowle, M.J. (1993) 'The economics of a reduction in smoking: a case study from Heartbeat Wales', *Journal of Epidemiology and Community Health*, vol 47, no 3, pp 215-23.

Phillips, C.J., Humphreys, I., Kendrick, D. et al (2011) 'Preventing bath water scalds: a cost-effectiveness analysis of introducing bath thermostatic mixer valves in social housing', *Injury Prevention*, vol 17, no 4, pp 238-43.

Pirmohamed, M., James, S., Meakin, S. et al. (2004) 'Adverse drug reactions as cause of admission to hospital: prospective analysis of 18820 patients', *British Medical Journal*, vol 329, pp 15–19.

Plsek, P.E. and Greenhalgh, T. (2001) 'The challenge of complexity in health care', *British Medical Journal*, vol 323, pp 625-628.

Rainer, T.H., Jacobs, P., Ng, Y.C. et al (2000) 'Cost effectiveness analysis of intravenous ketorolac and morphine for treating pain after limb injury: double blind randomized controlled trial', *British Medical Journal*, vol 321, pp 1–9.

Rawlins, M., Barnett, D. and Stevens, A. (2010) 'Pharmacoeconomics: NICE's approach to decision-making', *British Journal of Clinical Pharmacology*, vol 70, no 3, pp 346-9.

Romero, C. (1997) 'Multicriteria decision analysis and environmental economics: an approximation', *European Journal of Operational Research*, vol 96, pp 81-89.

Runge, M.C., Converse, S.J. and Lyons, J.E. (2011) 'Which uncertainty? Using expert elicitation and expected value of information to design an adaptive program', *Biological Conservation*, vol 144, pp 1214-23.

Sculpher, M.J., Pang, F.S., Manca, A. et al (2004) 'Generalisability in economic evaluation studies in healthcare: a review and case studies', *Health Technology Assessment*, vol 8, no 49, iii-iv, pp 1-192.

Seddon, J. (2008) *Systems thinking in the public sector: The failure of the reform regime ... and a manifesto for a better way*, Axminster: Triarchy Press.

Seldon, A. (2007) Foreword to W. Mansel, *Education by numbers: The tyranny of testing*, London: Politico Publishing.

Sen, A.K. (1985) *Commodities and capabilities*, Oxford: Oxford University Press.

Senge, P. (1990) *The fifth discipline: The art and practice of the learning organisation*, NY: Doubleday.

Stiglitz, J. (2002) *Globalization and its discontents*, London: Penguin Books.

The Economist (2000) 'The price of safety', 23 November. Available at http://www.economist.com/node/434618.

The Economist (2000) 'How not to run a railway', 23 November. Available at http://www.economist.com/node/433992.

Ueffing, E., Tugwell, P., Welch, V., Petticrew, M. and Kridtjansson, E., Cochrane Health Equity Field (2010) 'C1, C2 Equity checklist for systematic review authors', Cochrane Health Equity Field, Ottawa, Available at www.equity.cochrane.org/Files/equitychecklist.pdf.

Vincent, C., Neale, G. and Woloshynowych, M. (2001) 'Adverse events in British hospitals: preliminary retrospective record review', *British Medical Journal*, vol 322, pp 517-9.

Wagner, E.H. (1998) 'Chronic disease management: what will it take to improve care for chronic illness?', *Effective Clinical Practice*, vol 1998, no 1, pp 2-4.

Waldorp, M. (1992) *Complexity: The emerging science at the edge of chaos*, New York: Simon & Schuster.

White, L. (2000) 'Changing the "whole system" in the public sector', *Journal of Organizational Change Management*, vol 13, no 2, pp 162–77.

Wiffen, P., Gill, M., Edwards, J. and Moore, A. (2002) 'Adverse drug reactions in hospital patients: a systematic review of the prospective and retrospective studies', *Bandolier Extra*, June.

Williams, I. and Bryan, S. (2007) 'Understanding the limited impact of economic evaluation in health care resource allocation: a conceptual framework', *Health Policy*, vol 80, pp 135-43.

Williams, I., Bryan, S. and McIver, S. (2008) 'The use of economic evaluations in NHS decision-making: a review and empirical investigation', *Health Technology Assessment*, vol 12, no 7, pp iii, ix-x, 1-175.

Wilson, E.C., Rees, J. and Fordham, R.J. (2006) 'Developing a prioritisation framework in an English Primary Care Trust', *Cost Effectiveness and Resource Allocation*, vol 4, p 3.

Wilson, E.C., Sussex, J., Macleod, C. and Fordham, R.J. (2007) 'Prioritizing health technologies in a Primary Care Trust', *Journal of Health Services Research and Policy*, vol 12, no 2, pp 80–85.

Wilkinson, R. and Pickett, K. (2010) *The spirit level: Why equality is better for everyone*, London: Penguin Books.

Yokota, F., Thompson, K.M. (2004) 'Value of information literature analysis: a review of applications in health risk management', *Medical Decision Making*, vol 24, pp 287–298.

Zarkin, G., Dunlap, L.J., Hicks, K.A. and Mano, D. (2005) 'Benefits and costs of methadone treatment: results from a lifetime simulation model', *Health Economics*, vol 14, pp 1133-50.

SIX

The impact of evaluation on decision making

Impact theory

The generally agreed main purpose of formal evaluation in the public sector is to improve services. In order to achieve that broad objective, governments and public sector and voluntary sector bodies produce strategies that culminate in policies which, in turn, inform the design and operation of projects and programmes. In earlier chapters we have made a distinction between *outcome* and *impact*. Those who have carried out and written on the subject of evaluation are agreed that the term 'impact' refers to the cause–effect relationship between planned activities and the intended social benefit. Rossi et al (1999) use the phrase *impact theory* to sum up the 'beliefs, assumptions, and expectations' (p 78) about this relationship. Here again, we are inclined to discount a definition of a theory that relies on anything less substantial than a firmly evidence-based explanation.

On this point, and in relation to the issue of attempting to identify a cause–effect link between inputs–outcomes–impact, Pawson (2006) offers a rather radical realist perspective. His claim is that 'interventions are theories' (p 26). He notes that the conventional interpretation of interventions is to regard them as tangible items such as resources, equipment and personnel whereas, from the realist perspective, interventions are always based on a hypothesis that postulates:

> 'If we deliver a programme in this way or we manage services so, then it will bring about some improved outcome.' Such conjectures are grounded on assumptions about what gives rise to poor performance, inappropriate behaviour and so on ... (p 26)

In referring to the supposed 'theory' as a hypothesis, Pawson supports our assertion about the misuse of 'theory' in setting out to explain the process of outcome and impact assessments. However, what Pawson regards as interventions are more accurately known as 'inputs' – those resources – including sets of values – which are used to *generate* interventions. Interventions are neither theories nor hypotheses nor tangibles; they are *actions that form the process of interaction between participants.* Process as a key element in the usual configuration of evaluation research tends to feature less prominently in the literature than outcome and impact yet, in a sense, it can have a clear impact on, for example, intended beneficiaries of public services. For example, in an out-patients' department of a hospital, given the choice between being seen within a given period of time but being treated as little more than a number, or waiting longer for a more personal response, it is quite possible that many people would be prepared to wait a little longer if this meant that they each would be treated as an important individual. In short, they would in this context rate process above output.

Impact assessment

A full-blown theory to be applied to the process of assessing the impact of a particular policy, programme or project would be very useful. Whatever the context, decision makers could be confident that they would be able to isolate the factor or, more likely, factors that led to the outcomes. Then, having identified that cause–effect nexus, the evaluation commissioner and designer could look at the next stage in the evaluation process and identify the link between the outcome and its impact. What undermines the proposition that *impact theory* is a useful or even an essential weapon in the evaluator's armoury is that nowhere in the literature is there actually articulated an example of such a theory. That there is such a theory, therefore, remains something of a fabrication. In the real world where hard-headed decision makers need categorical assurances that (a) led to (b), 'beliefs, assumptions and expectations' are of no use.

In addition, the long-term effect – whether positive, negative or something of each – need not relate only to one group of people. In the planning of a piece of evaluation research, there will be potentially a number of different stakeholders. For example, a programme of staff development might have as its interim objective enhanced skills or competences among social workers engaged on child care cases. These enhanced skills and competences could then be assessed as an output measure. The hoped-for outcome might be improved communication between social workers and the staff of other agencies, with an expected impact of reduced risks of children being ill-treated or neglected. If there turned out to be a clear correlation between social workers' enhanced skills and competences and fewer incidents of maltreatment of children over a period of, say, five to ten years then a consequent impact could be improved levels of self-esteem, self-confidence and higher status for that particular cohort of social workers. One can conceive of other 'spin-offs' for the department and the collaborating agencies.

One of the methodological problems with assessing the longer-term effects of interventions after the conclusion of a project, programme or policy implementation is the very fact that some time will have elapsed between completion or implementation and the point at which some changes have been perceived and reported. As an example, we can return to our previous brief discussion of reconviction rates following a period or periods of imprisonment or after the successful completion of a community sentence. If, on the face of it, there would appear to be a reduction in criminal activity over a fairly lengthy period, how confident could the researcher be in attributing this statistic to previous sentencing decisions? It is in instances of this kind that the experimental research design would be advocated as the only means of controlling variables that in themselves might account for the decrease in offending behaviour. In a very real sense, it is this problem of attribution that is at the heart of debates about the utilisation of evaluation research findings.

The utilisation of evaluation research findings

Patton's solution

Perhaps the most accessible means of following Patton's ideas on this topic can be found on the website of the Evaluation Center of Western Michigan University, where under the section Evaluation Models he has posted his checklist ('Utilization-Focused Evaluation') on how to maximise the likelihood of 'primary intended users' taking heed of and adopting the research results (Patton, 2002). We have already noted in Chapter Two that Patton's main focus is on the commissioners of the evaluation research since they are the ones who have the power and authority to implement the course of action indicated by the findings. Central to the 'utilization-focused evaluation' (U–FE) approach is negotiation between the intended users and the evaluator in which those carrying out the evaluation offer 'a menu of possibilities within the framework of established evaluation standards and principles' (Patton, 2002, p 1). The whole process is one of interaction and collaboration in which the commissioners decide on the design and data collection methods which they consider most appropriate for their purposes. This assumes that the intended users will have a very clear idea of how they plan to use the findings.

Patton's 'model' derives from the perfectly reasonable belief that if decision makers are actively involved from the start they are more likely to feel ownership of the evaluation process and they will be more inclined to accept and act on the findings. To achieve this positive commitment, Patton recommends the performance of twelve tasks to be carried out by the evaluator. The first cluster of activities included under Task 1 is:

- explaining the nature and purpose of U–FE;
- finding out whether the client is committed to doing useful evaluation;
- assessing if the client is prepared to spend time and resources on the evaluation.

We shall pause here to ask whether it is conceivable that any clients would suggest at the outset that they were not really interested in 'useful evaluation'.

With regard to the third point, it is not clear whether this refers to the time and resources necessary for the collaborative involvement that this approach demands, or to the decision to commission a programme of evaluation research. However, logic demands that Patton means the former. He stresses that successful completion of this first task depends on the negotiating skills of the evaluator. Naturally, if this first step fails then either further negotiation takes place with a view to agreeing a modified approach or the client dictates the design, methods of data collection and time-frame for carrying out the evaluation. But how could it fail at this first stage and, if it did fail, would the evaluator(s) – presumably wedded to U–FE as the preferred if not the only option for conducting a 'useful evaluation' – withdraw graciously or bite their tongue(s) as it were and do the client's bidding?

Since the client is left to decide on which course to take among a 'menu of possibilities' it must surely follow that the client will indeed have the last word on how the evaluation is to proceed. The previous query about whether a client would admit to commissioning an evaluation other than to utilise the findings does not, of course, rule out the possibility that in reality the primary purpose of commissioning the research might have little or nothing to do with using the findings. We shall return to this point later in this chapter.

A basic assumption that informs Patton's checklist is that the primary intended user has a clear idea prior to the evaluation of how or whether to use the research findings. It would surely be presumptuous on the part of evaluators if they tried to predict that the results of the evaluation will be of such a nature that they will actually be 'useful'. This is analogous to drug companies seeking a commitment by medical practitioners that they will use a new drug before its efficacy has been rigorously tested and confirmed.

In Patton's schema, each of the twelve tasks and their accompanying activities rely on their performance on the successful achievement of the preceding task. The sequence is:

1. Program/Organizational Readiness Assessment.
2. Evaluator Readiness and Capability Assessment.
3. Identification of Primary Intended Users.
4. Situational Analysis.
5. Identification of Primary Intended Uses.
6. Focusing the Evaluation.
7. Evaluation Design.
8. Simulation of Use.
9. Data Collection.
10. Data Analysis.
11. Facilitation of Use.
12. Metaevaluation.

It would appear rather odd that Task 2 includes assessing the match between the evaluator's skills and what will be needed in the evaluation. It would indeed be unfortunate if – after the initial stage of informing and negotiating with the client regarding the format of the evaluation – those who are carrying out the research are found to be not up to the task. Perhaps to anticipate a possible criticism raised above about the difficulty of predicting the ways in which the findings will be used, Patton's Task 8 involves fabricating findings 'on the proposed design and measures' (Patton, 2002, p 5). Depicting various results will guide users to check whether the design and data collection methods need to be revised in order to increase utility. It remains unclear as to how the eventual design and methods should be changed if the array of potential results are merely simulated. What, one might ask, is Task 1 doing as the first stage in the evolution of the research design when this might all be changed after the completion of Task 8?

It should be instructive to imagine a scenario in which 'simulation of use' is being tried out. Consider a situation where a government is concerned with the increasing NHS expenditure on treating people who have brought on themselves quite serious health problems. The prevalence of hard drug use, of over-eating and the excessive consumption of alcohol are all seen as behaviour that is chosen by those who indulge in unhealthy practices. The government insists that the costs of treating such individuals could be spent much more productively treating victims of circumstances outside their control and which adversely affect their health. The government announces a policy to withdraw resources from treating preventable illnesses and to reduce money allocated to health education and health promotion, which appears to have little effect on the choices of lifestyle that people choose to follow. According to Patton, the evaluator then sets about 'fabricating realistic findings that show varying results' (Patton, 2002, p 5).

The varying results could be:

- more resources become available to treat non-preventable diseases;
- a public outcry demanding a reversal of the decision on the grounds of discrimination;
- the medical profession asserts its ethical duty to try to help all patients regardless of lifestyle;
- statistically significant reduction in self-harming lifestyles post-policy implementation compared with pre-policy implementation;
- no statistically significant reductions.

Clearly, the most favoured results from the government's perspective would be the first and fourth of the simulated results. In our scenario, the intention, prior to this U–FE stage, is to pilot the policy in two local authority areas over a period of five years. This amounts to a quasi-experimental research design, the data being collected through the records of GPs and hospital authorities. Items 2 and 3 would be unlikely to encourage reconsideration of the policy *design* nor, necessarily, would Item 5, other than to revise the timescale to a longer trial period on the ground that five years is too short a time for the policy measures to take effect. The basic design and data collection methods would not need to change. In any case, if the policy makers were faced with the first and last results they could well decide at the outset that the re-allocation of resources was to be given the highest priority and therefore the policy would be implemented despite its unpopularity in some quarters. Secondly, if some citizens were happy to continue using hard drugs, eating or boozing to excess then, the government would say: well, that's their choice. There might be examples where simulation of use could influence a re-think of the research design but Patton does not furnish us with any.

In short, we accept that Patton's checklist is a very worthy attempt to offer a template for the practice of evaluation which, he is confident, will lead to a much greater possibility that the results of the evaluation will be acted upon. In focusing on the use of evaluation results Patton is very much in line with the majority of academics.

The Rossi et al formula

Rossi, Freeman and Lipsey (1999) classify the use that is made of evaluation results into three categories. These are:

1. Direct or instrumental use.
2. Conceptual utilisation.
3. Persuasive utilisation.

The first type occurs when there is documented and specific use of evaluation findings by decision makers and other stakeholders. The authors provide two examples of this in the USA, one being the development of care programs for the poor.

'Conceptual utilization "refers to the use of evaluations to influence thinking about issues in a general way"' (p 432). The example they give relates to the evidence emanating from evaluation findings about the cost and efficacy of delivering health and welfare services. The authors conclude that 'These evaluations did not lead to the adoption of specific programs or policies but provided evidence that present ways of delivering were costly and inefficient' (p 432). The third form of use – 'persuasive utilization' – happens when politicians choose to defend or attack the status quo, drawing on the results of certain evaluations.

The important feature of the discussion by Rossi and his co-authors is that they are able to cite instances, documented by Leviton and Baruch (1983) and by Chelimsky (2001), where direct or conceptual use of findings has been .identified. They regret, however, that smaller-scale evaluations of projects and programs rarely find their way into the literature. Rossi and colleagues are not as pessimistic as many other evaluation analysts who lament the apparent non-use of evaluation findings. They maintain that there have been discernible examples of conceptual utilisation in the USA but admit that such examples are difficult to trace. One of the reasons for this is that, having completed their evaluation, evaluators move on to other enterprises and do not have the time to follow up on the question of how, if at all, their results have influenced or at least impinged on decision making. We shall return later in this chapter to discuss reasons why evaluation results might not be used.

We now turn to Rossi et al's (1999) formulation of how to maximise utilisation, in which potential barriers to utilisation are implicit. They base this section on the work of Solomon and Shortell (1981).

- *Evaluators must understand the cognitive styles of decision makers.* In other words, the reporting of the findings needs to be tailored to the intended consumers of the report. Busy politicians, for example, will be looking for a concise and clearly presented report rather than a detailed academic piece of work.
- *Evaluation results must be timely and available when needed.* Criteria governing the preparation of academic articles need to be set aside in favour of a quickly prepared document.
- *Utilisation and dissemination plans should be part of the evaluation design.* This guideline prefigures one of Patton's central tenets that ownership and utilisation of the results will be enhanced by a collaborative and interactive relationship between evaluator and primary intended users.
- *Evaluations must respect stakeholders' programme commitments.* Different stakeholders might hold different values and evaluators need to be aware of and sensitive to this. These should be made explicit before the beginning of the evaluation.
- *Evaluations should include an assessment of utilisation.* Evaluators and decision makers must agree on the criteria by which its successful utilisation may be judged.

It would be difficult to take issue with any of these five instructions. They do, however, relate to an idealised situation. Over the course of an evaluation circumstances might change, with the consequence that the consumers of the research might have to reconsider the ways in which the results will be applied in practice. To predict and commit to a firm agreement on utilisation is to pre-empt the nature of the findings. They could turn out to confirm or undermine the projected merit of the project, programme or policy. This predictive element in how to maximise the use of evaluation research *results* comes close to the depiction of evaluation as applying the persuasive mode of utilisation since it implies that the decision makers have made up their minds irrespective of the evaluation findings.

Utilising the findings: obscuring the issue

One of the merits of the text by Rossi and his co-authors is that their work is eminently readable. If evaluators coming from an academic background are not able to couch their research findings in a style and form that communicates rather than excludes, then – as noted above – the findings are not likely to influence decision making. The research carried out and reported by Cousins and Shulha (2006) is undoubtedly earnest and scholarly. Unfortunately, if they were to produce an evaluation report intended for use by those outside academia they would have to provide a glossary that would be not much shorter in length than their report.

Their central theme is the distinction between 'knowledge use' and 'evaluation use'. This culminates in what they term an 'exemplar' which lists the different characteristics of the two types of use. We take some examples of their writing style out of context but such phrases as 'heterophilous nature of participant group', 'reciprocal influence through sustained interactivity', and 'direct participation potency' are replicated throughout the paper. Other phrases, by no means confined only to one or two evaluation authors, such as 'epistemological challenges', and 'a knowledge system-utilisation perspective', have no currency except in the world of academic textbooks on evaluation. This largely arcane language does nothing, we would suggest, to encourage potential decision makers to become informed about the nature and purpose of evaluation by reading such texts. The riposte to this assertion would probably be that the book is not aimed at people who are employed in or elected to government and public service organisations. The intended readership is other academics. This is a perfectly fair response, and one that will be reviewed in the final chapter. Indeed, Mohr (1995) makes this point very clearly in the Preface to the first edition of his book on impact assessment. He states: 'This book is addressed to scholars' (p xvii). Mohr's concern is with experiments and quasi-experiments and a quantitative approach to the collection and analysis of data. His text is not for the numerately squeamish and carries numerous graphs, diagrams and equations. One example is his formulation of a mathematical definition of effectiveness (Mohr, 1995, p 7):

$$\text{Effectiveness} = \frac{R - C}{P - C} = \frac{10.5 - 15}{10 - 15} = \frac{-4.5}{-5} = \frac{-9}{\text{or } 90\%}$$

Other less comprehensible equations also appear, such as those expressed in Greek characters on p 143 and elsewhere in the book. This presumption of the positivist paradigm and its accompanying objective of quantifying the possibly unquantifiable has become somewhat out-dated as there has been a shift in the evaluation literature to methods adopted from social enquiry rather than mathematics.

Positioned somewhere between programme and policy evaluation as amenable to the generation of mathematical formulae and the real world of human experience and plain speaking is the relatively commonplace obscured behind a would-be intellectual or at least an academic façade. An example from Bhola (1998) is a worthy illustration. The abstract of his article entitled 'Constructivist capacity building and systemic evaluation and training in South Africa' begins:

> What follows is a discourse of coherence … through an epistemic triangle conjoining three epistemological traditions of systems thinking … and second, a praxeological triangle that unites planning, implementation and evaluation in one single act of reflective action with purpose. (p 329)

Clearly, this article – like the text of Mohr's book – is not intended for the lay reader but for other academics. However, the potential hazard in using this lexicon of specialist language is the inability to set aside this form of expression in report-writing for the commissioners of evaluations. Each profession has its own form of cant but those attempting to raise the practice of evaluation to a truly distinct academic discipline must be cautious not to over-complicate a process that, we would argue is, conceptually, a relatively straightforward activity.

Utilising the findings: the dissenters

Writing on the subject of the purposes and use of evaluation, Eggers and Chelimsky (1999) express opposing views. Eggers argues that all evaluations must identify the problems at the centre of a search for solutions and 'create sustainable benefits for given target groups' (p 93). He does, however, qualify his aspirations for the role of the evaluator as an agent of change. He admits that 'the evaluator must lead the horse to the water even if he cannot make him drink' (p 93). Eleanor Chelimsky, politely disregarding the single gender references in Eggers' statement, claims that there are many purposes of evaluation including accountability and efficiency, which do not necessarily aim at use.

In a speech at the UK Evaluation Society Conference in 1997, Chelimsky set out a number of useful aspects of evaluation which do not necessarily refer to the application of findings to actual practice (1997, pp 99-100). They are:

- measure and account for the results of public policies and pograms;

- determine the efficiency of projects, programs and their component processes;
- gain insights into public problems and into past or present efforts to address them;
- understand how organisations work and how they learn;
- strengthen institutions and improve management performance;
- improve agency responsiveness to the public;
- reform governments through the free flow of qualitative information; and
- expand the measurement of results from the national to the international scale.

In summary, she classified evaluation into three broad categories:

- Evaluation for accountability – for example, measuring results in terms of efficiency.
- Evaluation for development – helping to strengthen institutions.
- Evaluation for knowledge – obtaining a deeper understanding in some specific area or policy field.

Chelimsky claims that as far back as the 1960s, evaluators were complaining about the non-use of results but argues that 'use' would only be relevant for the third of her 'approaches'. Whether items cited in Chelimsky's list would be regarded as off-shoots of evaluation rather than purposes is a moot point.

In the same volume of the journal which contains the dialogue between Eggers and Chelimsky, Carol Weiss (1999) – although agreeing with Eggers – also concedes that policy makers often accept the findings only when the evaluation justifies the course of action that they already want to pursue and also admits that 'almost never does the choice of policy hinge on the absence of information' (p 471).

Such doubts about (a) the justification for commissioning and carrying out evaluation research and (b) its impact on decision making are further explored and explained by a few authors. Green and South (2006) make only passing reference to the exposure by Suchman (1967) of forms of evaluation that covertly rather than explicitly invite formal evaluations but without any intention of taking on board any of the results. These are labelled 'pseudo-evaluations'. The main types are:

- Eyewash – this focuses on surface experiences in that the design and methods of the evaluation seek only superficial data.
- Whitewash – a planned attempt to cover up programme failure.

- Submarine – the predetermined intention to undermine a programme.
- Posture – ritual use of evaluation with no intent to use findings.
- Postponement – evaluation undertaken to postpone or avoid action.

Some of these – we might dub them 'tactical evaluations' – resemble other ploys such as reviews, inquiries, reports, all of which could screen a decision not to decide. Hogwood and Gunn (1984) suggest a more extreme version of why decision makers might avoid action. They contend that:

> One paradox of evaluation is that it may only be possible
> to carry out monitoring or evaluation by promising not to
> use its results. (p 227)

The reasoning behind this seemingly controversial assertion is that many people who have a stake in the programme, such as staff and politicians, might regard the evaluation as a threat to the continuation of the programme. By co-operating with the evaluator, they fear that in a very real way they will be accessories to their own possible occupational demise.

What might be construed as rather cynical interpretations of occasional, perhaps more than occasional, instances of political chicanery are reminiscent of the aphorism attributed to the economist John Maynard Keynes, which sounds very much like a senior civil servant portrayed in a former situation comedy. According to Keynes:

> There is nothing a government hates more than to be well-
> informed for it makes the process of arriving at decisions
> much more complicated and difficult. (1937, p 409)

This is not an outlandish statement, as one of the authors of this book can testify. At a public meeting called to hear expert witnesses speak for and against an application to develop a former tipping site for housing, a local councillor rose to his feet and berated a scientist from Harwell with the words: "We don't want the facts!" Of course people who have the power to make decisions in the public sphere do not want information when they have already made up their minds. Facts become an irritant. To an extent this kind of ill-informed decision making was a criticism levelled at Tony Blair and George W. Bush who, their critics claimed, decided to invade Iraq whether or not weapons of mass destruction could be found. The assertions made by Suchman and by Keynes might sound subversive but they surely introduce a touch of realism to those models of the policy-making process that depict decisions as a detached and quasi-scientific analysis of decision choices.

Yet, as shall be seen, academic after academic has been inclined to lament the lack of evidence that confirms the utilisation of evaluation findings. This might be because: (a) the evidence has not been reported; (b) it is difficult to gain access to the information that would confirm or refute the utilisation; (c) it is difficult to perceive whether it was the evaluation findings or some other factors that led to a particular course of action; or (d) (an extreme form of (b)) the results were never made public.

Reasons for non-utilisation of findings

Drawing on some examples of previous events in which the results of what might broadly be called 'research' did not prompt the UK government of the day to take heed and act, we might suggest some reasons why the data generated by evaluations are not acted upon.

In the late 1970s the UK Labour government appointed Sir Douglas Black to chair a working group in order to determine whether the serious health inequalities among certain areas in Britain were correlated with income levels and general standard of living. The Black Report (1980) did indeed confirm the government's assumption that such inequalities did exist and that the appropriate action needed to be taken in order to redress this imbalance. However, just before the report saw the light of day there was a change of government. The incoming Conservative administration chose to shelve the report.

During the mid-1980s the Conservative government introduced planned changes in the formula by which householders' local authority rates were to be calculated. The new community charge came to be known as the *poll tax*. Because this proposed change was quite radical and there were immediate rumblings of dissent among opposition political groups and citizens, the government decided to pilot the scheme in Scotland in order to test its reception. The impact of the proposed change was extremely negative, to the point of large-scale demonstrations in many parts of Scotland. Despite these ominous signs of serious dissent, the prime minister, Margaret Thatcher, chose to ignore the results of the pilot scheme and implement the poll tax across the rest of the UK as well as in Scotland. This led to widespread civil disobedience and, in effect, the start of political manoeuvres to remove Mrs Thatcher from her position as the Conservative leader.

In both these cases, it was clear that certain politicians did not really want the facts, such was their ideological commitment to a predetermined course of action. These examples constituted a departure from the rational model of decision making. On a less controversial note, the occasional surveys carried out in order to discover whether the majority of the UK population are in favour of capital punishment for certain crimes, show that there is considerable support for this policy. Successive UK governments, however, have ignored the survey findings because of firmly held principles about State executions. It is possible, therefore, to extrapolate from these examples that decision makers might shy away from implementing policies indicated by the results of evaluation research because to do so would compromise the moral and ideological commitments that have shaped their political identities. At this level of decision making, it is usually quite clear why a certain course of action is not going to be followed because of statements made at the time by leading politicians. However, the reasons for non-take-up of indicative action might not be so easy to detect at the level of project or programme evaluations.

One example of a politician apparently ignoring the results of an evaluation can be provided by one of the authors of this book, who was involved in a pilot initiative to introduce automated pharmacy facilities in three hospitals in order to inform the decision whether to implement the scheme across other hospitals. The evaluation was due to be completed and reported on in March so that the results could be fed into the decision-making process in April. However, the Minister, on a visit to a hospital not included in the pilot sample, announced that the automated pharmacy scheme would be introduced in all hospitals over the following two years.

Projects, programmes and non-utilisation of findings

Rossi et al (1999) and Patton (2002), in setting out their ideas on how to facilitate the adoption and implementation of evaluation findings, argue that the key to success lies in (a) a collaborative and participative research design in which key users and stakeholders are involved from the beginning of the evaluation; and (b) good communication between evaluator and evaluation research commissioners. Other commentators, as shall be seen, lay their emphasis elsewhere.

Hogwood and Gunn (1984) adequately sum up the frustration expressed by a number of evaluation analysts:

> The newcomer to evaluation might assume that having carried out the necessary research and prepared a report on the findings, the implications of the report in terms of policy-making would immediately be taken up by decision-makers, especially if the evaluation had been commissioned by government. As a result the newcomer would be puzzled as to why in most cases nothing at all seemed to happen. (pp 237–8)

They go on to suggest that the tyro evaluator might then assume that it was the quality of the methodology that impaired the probability of the results being acted upon whereas, according to Hogwood and Gunn, the 'quality of methodology does not appear to be a particularly important determinant of whether evaluation research will be utilized' (p 238). The more likely obstacle to utilisation, they continue, is the inability of the evaluator to spell out clearly the policy implications of the findings with the result that the programme manager complains that the results are not relevant to the programme's needs. A further potential barrier is the use of technical language. They state that 'If evaluation research is to be utilized, it has to be communicated in a language comprehensible to those who have to make decisions on the basis of it' (p 238).

Hogwood and Gunn add two more potential reasons for non-utilisation:

- The evaluation results may not fit in with the timetable for decision-making. Lack of foresight about the need for evaluation might have led to a late start or a sudden crisis might have intervened. On the other hand, the research itself might have taken longer than anticipated, for example in the fieldwork and data analysis.
- An evaluation report might be regarded as threatening to certain key people within the organisation. Staff might be resistant to possible change in working practices and career structures. For these reasons the evaluation findings might not be seriously considered.

The potentially threatening aspect of some evaluation research findings has also been noted by Perloff and Rich (1986) in their discussion of the role of evaluation in the US education system. These authors also reiterate the need for effective communication between evaluators and managers in order to integrate evaluation into an organisation's decision-making process and the evaluator's access to key decision makers and the ability on the part of the evaluator to translate research results into language that the potential user can understand.

Hedrick (1988) claims that many evaluation studies are initiated primarily to confirm existing beliefs or an existing policy position. Furthermore, commissioning of an evaluation might be used as a delaying tactic when policy makers are reluctant to take action.

Finally, Veney and Kaluzny (1984) argue that it should not be assumed that the explicit programme objectives which are often dictated by government departments to 'run with' are, in fact, the primary motivation for commissioning an evaluation report:

> From the standpoint of rationality, a given program may be more a means of controlling resources, maintaining a particular elite in power, or providing a hope to special interest groups or disgruntled portions of the population than a way of actually eliminating or reducing the problem to which the program is manifestly addressed. (p 27)

As supporting evidence for this statement, the authors cite the Medicaid and Medicare programmes in the USA which purported to be aimed at reducing social injustices in access to medical care but which, according to Veney and Kaluzny, were initiated for political reasons. They make a distinction between legal, social and political bases for the instigation of programmes and technical criteria. Only the last named can be tested empirically. As a result, the evaluator can expect to have some impact on decision making if, for example, the main criterion is economic.

Their contention that programmes are likely to survive or fail because of the logic of political pragmatism is endorsed by Cronbach (1980) who regards all evaluation as a political activity involving a complexity of concerns and objectives. Rational decision making, he asserts, is a myth.

Finally, Guba and Lincoln (1981), referring to the 'hue and cry' about the non-utilisation of evaluation findings, are inclined to exonerate politics and politicians for apparently ignoring the results of evaluation research. They refer to the assumption by evaluators that non-utilisation is due to ignorance, laziness or side-stepping by responsible decision makers. Their view is that such apparent disregard is more likely to be because of the weaknesses in traditional evaluation that does not sufficiently take into account the concerns of stakeholders. With particular reference to the positivist paradigm which, in another volume, they vigorously reject (Guba and Lincoln, 1987), they claim that while such evaluations might produce information that is statistically significant, they do not produce worthwhile knowledge. 'Given their general level of triviality, it is probably a good thing that evaluation research has not been more widely used' (p ix).

They advocate a move away from objectives-focused evaluation to *responsive evaluation*. In dismissing the scientific paradigm of enquiry they propose an approach using ethnographic, anthropological and sociological field studies in order to study behavioural phenomena as a more *naturalistic* form of research (Guba and Lincoln, 1981).

The work of Carol Weiss

Carol Weiss has been a prolific contributor to the evaluation literature over many years. One of her main preoccupations has been the question of why evaluations do not seem to influence decision making. Although she contends that evaluation research is viewed as a way to increase the rationality of policy making, she recognises that one of its failings lies sometimes in unrealistic expectations of the potential of evaluations to bring about major change (Weiss, 1972). Another weakness is that the results often go unpublished.

Weiss, in the same volume, lists a number of possible factors inhibiting the use of findings. These are:

* organisational resistance to change;
* the findings are not acceptable;
* the findings may contradict or be alien to the existing ideology;
* unlike profit-making businesses, service agencies are not seriously penalised for failing to reach goals.

Weiss goes on to stress that evaluation will never provide all the answers and that 'Maybe the most practical use of evaluation findings is to provide hard evidence to support the proponents of change within the existing decision-making system' (1972, p 125). This statement would seem to introduce a tendentious element into the evaluation design and process. Alternatively, this could qualify as a perhaps rather cynical acceptance of who actually has the power and authority to make decisions within an organisation. Of course, an inherent danger in any political situation is that research data can be mis-used. The selection and suppression of findings can serve the purposes of either the proponents or opponents of change. This prompts the question, to be addressed more fully in Chapter Seven, of the extent to which the evaluator should strive to ensure that the outcome of the research is accepted as a real contribution to decision making. Weiss continued writing on the vexed question of (non-)utilisation during the 1970s (Weiss, 1978) and the following decades (Weiss, 1980; Weiss, and Bucuvalas, 1980; Weiss (ed), 1991).

In the main, Weiss is optimistic about the impact of evaluation on decision making. While accepting that 'For evaluators, awareness of the probable limitations of their influence has been particularly distressing' (Weiss, 1999, p 471), since utility, she asserts, is the primary purpose of evaluation, evaluators must be realistic about what they can hope to achieve. Although it might not be apparent that evaluation findings have had any impact on decision making, Weiss is confident that the results can and do lead to what she terms 'enlightenment' (Weiss, 1980). This term refers to 'the percolation of new information, ideas and perspectives into the arena in which decisions are made' (Weiss, 1999, p 471). Unfortunately, no evidence is produced to support this claim other than references to a number of social science research projects in parts of Western Europe. This is surprising in view of Weiss's long acquaintance with the attention given to evaluation studies in the United States.

An important contribution that Weiss makes to the debate on utilisation is to point out that decision making does not normally occur at one particular time and in one particular place. It is more likely that decisions take shape gradually with clusters of officials each taking small steps until – even without them being aware – a decision is reached. However, Weiss also acknowledges that evaluation commissioners might be aware of the fact that the researchers bring to the project their own values and biases that can mar the required objectivity. There are also commissioning agencies that will be able to recognise poor quality research; data that derives from flawed methods of data collection and inadequate analysis. Add to these problems the policy maker's adherence to firmly held beliefs and values, and the gap between receiving the findings and taking decisions indicated by them becomes even more problematic.

The pessimists

If Weiss sounds a positive note in the debate about the impact of evaluation on decision making, others are not so sanguine. Writing in the late 1970s, Imboden (1978) inveighed against the predominantly negative relationship between project managers and evaluators. Imboden presents the following criticism of the evaluation process:

- Because project managers often inflate the positive benefits that the service users receive, they regard the monitoring and evaluation of these effects as a threat.
- Evaluations are time consuming and skilled labour intensive. The results of the evaluation are often not available when they are needed by the management.
- Evaluations are not management oriented. They often 'have their own dynamics' (p 121). The questions they ask are not the ones in which management are interested.
- It often happens that project management resents the interference of outsiders who tend to burden them with requests for information and whom they consider as 'well-paid parasites who have no responsibility for the success of the project' (p 122).
- The evaluation reports are written in language that is not easily understood.
- The reports attempt to show what happened and why it happened but offer no recommendations as to what should be done.

Some of the shortcomings alluded to by Imboden appear in the writings of others – for example Rossi et al (1999) and Solomon and Shortell (1981) – on the issues of timeliness of reports; research geared towards the needs of management and lack of early agreement between evaluator and commissioner/manager on the likely use that will be made of the findings; and by Hogwood and Gunn (1984) on the fear by key staff about the possible implications of the evaluation findings on their work prospects. If there are faults that conspire to weaken the chances of evaluation impacting on decision making then the faults would appear to be on both sides: evaluator and commissioner.

Suet Ying Ho (1999), discussing the evaluation of urban regeneration programmes in Britain, lays the blame squarely at the feet of the politicians. On the positive side Ho points out that, since the mid-1980s, the British government has laid more emphasis on the monitoring and evaluation of existing and new policy initiatives. All new regeneration schemes launched in the 1990s were subjected to national evaluation studies, which was a welcome approach to tackling urban deprivation. On the negative side, claims Ho, 'there is little evidence to show that new regeneration initiatives have been formulated based on lessons learned from previous evaluation studies' (p 423). The main reason why previous evaluation studies seem to have had little or no impact on policy making, according to Ho, is that, at the time of writing, the British government's approach to evaluation pays more attention to the criterion of value for money and an audit of outputs rather than on assessing the impact of the various programmes. Ambrose (2005) corroborates Ho's critique by maintaining that the evaluation of urban regeneration programmes is too dependent on the criteria of top-down performance indicators.

This indictment of the political restrictions affecting the application of evaluation research to decision making is perhaps a consequence of the unrealistic expectations that Weiss (1999) referred to, namely the assumption that a decision would be taken at one point in time and that being very soon after the presentation of the evaluation research report.

Another disenchanted commentary on the topic of utilisation comes from Caplan (1979). He argues that there is poor communication between researchers and policy makers. They live in different worlds and speak different languages. This viewpoint presents a particularly pessimistic assessment of the future role of formal evaluation in organisational and political decision making. It would appear, indeed, to have no future if the two parties are so philosophically and culturally divided. In the opinion of Nutley et al (2007), Caplan's statement is too simplistic because it ignores the wider organisational contexts that shape and contain individuals' actions. In their view, Caplan also ignores the overlap between the two groups. Policy networks can involve academics and analysts inside and outside governments, all sharing specialised knowledge and experience of a particular policy domain.

Caplan's reference to 'different worlds' and 'different languages' can be construed as metaphors for something less dramatic than irreconcilable differences. Of course external evaluators and politicians or management operate in very different milieus and mould their means of communication to different audiences but that does not mean that they are aliens one to another.

In their review of the impact of evaluation research in the field of crime and police work, Alpsten and Clarke (1974) concluded that change is not readily achieved in a system that is complex, diverse, that suffers from inertia and which has to serve various objectives. Furthermore, 'Administrative control is often weak and indirect, knowledge is in short supply, beliefs are strongly held, and emotions run high. In short, anyone who wishes to introduce change must be prepared for a slow and complex road to success' (p 78).

Perhaps bridging the gap between the pessimists and optimists or, perhaps, more accurately 'realists' is the imperative of Shadish, Cook and Leviton, quoted by Dickinson (2008, p 6), that 'evaluators need to be more active in ensuring that their findings are acted upon'. This clearly assumes a degree of persuasion and leverage that several other commentators would support but not necessarily agree was feasible.

Eleanor Chelimsky and the real world

In a relatively rare explicit example of an academic co-existing fruitfully with politicians in the world of evaluation research, Chelimsky draws on her experience in the USA of working on evaluations for Congress. She offers both a positive and realistic account of how to improve the chances of evaluation findings having an impact on decision making. At the first meeting of the American Evaluation Association in 1986, she presented a paper on the politics of programme evaluation (Chelimsky, 1987).

One of her most surprisingly novel, yet fundamentally obvious acts was to ask politicians why they might not take action on the results of evaluations. Referring to previous literature which addressed the same question but with no empirically derived data, Chelimsky listed the presumed reasons for non-utilisation. These were:

- some evaluations were simply not good enough (Bernstein and Freeman, 1975);
- perhaps the results of an evaluation *were used*, but it was difficult to trace any link because evaluation was just one of many factors influencing decision making (Chelimsky, 1985);
- that there were many ways in which to interpret the term 'utilisation' (Weiss, 1979).

The reasons why policy makers appeared to ignore evaluation findings came out of a symposium attended by politicians and evaluators representing a range of academic disciplines. According to Chelimsky, many of the reasons given were shocking to the evaluators present. They learned that evaluations were not used because:

- there were agency and bureaucratic conflicts;
- some programme managers preferred to remain ignorant (thus echoing the opinion of Keynes, 1937);
- evaluations will be used only if managers wanted them to be;
- to some of its potential users the evaluation emerged from what was called an 'ivory tower' process;
- the report was too late to be useful;
- the report was too full of jargon to be understood;
- the report was too lengthy for the user to read;
- the evaluation attempted to answer a question that was quite different from the policy question originally posed.

Chelimsky claims to have tangible evidence that evaluations carried out by herself and colleagues have been used in a variety of ways. One of these is informing debate about policies and legislation.

> Evaluation's main value to policy in the long run is not its capacity for political influence but its contribution of systematic, independent, critical thinking to the decision making process. (1987, p 11)

In order to enhance the likelihood of the findings having some discernible influence, if not on the decision itself but on *the process of decision making*, Chelimsky – drawing on her own experience working with and for powerful politicians – recommends the following:

- Independent analysis that is strong methodologically and seeks to be as objective as is humanly possible.
- Early discussion with the evaluation commissioners about the research design, including reaching agreement on the time taken to complete the evaluation; what data collection methods will be used; how likely it will be to get answers to the questions posed; how credible the study is likely to be and what types and numbers of reports will be produced.
- The appointment of panels to critically review the evaluation.
- The use of as much oral presentation of findings as possible.
- Banish evaluation jargon; present the findings so that they will be intelligible to several audiences.
- Make sure that the production of the report coincides with key points in the political calendar.
- The evaluator must have mastered a wide variety of evaluation approaches in order to address the diversity of policy questions that political debates engender.
- Prioritisation of the evaluation findings; highlight those findings that will give rise to policy action. 'Telling all is tantamount to telling nothing' (Chelimsky, 1987, p 19).

There is no indication that Chelimsky is offering this list as either exhaustive or prescriptive for other evaluators in what might be different political milieus or eras. Its strength is that it derives from practical experience. In reaching this stage of evaluation development Chelimsky pays tribute to earlier commentators who raised the issue of non-utilisation such as Weiss (1973) and Cronbach (1980). She certainly responded positively to the assertion by Weiss that 'only with sensitivity to the politics of evaluation research can the evaluator be as strategically useful as he (*sic*) should be' (Weiss, 1973, p 40).However, after more than 20 years since Chelimsky wrote optimistically about 'the very difficult problem of integrating the disparate worlds of politics and evaluation research' (Chelimsky, 1987, p 7), the 'problem' still features prominently in evaluation literature.

Evaluation and decision making: facts or assumptions?

Despite half a century or more of journal articles and books on formal evaluation there remains a substantial gap in the literature reporting on whether the results of the research projects have had an impact on decision making: whether this be a decision to continue with projects or programmes in their present form; to modify them or to abandon them. Similarly, there is very little information about the extent to which government policies in the UK have been shaped, informed or influenced in any way by the information produced by evaluation research. This is very disappointing because follow-up studies that managed to elicit this type of information could greatly assist in improving the connection between academic activity and the world of managerial and political action or, indeed, inaction.

This lamentable dearth of post-evaluation research could have resulted from a number of negative circumstances.Yet, because there is also a noticeable gap in the literature that manages to explain why such follow-up studies have not taken place, we can only make uninformed guesses as to the reasons – rather like the welter of uninformed conjecture that has been offered as to why evaluation research findings have apparently fallen on deaf ears. If this is the case, it is difficult to understand why formal evaluations continue to be commissioned or why the stream of academic articles and books continues to flow. In effect, much of the literature referenced in this chapter is proclaiming that evaluation is of no use.That is only a rather blunt way of referring to 'the non-utilisation of findings'.This rather simple logical inference can only be gainsaid if the main purpose of evaluation is not agreed to be of use to decision makers. However, a review of the evaluation literature confirms that the majority of writers on the subject believe this to be the case.

Let us, at this point, consider the various suppositions drawn from the literature about the possible reasons for the non-utilisation of findings and, therefore, the lack of impact that such research has had on decision making.The list is almost embarrassingly long.Where no reference is attached, to an item, that stands as our own additional suggestion as to a possible reason for the apparent non-utilisation of evaluation findings.

- The evaluation report gave unclear recommendations about what action was needed – or offered no recommendations at all (Clarke, 1999).
- The report was poorly presented (Weiss, 1999).
- The report was not completed in the time originally allocated; therefore events overtook the implications of the findings (Imboden, 1978; Hogwood and Gunn, 1984; Clarke, 1999).
- The evaluator may have departed from the original intention of the evaluation.
- The quality of the research was not of a high standard and therefore the data produced was not considered acceptable (Weiss, 1999).
- The implications of the findings might not have been acceptable because of vested interests of certain key stakeholders (Weiss, 1972; Hogwood and Gunn, 1984).
- Because of changed financial circumstances, there were insufficient resources to act on the evaluation report's findings/recommendations (Alexander, 2003).
- The person who commissioned the evaluation had left the organisation.
- The evaluator and decision makers were working to different time-scales (Hogwood and Gunn, 1984; Clarke, 1999).
- There was inter-personal friction that impaired the evaluation's progress.
- There was lack of co-operation from certain informants because they saw the evaluation as a threat (Hogwood and Gunn, 1984).
- The evaluation was only a 'symbolic' commission to convince interested parties that action was being pursued (Suchman, 1967; Owen, 1993; Clarke, 1999).
- There was a change of administration/government during the course of the evaluation.
- The evaluation was commissioned in order to 'prove' that the project, programme or policy need not be changed (Imboden, 1978; Clarke, 1999; Weiss, 1999).
- The evaluation report was written in a form that was not sufficiently accessible to its intended readership (Solomon and Shortell, 1981; Hogwood and Gunn, 1984).
- The evaluation did not come up with the results that the commissioner(s) wanted (Weiss, 1972; Chelimsky, 1987).

- There was disagreement among important stakeholders as to what action should be taken as a result of the evaluation findings (Solomon and Shortell, 1981).
- Poor communication or misunderstanding between evaluator and commissioner(s) at the outset about the purpose of the evaluation (Imboden, 1978; Caplan, 1979).
- The evaluator did not adequately consult certain key stakeholders prior to designing the evaluation research and its objectives (Patton, 1997; 2002).
- The results of the evaluation were such that there was no indication that any decision needed to be taken.

Conjecture, after all, relies on what might be called 'logical imagination'. It could be argued that all of these hypothetical obstacles to the use of evaluation findings could be prevented. We shall deal with each in turn.

Recommendations unclear or no recommendations made

It should be agreed at the outset between evaluator and commissioner whether, first of all, there is a need for the eventual report to include recommendations based on the research data. Preferences might differ between decision makers as to whether they prefer reports to include recommendations or merely to report the findings. Criticisms contained in the literature about a lack of consultation and communication (Caplan, 1979; Patton, 2002) are hard to understand when money is being spent on research that is intended to produce useful results.

The report was poorly presented

This occurrence indicates that during the course of the evaluation there was no interaction between all those key people involved in the evaluation; that there was just a final report that was not scrutinised *en route* by anyone other than the person(s) carrying out the evaluation. Wye and Hatry (1988) described the continuous interaction between evaluators and the agencies whose programmes were being evaluated in certain states in the USA. The responsibility for carrying out the evaluations rested with government executive branch units. Their emphasis on interfacing effectively with personnel operating in the programme increased the likelihood of implementation of the evaluation report suggestions. In addition, staff in the agency programme participated in the evaluation teams and were, therefore, able to comment on the development of the research and on the evolving report. As a result of this collaborative approach advocated by Patton (2002) the research findings were seen to 'affect government decisions and actions regarding the programs evaluated' (Wye and Hatry, 1988, p 4).

The report was not completed on time

Again, this drawback indicates a lack of ongoing communication between evaluator and commissioner. To let this situation arise suggests a surprising attitude of *laissez faire* on the part of those paying for the evaluation. Of course, unforeseen obstacles to the progress of the research might well occur but even if such a problem did arise, it would not be impossible to make allowances and agree a modification of the evaluation. On the other hand, this hypothetical situation could reflect on the ability of the evaluator to work to deadlines. In this case, in most contractual arrangements, the commissioning authority would insert a penalty clause which would reduce the agreed fee payable to the evaluator. While this would not entirely remedy the problem it would, to an extent, alleviate it.

The evaluator departed from the original intention of the evaluation

This is really another example of a serious lack of interaction between the two parties. It is not necessarily indicative of a fault on the part of the evaluator. There might be good reasons for the main purpose or objective of the evaluation to be modified *en route*. That is one advantage of embedding a formative component into the evaluation. Provided that such a deviation from the agreed purpose is endorsed by participants, stakeholders and the commissioner, this alone need not prevent the findings being utilised.

The quality of the evaluation was not of a sufficiently high standard

As we have noted, Hogwood and Gunn (1984) claim that the non-utilisation of evaluation findings is rarely due to poor data collection or inferior research design or analysis. Weiss. however, disagrees:

> Some evaluation is poorly conceptualised, poorly conducted, inadequately interpreted and afflicted with the researchers' biases ... and provides a poor guide to subsequent action. (1984, p 479)

None of the authors supports their assertion with any referenced examples, so neither statement can be tested. Weiss, to some extent, qualifies her argument by claiming that because officials are not always able to tell a good study from a poor one they become wary of the whole enterprise. This last statement is somewhat difficult to accept. It assumes that some officials are so unaware of the criteria by which to judge a piece of evaluation research they would presumably be very likely to select the wrong bidder among those agencies that responded to the invitation to tender. Few evaluations come cheap and to delegate the responsibility of choosing an evaluator with a good prospect of delivering high quality research to persons unacquainted with the practice of research seems very unlikely.

The findings are not acceptable because of the vested interests of stakeholders

This is quite possible. We have made the point earlier in this chapter that to attempt to agree on how the evaluation findings will be adopted for decision making is to anticipate the nature of the outcome of the research before the process begins. This approach strongly implies that the key stakeholders – senior officials, politicians, service user groups, perhaps – intend to approve of the findings only if they conform with certain unyielding positions and perspectives. The logical inference from this scenario is for the stakeholders to inform the evaluator in advance what they wish the results to show. Hopefully, this is an improbable scenario. The more likely event is that those who have the authority to act on the findings will conceal their expectations of what they believe the research will come up with and then, if the results conflict with this, they will leave the report in the pending tray or, more logically, in the bin.

Insufficient resources to act on the evaluation's findings

This, as a potential obstacle to taking action as a result of the evaluation's findings, has been confirmed by Helen Alexander (2003). She reviewed the reports of three health service evaluations carried out in Scotland and found that one reason for non-implementation was lack of funding. She interviewed four key informants from each evaluated project. Although other negative responses were forthcoming – for example, in one project there was disagreement with the evaluation results; the changes recommended were going to happen anyway; and in another, the evaluation simply validated existing practice – several respondents considered the evaluations to be 'useful'. It is not made clear why there were insufficient resources to implement the recommendations for two of the projects. Some possible reasons could be:

- the recommendations, if actioned, could have required a level of funding not anticipated by the health organisation sponsoring the evaluation;
- there was an unstated hope that the results of the evaluations would rubber-stamp existing practice and not require additional funding;
- the evaluators' recommendations were unrealistic.

The person who commissioned the evaluation has left the organisation

This should not present an intractable problem provided that the individual concerned has communicated with other key persons in order to further the progress of the evaluation. There would surely be correspondence between commissioner and evaluator leading up to the appointment of the evaluator, and records of meetings held between the key partners during the course of the evaluation. If provisions to deal with a change of personnel were not put in place then the commissioning agency would be the loser and rightly so.

Evaluator and decision makers were working to different time-scales

Milestones and deadlines should have been negotiated and mutually agreed before the start of the evaluation. Here again, communication between the evaluator and commissioner is vital at all stages of the evaluation process. As in any research enterprise, setbacks do occur and the best-laid plans can go awry without anyone being at fault. For example, the unforeseen absence or change of key personnel, including change of the politician in charge or change of government, could delay the completion of the fieldwork and/or the final report. If the commissioner insists on a shorter time-scale than was previously agreed, then the evaluator will need to spell out the possible consequences in terms of the validity or representativeness of the findings.

Inter-personal friction impaired the progress of the evaluation

The possibility of some participants in the evaluation feeling threatened by the whole process has already been mentioned. Although the purpose of evaluation is almost universally agreed to be aiming to improve service provision and quality and, particularly at macro-policy level, to improve people's quality of life and to ensure greater value for money, putting a particular project, programme or policy under the microscope, so to speak, can easily be interpreted as seeking to reduce their scope or duration. Of course, inter-personal friction could stem entirely from a clash of personalities. Where the co-operation of certain participants is crucial to the successful gathering of data, efforts have to be made to resolve the problem. That might not be an easy task. Anxieties about the possible outcome of the evaluation can be allayed – if those anxieties are made manifest – by an honest official statement about the expected benefits to be delivered depending on the evaluation's findings. If, indeed, the primary purpose is to save money, this might prompt the involvement of trade unions. The ethics of any form of research demands a high level of openness and honesty. Being open and honest at the outset about purpose, about staff anxieties and about personality issues should either clear the way towards utilising the findings or jeopardise the entire evaluation. Happily, such a hypothetical obstacle has not featured in any reported evaluations.

The evaluation was only 'symbolic'

If this were indeed the case, then it is obvious that the results and, if requested, recommendations of the evaluation research, would not be utilised. We would suggest that it would be highly unlikely that this barrier affecting decision making would be openly admitted by any commissioning body. Cynics (or realists) would probably draw attention to various reviews and inquiries called for by government ministers that inspired no action or change in policy. Politicians called to account for apparently ignoring the findings of reviews, inquiries or evaluations are able to provide very plausible reasons for not acting: economic circumstances have changed; other policy areas must now take precedence; the findings are not sufficiently persuasive. It is barely imaginable that any figure of authority would declare that the evaluation was funded just to make it look as though it was considered important. That said, one can do no more than surmise in particular cases that such was the actual intention.

A change of administration/government

As noted earlier in this chapter, the results of often lengthy and painstaking research can be ignored because those with the power and authority to take action, be due to it a change of government, a change of political complexion at local authority level or a newly appointed senior official, decide not to act on the findings or recommendations. This could be for a number of reasons other than because of ideological differences. Whatever the reasons – spoken or unspoken – those who have carried out the evaluation task have to accept the reality of the situation.

The evaluation was commissioned to preserve the status quo

In the reference above to the work of Alexander (2003), one of the projects evaluated resulted in findings that confirmed that the existing project or programme did not need to be changed but was achieving what it was intended to achieve. This, of course, is not the same as a presumption on the part of an observer or evaluation analyst that those who funded the evaluation wanted it to prove that no change was needed. If the findings vindicated this (unstated) objective then the report would no doubt be hailed as a very welcome summary of the research. Alternatively, findings that indicated the need for change would not be found to be acceptable for reasons other than an explicit disavowal of findings that did not support the status quo.

The evaluation was not sufficiently accessible for the intended readership

One of the authors of this book was made to realise soon after appointment as a researcher in local government, that senior managers were not looking for a mini-PhD when they asked for a research-based report on a particular aspect of the department's services. What they wanted was a short report that was very readable and not replete with graphs and references. As a result, the decision was made to supply senior management with the executive version and keep the more detailed account for reference if any councillor wanted to analyse the content in greater depth – a ploy recommended by Clarke (1999). Seasoned evaluators should be aware of the potential pitfall of producing a report that – although well-researched – is expressed in language and format that obscures rather than reveals the findings. Since many formal evaluations are carried out by university academic staff, it could be all too easy to fall into the trap highlighted by Imboden (1978) that the eventual report is more geared towards an academic readership than 'real world' decision makers.

The evaluation did not come up with the results that the commissioners wanted

This is similar to the charge that the evaluation was commissioned in order to preserve the status quo. The difference here is that the commissioner or commissioning agency might have wanted the evaluation to 'prove' that the project, programme or policy needed to be changed or even abandoned. This possible scenario would seem to call into question the approach favoured by Patton (2002), in which the evaluator and commissioner agree on how the results will be utilised prior to the research being carried out. Two inferences can be drawn in this instance. Either the commissioner takes a risk – and possibly a costly one – that the results will confirm the desired outcome or the two parties collude so that the desired outcome is assured. We would suggest that neither is likely to happen. However, in the absence of any empirical data, this assumption is no more convincing than any other groundless suppositions.

Disagreement among stakeholders about what action should be taken

This, undoubtedly, could happen. Now that more and more emphasis is being laid in the UK on multi-agency working practices (Department of Health, 2005; Department for Education, 2011) the possibility of conflicting views on what action should follow the evaluation can not be discounted. For example, projects aimed at reducing anti-social behaviour are likely to involve co-operation and joint planning among the police, local authorities, the third sector and the probation service, acting in accordance with an over-arching central government policy. Local communities too will have their own ideas as to what constitutes priority action that needs to be taken. Potential disagreement or disputes can only be prevented or resolved by open, honest dialogue. There is much less likelihood of different perspectives stifling or delaying post-evaluation decision making if collaborative working practices are firmly structured and ongoing rather consisting of meetings of different organisations which are convened for ad hoc or one-off projects.

Misunderstanding about the purpose of the evaluation

It is not impossible to conceive of a situation in which one of the key participants has some misconceptions about the purpose of the evaluation. We have already drawn attention to the hypothetical situation in which the commissioner harbours a hidden agenda –

an unstated objective which is essentially dishonest or, to use a less pejorative term, 'politically motivated'. Other than this possible scenario, it is difficult to imagine a situation arising in which the key players have not thoroughly scripted and clearly agreed on the reason(s) why the project, programme or policy is the subject of an evaluation. Without such an understanding, it would not be possible to design the format, methodology and time-scale of the research.

Inadequate consultation with stakeholders prior to the evaluation

This lack of consultation could be the cause of a misunderstanding of the purpose of the evaluation, as discussed above. For whatever reason, the evaluation commissioner might want the research to be confined to a narrow range of stakeholders rather than to include all interested groups. Limiting the scope of the evaluation in this way could be because of a need to restrict the time-scale and/or resources, knowing, perhaps, that the findings might only provide a partial set of data. It is to be hoped that, given a free rein, the evaluator would consult with all stakeholders at the outset and during the course of the evaluation.

Evaluation results did not indicate the need for a decision to be made

This is not as fanciful as it might appear, and possible reasons may be:

- The results could be presented as only interim findings – as the preliminary stage in a two- or three-phase evaluation.
- It became apparent that certain stakeholders were not involved as participants and therefore a decision was deferred until after they had been consulted.
- No decision needed to be made because the findings were considered to be the result of a poor standard of research and not worth acting upon.

The impact of evaluation on decision making: what do we know?

Before attempting to answer this question, we need to look again at the concept of 'impact'. In contradiction to Scriven (1991), who did not perceive any difference between *outcome* and *impact*, we have chosen to interpret outcome as the result of a whole process involving the application of inputs geared towards the achievement of an objective or objectives; impact is the longer-term effect of the outcome – on an individual, organisation, a community or a whole nation. Thus, a policy followed by action to reduce the budget deficit could result in achieving that aim but, in the longer term, might increase the level of unemployment, lead to public demonstrations, bring forward the announced date of a general election, or have little or no impact in a negative or positive sense.

In depicting 'impact' in this way, it brings into focus one reason why there is little empirically derived evidence about whether evaluation findings bring to bear any influence on decision making. As noted earlier in this chapter, the policy-making process, for example, is highly unlikely to follow some sequential, linear trajectory. Moreover, it usually takes time for an actual decision to be implemented. There is, for instance, often a substantial time gap between the drafting of policies and publication in a manifesto and the action taken to put the policy into practice. Neither is it highly unusual for a manifesto promise to be watered down, greatly delayed or forgotten about. In one sense, the very term 'impact' is its own worst enemy. It has connotations of immediacy and of forcefulness. It might, after all, be more accurate to talk about the *influence* of evaluation on decision making. Henkel (1991) makes a telling contribution to the argument. She asks: 'What counts as impact or evidence of impact?' and 'At what intervals of time should judgements on these be made?' (p 213). She continues:

> The metaphor of policy impact is unsatisfactory for a number of reasons. It reifies and simplifies human action in a highly complex political system. The impact metaphor derives from mechanical theories of physics. It suggests unidirectional processes in which evaluative bodies themselves rather than those evaluated cause change. It assumes that impact is directly observable and attributable. (p 213)

Could one of the solutions be to return to the classic research design of the experimental and control group in order to increase the probability of identifying a cause and effect relationship within the evaluation process? On the face of it this would seem a sensible if not in every context a practical or ethical solution. However, in the world outside the laboratory, problems begin to present themselves as time passes between assessing the result of an intervention – be it a surgical operation, a test of chemical or nuclear weapons or the application of a new drug – and any damaging or beneficial side-effects. Towards the end of 2010, for example, the Ministry of Defence in the UK was refusing to accept that various cancers in service personnel were caused by those individuals having witnessed and been in proximity to nuclear tests many years previously. The argument against acknowledging a cause–effect phenomenon is that over such a lengthy period of time, other factors (in textbook terminology, intervening or confounding variables) could have been responsible for the deterioration in health.

Where the intervention is a piece of evaluation research carried out with people working in an organisation and often with a number of other stakeholders an attempt to disentangle the 'true cause' from other possible causes or influencing factors becomes even more difficult. The fact that we have chosen not to discount the possibility of evaluation commissioners not even considering the utilisation of the findings underlines how seemingly perverse human beings can be. Predictability can rarely be assumed during the course or after the conclusion of an evaluation.

According to Clarke (1999), evaluations are more likely to have a direct impact on programme decisions in local, small-scale studies where there is a close, collaborative relationship between the evaluator and the programme managers. He asserts that those who are responsible for making decisions also use information gained from sources other than an evaluation, such as professional journals, conversations with colleagues and feedback from service users.

The frustration in reading comments like these from Clarke and too many other writers on evaluation is that they provide no empirical evidence for their statements but merely recycle similarly unsubstantiated opinions of other evaluation 'theorists'. The main organ for the dissemination of articles on the subject of evaluation in the UK is the journal *Evaluation*, first launched in 1995. A search through the past 16 volumes up to 2010 reveals that out of the total of 359 published papers only 42 reported on the results of analysing evaluation case studies. Furthermore, only five set out to establish whether the evaluation findings had any impact on decision making. In contrast, the American journals, for example *Evaluation and Program Planning* and *Evaluation and Practice*, include a relatively high percentage of articles reporting on evaluation research projects.

One plausible reason for the lack of such follow-up research is that, having carried out an evaluation, the evaluator moves on, his or her mission accomplished. It would be desirable, however, for the possibility of a follow-up period to be written into the evaluation contract or less formal agreement. It would be important not to try to negotiate this proposal in a challenging way – as if the evaluator were to give the impression that he or she expected the results to be acted upon and would want to know, if no decision had been a consequence of the evaluation, as to why this was the case. The whole momentum of formal evaluation has started from modest beginnings into what has been described as a 'growth industry' (Weiss, 1977). Perhaps a new generation of evaluation research should now receive support to redress the present imbalance between practice-based research articles and those that are intended to stimulate academic debate. The two kinds are not by any means incompatible. Perhaps we need to apply what Weiss (1972) conceived as the essence of evaluation – judging merit against some yardstick – to the impact of the evaluation literature and ask: *To what extent has evaluation literature had a discernible impact on the development and practice of evaluation research?*

Concluding note

Identifying the possible impact of evaluation research on decision making, particularly at the level of central government policy making, remains problematic despite something approaching half a century of evaluation studies. Without sufficient evidence, either in quantity or in quality, relating to whether or not the results of evaluations have influenced decisions we are left to ponder on whether there is any way to remedy this apparent failure of formal evaluations – rather than other forms of judging merit against some yardstick, such as inspections, audit and accreditation – to make a recognisable impact.

In the next chapter, we shall discuss some possible approaches to enhancing the value and reputation of evaluation in the realms of academia and politics.

References

Alexander, H. (2003) 'Health service evaluations: should we expect the results to change practice?', *Evaluation*, vol 9, no 4, pp 405-14.

Alpsten, B. and Clarke, E.V.G. (1974) *Methods of evaluation and planning in the field of crime*, Strasbourg: Council of Europe.

Ambrose, P. (2005) 'Urban regeneration: who defines the indicators?', in D. Taylor and S. Balloch (eds) *The politics of evaluation*, Bristol: The Policy Press.

Bernstein, I.N. and Freeman, H.E. (1975) *Academic and entrepreneurial research: The consequence of diversity in federal evaluation studies*, NY: Russell Sage.

Bhola H.S (1998) 'Constructivist capacity building and systems evaluation and training in South Africa', *Evaluation*, vol 4, no 3, pp 329-50.

Caplan, N. (1979) 'The two-communities theory and knowledge utilization', *American Behavioral Scientist*, vol 2, no 3, pp 459-70.

Chelimsky, E. (1987) 'What have we learned about the politics of program evaluation?', *Evaluation Practice*, vol 8, no 1, pp 5-21.

Chelimsky, E. (1991) 'On the social science contribution to governmental decision-making', *Science*, vol 254, Oct, pp 226-30.

Chelimsky E (1997) 'Thoughts for a new evaluation society', *Evaluation*, vol 3, no 1, pp 97-109.

Clarke, A. (1999) *Evaluation research: An introduction to principles, methods and practice*, London: Sage.

Cousins, J.B. and Shulha, L.M. (2006) 'A comparative analysis of evaluation utilization and its cognate fields of inquiry: current issues and trends', in I.F. Shaw, J.G. Greene and M.M. Mark (eds) *Handbook of evaluation: Policies, programs and practices*, London: Sage.

Cronbach, L.J. and associates (1980) *Towards reform of program evaluation*, San Francisco, CA: Jossey Bass.

Department for Education (2011) *Children and young people: Multi-agency working*, London.

Department of Health (2005) *Partnership and regulation in adult protection: The effectiveness of multi-agency working and the regulatory framework in adult protection*, University of Sheffield/King's College London.

Department of Health and Social Security (1980) *Inequalities in health: Report of a research working group* ('the Black Report'), London: DHSS.

Dickinson, H. (2008) *Evaluating outcomes in mental health and social care*, Bristol: The Policy Press.

Eggers, H.W. and Chelimsky, E. (1999) 'Purposes and use: what can we expect?', *Evaluation*, vol 5, no 1, pp 92-6.

Green, J. and South, J. (2006) *Evaluation*, Maidenhead: Open University Press.

Guba, E.G. and Lincoln, Y.S (1981) *Improving the effectiveness of evaluation results through responsive and naturalistic approaches*, San Francisco, CA: Jossey Bass.

Hedrick, T.E. (1988) 'The interaction of politics and evaluation', *Evaluation Practice*, vol 9, no 3, pp 5-14.

Henkel, M. (1991) *Government, evaluation and change*, London: Jessica Kingsley.

Ho, S.Y. (1999) 'Evaluating urban regeneration programmes in Britain', *Evaluation*, vol 5, no 4, pp 422-38.

Hogwood, B.W. and Gunn, L.A. (1984) *Policy analysis for the real world*, Oxford: Oxford University Press.

Imboden, N. (1978) *A management approach to project appraisal and evaluation*, Paris: Development Centre of the Organisation for Economic Co-operation and Development.

Keynes, J.M. (*The Times*, 11 March 1937) from *Keynes' collected writings*, vol 21, p 8409.

Leviton, L.C. and Baruch, R.F. (1983) 'Contributions of evaluation to educational programs', *Evaluation Review*, vol 7, no 5, pp 563-99.

Mohr, L.B. (1995) *Impact analysis for program evaluation*, Thousand Oaks, CA: Sage.

Nutley, S.M., Walter, I. and Davies, H.T.O. (2007) *Using evidence: How research can inform public services* Bristol: The Policy Press.

Owen, J.M. (1993) *Program evaluation: Forms and approaches*, St Leonards, NSW: Allen and Unwin.

Patton, M.Q. (1997) *Utilization-focused evaluation: The new century text* (3rd edn), Thousand Oaks, CA: Sage.

Patton, M.Q. (2002) *Utilization-focused evaluation (U-FE) checklist.* Available at www.wmich.edu/evalctr/checklists

Pawson, R. (2006) *Evidence-based policy: A realist perspective*, London: Sage.

Perloff, R. and Rich, R.F. (1986) 'The teaching of evaluation in Schools of Management', in B. Gross Davis (ed) *Teaching of evaluation across the disciplines*, San Francisco, CA: Jossey Bass.

Rossi, P.H., Freeman, H.E and Lipsey, M.W. (1999) *Evaluation: A systematic approach*, Thousand Oaks, CA: Sage.

Scriven, M. (1991) *Evaluation thesaurus*, Newbury Park, CA: Sage.

Shadish, W., Cook, T. and Leviton, L. (1991) *Foundations of programme evaluation*, London: Sage.

Solomon, M.A. and Shortell, S.M. (1981) 'Designing health policy research for utilization', *Health Policy Quarterly*, vol 1 (May), pp 261-73.

Suchman, E.A. (1967) *Evaluative research: principles in public service and action programs*, NY: Russell Sage.

Veney, J.E. and Kaluzny, A.D. (1984) *Evaluation and decision making for health services programs*, NJ: Prentice Hall.

Weiss, C. (1972) *Evaluation research: Methods for assessing program effectiveness*, NJ: Prentice Hall.

Weiss, C. (1973) 'Where politics and evaluation research meet', *Evaluation*, vol 1, no 3, pp 37-45.

Weiss, C. (1977) *Evaluating action programs: Readings in social action and education*, Boston, MA: Allyn and Bacon.

Weiss, C. (1978) 'Improving the linkage between social research and public policy', in L.E. Lynn *Knowledge and policy: The uncertain connection*, WA: National Academy of Science, pp 23-81.

Weiss, C. (1979) 'The many meanings of research utilization', in E. Chelimsky (1985) *Program evaluation: Patterns and directions*, WA: American Society for Public Administration.

Weiss, C. (1980) 'Toward the future of stakeholder approaches in evaluation', *New Directions for Program Evaluation*, vol 1983, no 17, pp 83-90.

Weiss, C. (1999) 'The interface between evaluation and public policy', *Evaluation*, vol 5, no 4, pp 468-86.

Weiss, C. and Bucuvalas, M.J. (1980) *Social science research and decision making*, NY: Columbia Press.

Wye, C.G. and Hatry, H.P. (eds) (1988) *Timely, low-cost evaluation in the public sector, New directions for program evaluation No 38*, American Evaluation Association, San Fransisco, CA: Jossey Bass.

SEVEN

The future for evaluation

In previous chapters there has been a good deal of discussion about 'theory-driven' and 'theory-based' evaluation. This approach, coupled with a degree of despondency among several evaluators about the apparent non-utilisation of evaluation research findings, has led to a fairly recent attempt to enhance the status of evaluation as an academic/professional activity. Ironically, although the present 'generation' of evaluators and writers on evaluation have almost as one discarded the experimental research design as something of a 'gold standard' to which all designs should aspire, the quest for evaluations to be taken more seriously by decision makers has turned to a predominantly quantitative system of verification.

To what extent this approach has moved or is likely to move evaluation into a new 'generation' or higher level of academic and professional endeavour will be examined later in this chapter. To assert that one of these modes of enquiry – meta-evaluation – is recent is somewhat deceptive since it is generally agreed that the term was coined by Scriven in an article published in 1969 (Scriven, 1969). Interest in meta-evaluation has appeared only spasmodically in evaluation texts and articles until a revival of interest in the topic during the last two decades. Yet, in the book by Rossi et al (1999), out of the 500 pages the topic of 'meta-analysis' takes up the equivalent of just half a page. Similarly, the voluminous text by Shaw et al (2006) devotes little more than one page to meta-evaluation or meta-analysis in all its 608 pages, while the general text on evaluation by Green and South (2006) does not mention either meta-analysis or meta-evaluation.

Interestingly, the paper by Scriven (1969) preceded the seminal work by Cochrane (1972) in which he pioneered the development of evidence-based medicine through his advocacy of the randomised controlled trial (RCT) as the most reliable means of producing valid data. Although, as noted in Chapter One, there was some initial opposition to what a few in the medical profession regarded as an unacceptably mechanistic foundation for clinical decision making, Cochrane's stimulus towards increasing efficiency and effectiveness within the health care system is now central to decisions about expenditure on new drugs and other clinical interventions. The experimental and control group research design is now firmly entrenched throughout medical research and an important adjunct to this mode of research is the systematic review.

Systematic reviews

Gomm et al (2000b) define the systematic review as an activity centred on:

> ... reviewing a number of pieces of research on approximately the same topic, using a stringent set of quality criteria, evaluating each in relation to each other in terms of its credibility, and discerning to where the combined evidence points, if anywhere, and identifying gaps in knowledge as priorities for further research. (p 37)

Within the health care system, a systematic review is a boon to practitioners. It enables them to keep up to date with research without spending an inordinate amount of time searching through published papers. Those who carry out the reviews set out the evaluation criteria used in order to check whether the published study merits inclusion. The primary criterion is whether the research is founded on the RCT design. This involves treating one group of people with a particular drug or other kind of intervention while another group – matched as closely as possible with the experimental group – foregoes the drug or other intervention. In this way, certain factors that might mar the possibility of identifying a cause-effect relationship can be controlled. These factors – as noted in Chapter One – are known as 'confounding variables'. Later in this chapter we shall be looking at whether the systematic review approach to accumulating data on aspects of health and health care can be applied to evaluation research under the banner of 'meta-evaluation'.

In order to do this, it is necessary to spell out the various stages in preparing to carry out a review. These are listed in another text by Gomm and co-editors (2006: p 138):

- Define precisely the question that the review is addressing.
- Search as exhaustively as possible for all studies that address the question.
- Assess the quality of these studies using pre-defined criteria.
- Exclude studies that fail to meet the criteria.
- Provide an overview of the results of the included studies.
- Interpret those results in terms of implication for practice.

One essential criterion to apply is whether the researchers have communicated clearly how they carried out the study. By what method did they arrive at their samples of subjects involved in the experiment or trial? Was the sampling method truly random, for example using every tenth name on a register or voting list, etc? Was the sample large enough to be representative of an even larger population? Was the purpose of the research made absolutely clear? Was it possible to control all potential confounding variables? How and by whom was the data collected and by what method or methods was the data analysed? How cogent are the results of the research in terms of informing practice? Many of these questions are, of course, applicable to research outside the clinical domain, including evaluation research.

It can be argued, however, that one particular confounding variable besets the world of systematic reviews. If Gomm et al are correct, there is a bias in medical research literature towards publishing those pieces of research that have come up with positive results and to ignore those 'with neutral or negative results' (p 138). It might also be true that researchers whose results turn out to be neutral or negative are not inclined to submit a paper for publication. It would be difficult, but not impossible, to confirm or refute this possibility.

While systematic reviews can not necessarily identify or rectify any bias in the corpus of published research studies, they have a role to play in communicating the findings of researchers who have exposed intentional deception in the presentation of findings that – through the efforts of other researchers – have been proved to be false. A fairly recent example of this was the much publicised link between MMR (measles, mumps and rubella) injections for children and the development of autism. In the UK, the author of a paper published in *The Lancet* in 1998 gained considerable publicity and, apparently, considerable amounts of money from campaigning groups from his assertion that MMR jabs caused autism in young children. Further studies and systematic reviews emanating from the Cochrane Library disproved the author's findings. Despite this counter-evidence, the discredited 'link' continued to receive publicity. Chivers (2010) complained that 'For years newspapers … reported any tiny case study that hinted at a link, while often ignoring huge meta-analyses and case studies that confirmed there was none. You can see why this happens – "vaccine may cause autism!" is a much better headline than "vaccine doesn't cause autism!"'.

Moynihan (2004), while accepting the value of systematic reviews in the context of health care, points to some of their limitations. These are:

- There is often not enough strong evidence to support or refute a promising treatment or intervention.
- The methods of synthesising the results of different studies are still evolving and are by no means flawless.
- Systematic reviews can be of varying quality.

Many trials do not adequately report potential or actual side-effects and this omission will also be reflected in the systematic review.

In a sense, systematic reviews rely for their findings on the quality of the trials that they are perusing. The counter-argument to this is that the reviewer should be able to discern weaknesses in the reported trials and accord to those the value that they deserve.

Meta-analysis

Chelimsky (1987) recommended meta-analysis as a major tool in helping decision makers make sense of conflicting evaluation findings and improve the quality of information available to them. There is a potential 'infinity factor' with regard to reviews and other forms of seeking to establish scientific truths, theories and laws. By this we mean that, for example, systematic reviews themselves can be subjected to analysis to find out whether they were carried out in a manner that will generate confidence in their own methodology. Meta-analysis fulfils this function. This, according to Gomm et al (2000b), involves pooling the results of several studies as if each were just part of a much larger study including them all. However, they point out that meta-analysis can be controversial in three ways:

- Studies are likely to have some differences, for example, in the subjects entering the trial, somewhat different interventions and producing different kinds of baseline and outcome data. Hence like may not be being pooled with like.
- Different studies may have involved different kinds of statistical calculations to produce their results; therefore there are good mathematical reservations about adding them together.
- There is a possibility that a large, but badly conducted trial will over-influence the pooled results, despite reviewers' attempts to eliminate poorly conducted trials from the review using quality or inclusion criteria.

This last point does indeed suggest the need for a further analysis of the results of a meta-analysis. Stufflebeam (2001) makes this same observation: '… a meta-evaluation can and should be conducted to assess the merit and worth of the completed meta-analysis study' (p 187).

Stufflebeam (2001) makes the point that meta-evaluation and meta-analysis are sometimes regarded as equivalent. Whereas meta-evaluation assesses the merit of an evaluation, meta-analysis is 'a form of quantitative synthesis of studies that address a common research question. In programme evaluation research this usually involves a treatment-control … comparison. Across a similar set of studies, the investigator calculates and examines the magnitude and significance of effect 'sizes' (p 187). This tendency to conflate the two procedures is exemplified in an article by Ashworth et al (2004). Under the paragraph headed 'What is meta-evaluation and how is it done?', Ashworth at al proceed to discuss 'The principles of meta-analysis' (p 195). To an extent, a certain amount of confusion appears to be pardonable. On the one hand, the statement is made that meta-evaluations have applications in meta-analysis studies – for example in order to determine which studies qualify for inclusion in a meta-analysis database; while, in the same paragraph, the author asserts that 'The meta-analysis technique is rarely applicable in a meta-evaluation, since most evaluations do not involve multiple comparative studies in a particular program area' (Stufflebeam, 2001, p 187).

Another dimension in the discussion attempting to distinguish between systematic reviews, meta-analysis and meta-evaluation is the work by Morley et al (1999). They record a systematic review and meta-analysis of randomised controlled trials of the effect of cognitive behavioural therapy and other forms of therapy on chronic pain. In their research they used systematic reviews as the preliminary stage in a meta-analysis. The review identified 33 papers after consulting various databases including Medline, PsychLit and Embase. In the meta-analysis stage statistical measures were used to study reliability and outcomes.

One definition of meta-analysis is that offered by Hattie and Hansford who describe it as 'a quantitative way to reduce the findings of many disparate studies to a common metric' (1984, p 239). The mathematical basis of meta-analyses has also been made clear by Egger and Smith (1997) in the context of medical research:

> meta-analysis is a statistical procedure that integrates several independent studies considered to be 'combinable'. (p 1533)

They echo the statement by Stufflebeam (2001) that biases can occur because of the exclusion of relevant studies and/or the inclusion of inadequate studies.

Meta-evaluation

To what extent can meta-evaluation conform to the principles and methods of systematic reviews and meta-analyses? If, as Guba and Lincoln (1989) initially showed, evaluation research has proceeded from a reliance on the experimental research design towards much more naturalistic, practical and realistic approaches, is it possible to consolidate the findings of evaluation studies? Stufflebeam (2001) defined meta-evaluation as:

> The process of delineating, obtaining and using description and judgmental information about an evaluation's utility, feasibility, propriety and accuracy and its systematic nature, competence, integrity/honesty, respectfulness and social responsibility to guide the evaluation and publicly report its strengths and weaknesses. (p 183)

This is a rather more elaborate definition than the one offered in a much earlier publication (Stufflebeam, 1981) which referred only to 'utility, practicality, ethics and technical adequacy of an evaluation' (p 151) or that of Greene who described it as the 'art and science of evaluating evaluations' (Greene, 1992, p 71).

These definitions contain two approaches to meta-evaluation: pre- and post-evaluation. In the first instance, the meta-evaluator(s) pass judgement on the key aspects of the evaluation before the evaluation takes place; for example, appropriateness of the research design, data collection methods, sample of interviewees and time-scale. At this preliminary stage the external third party acts as a consultant to those commissioned to undertake the evaluation of a project or programme. In the context of examining whether evaluations have influenced the policy-making process and political or organisational decision making, the post-evaluation position is the more relevant.

The criteria listed by Stufflebeam can be allocated to either or both of these types of meta-evaluation. For example, the *feasibility* of an evaluation refers to its capacity to be successfully carried out; that is the project's or programme's *evaluability*. 'Utility' relates to the evaluation's potential to be useful to the commissioner and 'propriety' to whether the evaluation is likely to raise any problems of an ethical nature such as intrusion into people's privacy. The other criteria that Stufflebeam lists – *systematic nature, competence, integrity/honesty, respectfulness* and *social responsibility* – could apply either to the pre-evaluation or post-evaluation stage.

However, not everyone would necessarily agree that Stufflebeam's criteria cover all concerns of meta-evaluators or that they are all relevant. Schwandt and Halpern (1988), for example, maintain that any proposed criteria to be applied in a meta-evaluation are themselves linked to a particular *paradigm* which is fairly accurately defined as a *conceptual framework*. This is an important observation made by Schwandt and Halpern because it raises not only the question of objectivity in relation to meta-evaluations but also to the design and methodology of individual evaluations. To extend this discussion it will be necessary to extend the above brief definition of 'paradigm' to its sociological origin and its relevance to understanding some of the reasons why the results of evaluations might not be utilised.

Thomas Kuhn (1962) introduced the argument that science was characterised by a commitment to a scientific paradigm. By 'paradigm' he was referring to a set of beliefs shared by a group of scientists about what the natural world is composed of, what counts as true and valid knowledge. It is a complete theory and framework within which scientists operate. It guides what evidence is collected, how it is collected and how it should be analysed.

> When scientists work within a paradigm, they tend to look for data that supports and refines that paradigm … they see the world in ways that are consistent with the paradigm … Consequently, scientists may ignore evidence that does not fit 'their' paradigm. (Haralambos and Holborn, 1995, p 859)

Bearing in mind Kuhn's interpretation of how scientific enquiry operates, we might expect meta-evaluations to identify the paradigm or 'world view' to which both the evaluator is committed and which – once the evaluation findings are disclosed – might or might not resemble the 'world view' of the commissioning agency or political institution. This phenomenon has also been registered by Georghiou (1999) in relation to the selection of performance indicators used in monitoring programmes within the European Framework Programme. Kuhn's thesis can also apply to the criteria applied by meta-evaluators. If we return to Stufflebeam's later definition of meta-evaluation (Stufflebeam, 2001) we can subject his criteria to a 'paradigmatic scrutiny'.

His predominant referents have to do with *process*, with the manner in which the evaluation was conducted. Compared with his earlier set of meta-evaluation criteria, he latterly places more emphasis on acceptable social interaction rather than levels of professional skill and competence although these would play their part. We can compare Stufflebeam's criteria with those advocated by Chelimsky (1983) when addressing the interpretation of what is meant by 'quality' as central to the assessment of an evaluation study. Her focus is on technical adequacy:

- Appropriateness of the evaluation design for answering the questions within its limitation of time and cost.
- Appropriateness of the evaluation's execution to the design selected and the resources available.
- Absence of major conceptual errors, inappropriate technical procedures and improper references or conclusions.

There is little doubt that Chelimsky would also prescribe an adherence to the codes of conduct that should be the hallmark of research activities (Palfrey and Thomas, 1996). Having said that, these two examples of criteria to be applied in a meta-evaluation do ostensibly confirm Kuhn's exposition of different research paradigms. On the one hand we have a concern tending towards the nature of social interactions; on the other hand the main focus is on technical awareness and competence. Certainly, it could be argued, that failings in either of these two approaches to evaluation are likely to produce questionable data.

Meta-evaluation of single evaluations and sets of studies

Single evaluations

Assessing the quality of a single evaluation has been likened to the process of financial auditing. Schwandt and Halpern (1988) regard meta-evaluation as an activity that is conducted for the same reasons as an audit; that is to provide users of the evaluation report with an outsider's opinion on the quality of the inquiry design, implementation and analysis. Stufflebeam (2001) makes the same point. 'Evaluation consumers, much like users of financial statements, seek assurances that evaluation procedures were appropriate and that findings were trustworthy and accurate' (p 25). Schwandt and Halpern (1988) list three key areas of enquiry that the meta-evaluator – the 'evaluation auditor' – would need to focus on. These are:

- *The evaluation **process***

Typical questions would be:

- – 'Was the information collected during the evaluation responsive to the needs of various audiences?'
- – 'Were the procedures used to gather data reliable, valid and within the scope of accepted practices?'
- – 'Were the rights of persons participating in the evaluation protected?'

- *The evaluation **findings***
  - – 'Was the final report released in a timely manner?'
  - – 'Was the report made available to all relevant parties?'
  - – 'Did the report clearly explain the object of the evaluation, the context and the findings?'

- Both ***process*** and ***findings***
  - – 'Were steps taken to enhance the utility of the findings?'
  - – 'Were cost-effective procedures employed?'
  - – 'Were resources used effectively during the evaluation?'
  - – 'Were the evaluation findings and conclusions supported by the data?'

To those principles and criteria for conducting meta-evaluations set out by Chelimsky (1983), Schwandt and Halpern (1988) add 'usefulness' or 'utility' in the words of the evaluation principles and standards decreed by the American Evaluation Research Society. Both Chelimsky and Schwandt and Halpern agree that the criteria applied in evaluating evaluations are relative to the paradigm to which the evaluator and 'auditor' are committed. What if the two 'world views' are not entirely compatible? What if the evaluator is primarily or even exclusively concerned with achieving a high standard of research whereas the meta-evaluator prizes the inclusiveness of the research design and process in its involvement and sensitive interactions with research participants? Furthermore, how clear are both evaluators about the preferences and expectations of the evaluation commissioners? They might be inclined towards either one of the two sets of values held by the evaluators or insist on a true amalgam of both sets.

Sets of studies

In their discussion of meta-evaluation Cooksy and Caracelli (2005) concentrate on the evaluation of sets of studies and help to clarify the functions of reviews and meta-analyses. They state that reviews of sets of studies have two main purposes.

First, the knowledge about evaluation quality that results from evaluation of multiple evaluations can be used to inform researchers' decisions about which studies to include in evaluation syntheses (Cook et al, 1992; Wortman, 1994). *Evaluation syntheses* combine information from more than one study in order to come to general statements about a particular intervention. *Qualitative syntheses* are generally known as *narrative reviews* while *quantitative syntheses* are called *meta-analyses,* which, as noted earlier, is a statistical approach towards drawing conclusions about the effectiveness of a kind of intervention and its overall impact. The intention is that, by applying standards of quality, meta-evaluation will eliminate those studies that display defects in certain aspects of the design and methodology.

Secondly, identifying weaknesses in evaluation research can help in developing high quality evaluation practice (Lipsey et al, 1985; Vedung, 1997). Lipsey et al (1985) and Bickman (1997) concluded after evaluating a very large number of published evaluation studies that the quality of the research was generally in need of improvement. Again the question arises as to a wide variety of attributes assigned to the concept, and Cooksy and Caracelli (2005) list a number of these. They also confirm what is an important consideration in meta-evaluation; that on the one hand the meaningful engagement of all would be valued under a deliberative, democratic approach but would perhaps be less emphasised from a post-positivist perspective.

A recognition that, in the words of Cooksy and Caracelli (2005), different evaluations are likely to be 'conducted under diverse paradigmatic stances' (p 15) must call into questions attempts to prescribe a definitive set of quality standards for carrying out evaluations. For this reason, disagreement about what constitutes a quality evaluation is 'a potential pitfall of meta-evaluations' (p 15). As far as the opposite of a quality evaluation is concerned, Stufflebeam (2001) provides a catalogue of the potential defects of evaluations that meta-evaluations might reveal. Evaluations might be flawed by:

- inadequate focus;
- inappropriate criteria;
- technical errors;
- excessive costs;
- abuse of authority;
- shoddy implementation;
- tardy reports;

- biased findings;
- ambiguous findings;
- unjustified conclusions;
- inadequate or wrong interpretations to users;
- unwarranted recommendations; or
- counterproductive interference in the program being evaluated.

Meta-evaluation in the UK

There is little evidence in the literature of meta-analyses or meta-evaluations having been carried out in the UK. One possible reason is that there are probably few programmes that include a significant number of individual projects that are similar in nature, scope and objectives. Even though Ashworth et al (2004) include three of the four co-authors who were attached to British universities, the meta-evaluation that they report relate to welfare-to-work programmes in the USA. They surveyed 24 such schemes. Having listed the key stages in conducting a meta-evaluation, they conclude with the final stage, which is to perform a regression analysis to explain variation in the effects of the various welfare-to-work projects. The results of the meta-analysis are then used as the data on which the meta-evaluation is founded.

In their article, Ashworth et al provide counter-arguments to the criticism of meta-analysis made by Pawson (2002a). Pawson first defines the procedure as he understands it:

> The basic locus of analysis is a particular 'family of programmes' targeted at a specific problem ... The overall comparison is made by calculating the typical impact (mean effect) achieved by each of the sub-types within the overall family. (p 161)

This procedure leads to the drawing up of a league table of effectiveness. Each individual intervention is then reduced to a single measure of effectiveness, which he regards as an oversimplification of programme outcomes which leads to a 'spurious precision' (p 162). This, Pawson reasons, is because meta-analysis does not allow for individual and contextual variations. For example, certain negative outcomes for individuals in an otherwise 'effective' programme are masked by a general outcome measurement. As a result, 'Vital explanatory information is ... squeezed out automatically in the process of aggregation'.

Pawson readily concedes that the American case study might not be the best example of a piece of meta-analysis and that other examples of *secondary analysis* might provide more convincing evidence for policy making.

Pawson dismisses meta-analysis and narrative or systematic reviews as offering the most satisfactory means of synthesising a collection of research studies and in their place he puts forward 'realist synthesis' (Pawson 2002b). In brief, his framework for analysis focuses on the cause-effect relationship which is, in most examples of evaluation, the primary focus of attention. Rather than evaluating programmes or a family of programmes, Pawson maintains that a different approach is required. It is not programmes, he argues, that work (or do not work); it is the underlying reasons or resources that they offer to their subjects that generate change. Causation is contingent, so evaluators should be trying to identify what works for whom and in what circumstances.

Ashworth and colleagues do not disagree with this recommended framework for analysis (Ashworth et al, 2004). However, they assert that quantitative meta-evaluation has the potential to be far more than the simplistic parody suggested by some critics (Pawson, 2002a; Pawson, 2002b, p 211). With further reference to these two articles by Pawson, Ashworth et al maintain that 'a quantitative meta-analysis is not the endpoint of evaluation but part of the ongoing process; the outcome is not the mean of means based on crass empiricism' (p 213). Furthermore, they assert, meta-analysis is capable of generating theories about how programes work for whom and in what circumstances – a direct refutation of Pawson's critique.

The future of meta-evaluation

There is an undoubted clash between the advocates of a meta-analysis approach to identifying the effectiveness and impact of evaluation research on policy making and those who wish to move away from the quantitative/positivist framework for carrying out evaluations. Meta-analysis, as we have noted, depends on the availability of a fairly large number of evaluations that feature similar projects that can be classified as forming a distinct programme or, at least, a kind of 'family network'. Because of the scale of evaluation activities in the USA, reports of meta-evaluations using meta-analysis as the main instrument of review have appeared in the evaluation literature. This coverage has not been replicated in the UK.

However, meta-evaluations either of the formative or summative kind originally described by Scriven (1969) have also been lacking in the literature. If, as many commentators have suggested, the main reasons for non-utilisation of evaluation findings are to do with faults in the evaluation process, methodology, timeliness of reports and other technical, research-related factors (Clarke, 1999; Weiss, 1999) then it would follow that (more) use needs to be made of single study meta-evaluation. The appointment of a third party evaluator to monitor and advise on the design and overall approach prior to the start of the evaluation could pre-empt the possibility of a flawed evaluation. Alternatively, an evaluation of the research after its conclusion might also be of value in recommending the report as it stands or in suggesting modifications or expressing reservations about the process and/or validity of the findings. Naturally the inclusion of an additional evaluator would mean additional costs to the commissioner but arguably this extra funding could prove its worth in terms of the meta-evaluation's cost-effectiveness. Chitty (2000) is certainly in favour of some form of aggregated evidence to inform policy makers. He maintains that there is a need to ensure that all the currently available research and evaluation evidence is thoroughly reviewed and synthesised and used to inform policy thinking and appraisal. According to Sanderson (2002), the Department for Education and Employment recognised the importance of review and synthesis of research evidence. Unfortunately, in the view of Sanderson (2002) there are grounds for concern about the nature of evaluation evidence since it fails to provide the basis for a theoretically grounded understanding of transferable lessons about what works and why.

The technical shortcomings of some evaluation research reports in other countries have been highlighted. For example, in Canada, the Treasury Board of Canada arranged for a meta-analysis of 130 evaluation reports produced for different government departments and concluded that 50% of the reports lacked credibility because the results were not based on information relevant to the aim of the evaluation, and in 32% of cases, the supporting arguments were not sufficient to generate a judgement (Treasury Board of Canada, 2004). The limited usability and utilisation of evaluation findings have been substantiated by other studies in the USA (House, 1980; Fournier and Smith, 1993; Datta, 2006) while a more recent meta-analysis of 40 programme evaluation reports (Hurteau et al, 2009) lends weight to the assertions of Guba and Lincoln (1972) and Scriven (1995) that programme evaluation has to be questioned as an original process that 'produces legitimate and justified arguments' (Hurteau et al, 2009, p 317).

In the domain of medical research, systematic reviews, meta-analyses and meta-evaluations are much more likely to be used appropriately because of the ability to control potentially confounding variables. Those social programmes subjected to meta-evaluations in the USA have also used the randomised controlled trial as the medium for the research. It would not be impossible to replicate this approach in the UK and, indeed, the relative dearth of reported instances of meta-evaluations of sets of studies sounds a discordant note in the light of successive governments' apparent commitment to evidence-based policy.

A return to the experimental design?

We have noted in previous chapters that the experimental evaluation research design has become somewhat discredited along with the positivist paradigm in which it was set. However, in view of the sustained *angst* about the apparent defects in evaluation studies and, as a possible consequence, the non-adoption of the research findings by decision makers, it would seem to be a logical step to reconsider the application of the experimental model to formal evaluations. Could there be any circumstances in the field of social research where something approaching a randomised controlled trial could be both practical and ethical? It could be argued that withholding a potentially effective clinical intervention from a control group of people is no more ethical than offering a series of counselling sessions to one group of young offenders while denying it to another similar group. If it proved practical to use the RCT design in, for example, a community setting such as a school, a playgroup or a housing estate, what would be the possible problems or objections? Sanderson (2002) has argued that in national initiatives such as the New Deal programmes in the UK, the use of control groups was not practical due to ethical objections to denying to some eligible people the benefits of the initiative. He suggests that 'In such situations, a range of quasi-experimental approaches can be pursued ... but these will not provide the kind of unequivocal results that policy makers seek' (p 12). However, testing such an initiative first in a pilot programme – a topic pursued by Sanderson – would probably be considered more acceptable than trying out a new policy nationwide if there was no guarantee that it would be of any benefit to the participants.

The dominance of the experimental design for evaluations was initially the result of the work of Campbell and his co-author Stanley in the 1960s (Campbell and Stanley, 1966). Campbell, in particular, was keen to apply his mode of research as a psychologist to the field of evaluation research. (Campbell, 1969). This attachment to the transference of a positivist scientific framework for research in the domain of social research continued well into the 1970s and 1980s. Weiss (1972) acknowledged the experimental–control group structure as an important framework for evaluation, as did Epstein and Tripodi (1977). Fitzgibbon and Morris (1987) continued to stress the classic randomised-controlled group design, but in the same year Patton (1987) was advocating greater use of qualitative data, although he accepted that both qualitative and quantitative data collection methods could be applied in a design that partook of both the positivist and constructivist paradigms.

By the 1990s commentators on evaluation were ready to discount the experimental design as inappropriate for research focusing on social groups within a community setting. Nutbeam (1998) summed up a general negative attitude:

> … the artificial assignment of individuals in communities to intervention and control groups is not only often impractical, but frequently impossible as it places quite unrealistic constraints on the evaluation design. (p 36)

Green and South (2006) have, more recently, suggested that a compromise might be possible. Instead of randomly assigning individuals to one of two groups, 'it may be more feasible to allocate naturally occurring units such as schools, hospitals or communities' (p 22) in what would be termed a quasi-experimental design. While allowing that small-scale and medium-scale projects and programmes will not consider an experimental design to be feasible, Green and South contend that just such a design could still be an option where there is a central issue of providing strong evidence of effectiveness and 'in those rare situations where it is possible to control for external factors' (p 73).

Referring to the arena of health promotion, Campbell and Stanley (2000) and Hawe et al (2004) agree that even in complex intervention programmes the randomised controlled trial might be a practical option. However, as Tilley and Clarke (2006) have pointed out, to achieve the 'double blind' element in a randomised controlled trial where neither the experimental nor the control group knows which is which would probably be impossible within the wider context of a neighbourhood or community – however that concept is interpreted. An additional problem is that of generalisability (*external validity*). Attempting to infer from a community-based intervention that the same result would occur in another comparable setting elsewhere is highly questionable. Tilley and Clarke maintain that 'Findings about effects are not generalisable across time, place and subgroup: external validity should not be assumed' (p 521).

The question of ethics mentioned earlier in this section is also an important consideration when contemplating the practice of randomly assigning individuals, groups, institutions or communities to an experimental or control group. The issue of gaining informed consent from potential research participants becomes more of a hurdle where large numbers are involved. Of course, not all projects or programmes depend for their evaluation on mustering large populations. Yet this distinction presents something of a paradox. If the intention of an evaluation is to provide evidence of a cause–effect relationship between a specific intervention and a particular outcome, then the greater the number of subjects involved the greater the chances of generating hard evidence. However, the methodological pitfalls inherent in such an experimental design makes a compromise more attractive and feasible. However, the smaller the numbers the less likelihood there is of the research producing generalisable results. Orr (1999) who, like Boruch (1997), is an advocate of the experimental design, makes this point emphatically:

> Random assignment of program participants cannot provide estimates of program effects on broader aggregations of individuals, such as neighbourhoods or entire cities. (p 15)

One of the useful functions – according to Orr – that a relatively small-scale social experiment can perform is to act as a pilot programme in order to create what he calls a 'working model' (1999, p 2) of the intended programme to be evaluated. A very telling point that Orr makes in the context of the evaluation sector in the USA is that his reason for writing a book on the subject of social experiments and programme planning is because this form of evaluation design is the least covered in the existing literature. This is so despite the fact that 'experimental designs have become the preferred method of program evaluation among most of the policy research community' (p 17). His statement exposes a disconcerting gap between actual evaluations 'out there' and the reporting of them in the literature consumed by academic researchers.

Our comment in Chapter Six concerning the relative dearth of reported evaluations in the UK literature is counteracted by the volume of articles on evaluations published in what might broadly be termed public service journals. A fairly random search of the internet will discover scores of such articles in, for example, the *Local Government*

Chronicle, Educational Review, Critical Public Health and the *British Journal of Social Work.*

So where does this leave us on the issue of whether modern-day evaluators should consider returning to a more scientific approach to evaluation practice? Even in the world of medical research – as we have noted in the case of the unfounded claims relating to MMR – those who carry out RCTs would probably rarely admit that their findings were incontrovertible. In fact, as Goldacre (2009) has ably demonstrated, sometimes the louder the claim the more likely it is to be based on counterfeit evidence. What is more, of course, treatment with drugs, while manifestly having a positive outcome on the patient, can also induce negative side-effects. In that event, it would not be enough just to announce that the intervention had produced the desired outcome. It would also be ethically imperative to draw attention to any undesirable consequences of taking the medication.

That is why we consider that there is a meaningful distinction to be made between the short-term *outcome* and the longer-term *impact*. However, in the context of discussions on the experimental research design, the phrase *impact assessment* refers to the effect that the intervention has been shown to have on the *outcome* – that is, that a cause–effect relationship has been established beyond a reasonable doubt. In RCTs, as in meta-analyses, tests of statistical significance will be applied in order to indicate the strength of connection between the input and outcome. Statistical tests can only be appropriate if the experiment is constructed in such a way that all other factors that might have contributed to the outcome have been eliminated. This involves meticulous sampling techniques in order to compare like with like between the experimental and control groups. To employ the next best option – a control and comparison group arrangement – will inevitably reduce the strength of any identified correlation between the intervention and eventual outcome.

Just such a contingency was encountered in the evaluation programme carried out by the authors of this book, outlined in Chapter Three. The initiative was already underway when we started on the evaluation. We therefore had to match as closely as possible the elderly service users in our comparison group with those in the experimental cohort. Random allocation per group was not possible. This quasi-experimental design was further weakened by the length of the programme – three years. Over this period the chances of extraneous variables influencing the course of the individuals' experience became increasingly high. In such circumstances, drawing any inferences from the accumulated data becomes an increasingly tenuous aspiration. We are then left with information that 'suggests' rather than 'proves'; that indicates a cause–effect nexus that is not 'beyond reasonable doubt' but that complies with the degree of convincing evidence applied in a civil court – that of 'the balance of probabilities'.

To some extent we are faced with a dilemma. On the one hand, it might be assumed that decision makers would ideally wish to be presented with evidence that is firmer than that which a civil court would require as a minimum for reaching a decision. Therefore, a more concerted effort on the part of evaluators to construct a form of social experiment that would hopefully provide evidence that goes beyond reasonable doubt would appear to be called for. Alternatively, it could be argued that since politicians, in particular, are just as likely to take decisions that fly in the face of otherwise persuasive information, those commissioned to undertake formal evaluations might opt for less methodologically demanding research designs.

Evaluating 'process'

Meta-analysis and the experimental research design are both focused on outcomes. In Chapter Two there was considerable discussion about forms of assessment such as audits, inspections and accreditations that were primarily interested in the achievement of measurable indicators of *outputs*, such as numbers of patients treated, numbers of high grades achieved in examinations or numbers of certain age groups unemployed. The missing component in any project, programme or policy is *process*, by which we mean the *manner in which a project, programme or policy operates* including formal procedures, rules and regulation; the nature of staff relations; management styles; regime (democratic/participative; autocratic/top-down). Gomby and Larson (1992) offer this definition of *process evaluation*:

> A process evaluation focuses on what services were provided to whom and how. Its purpose is to describe how the program was implemented, who was involved and what problems were experienced. A process evaluation is useful for monitoring program implementation, to identify changes to make the program operate as planned, and, generally, for program improvement. (p 71)

Hansen (2005) listed *process evaluation* as one of six types of evaluation and described it as discovering how the project or programme was viewed by clients and stakeholders.

On the one hand, it is not surprising that evaluators and those who commission evaluations have been interested predominantly in outcomes; on whether the intervention has achieved the desired objectives. However, the means by which the objectives were fully, partly or not achieved is surely a crucial aspect of any evaluation. That is why, we would argue, the process element in an evaluation has been largely ignored in the literature. In Chapter Three, we referred to an initiative which aimed to enable physically disabled service users to play a more active role in two centres' organisation and service delivery, where one of the present authors acted as an external observer. During the course of the initiative, feeding back to the participants was crucial in order to make progress towards achieving the project's objective.

After several weeks in which the head of the day centre took it upon himself to chair the group's meetings, a female day centre client was elected to chair the group. On one occasion when she was away, the day centre head took the chair. When the external observer pointed out to him after the meeting that no-one had invited him to take over he admitted that 'old habits die hard'. The role of the observer was, in essence, to monitor progress towards greater client autonomy and collective emancipation by feeding back to members of the group the positives and set-backs that, in his view, had occurred during each meeting. Without this continuous assessment of the way in which the group operated, it is likely that it might have taken much longer to reach the agreed outcome or, at worst, the project would have been abandoned or the overall aim watered down.

One example of this possible scenario was the opportunity granted by management to the clients to have more say in their day-to-day experience either in the day centre or residential centre. It became clear to the observer that management's concept of 'more say' was greater choice of which day(s) to attend the day centre and a wider range of menus to choose from. There was almost an audible intake of breath on the part of the department's staff when the service users asked to be represented on the staff appointments panel. Discussions between staff and the observer managed to reveal to some members of staff that meetings and expectations were metaphorically and literally conforming to the agenda of the staff members, which was not the expressed *modus operandi* when managers first introduced the project to service users.

It would seem to be nothing more than sheer common sense for the process of projects, programmes and policies to be subjected to scrutiny *en route* to what is hoped will be a favourable outcome. Process evaluation – or monitoring – must be intended to prevent failure.

At its best it is a form of *action research* in which all key participants/ stakeholders reflect on stages in the process of implementing the contents of the initiative. In this way, matters can be adjusted. Costs can be reviewed and, if necessary, aspirations modified. Obstacles, such as staff attitudes to change, can be overcome or reduced. Additional time to complete the initiative might be open to negotiation. Ultimately, the purpose of process evaluation is to avoid having to ask at the end of the journey 'Where did it all go wrong?' or 'How did we manage to achieve all that?'. An additional potential benefit for many evaluators of carrying out process evaluation is that it could contribute to theory-building; on how positive outcomes can be attained in complex organisations and social systems.

In search of theory

In the evaluation literature the commitment by many authors for theory-driven evaluation is well-documented (Chen, 1990; Pawson and Tilley, 1997; Madison, 2002). In many areas of research activity the need for theory-building has consumed much time and energy. In the natural sciences, the mode of enquiry runs a course of observation, description, testing and re-testing towards an explanation of how and why certain phenomena occur. The quest is and always has been for predictability by noting repeated events, such as the sun rising in the same location, and by observing and/or creating certain conditions, then observing what follows as a direct consequence. The methods of natural science became the hallmark of rigorous research. The object of scientific enquiry was to discover laws through the process of testing hypotheses (*informed suppositions*) and developing theories (*explanations, proved or yet to be proved*).

Since evaluation research is a form of social research, we could usefully look at sociological theories to discover how they came into being. Haralambos and Halpern (1995) define a theory as 'a set of ideas that claims to explain how something works. A sociological theory, is, therefore, a set of ideas that claims to explain how society or aspects of society works' (p 7). It is not coincidental that many sociologists would prefer to be called 'social scientists' since the status of research-informed activities and their practitioners is enhanced by defining it as a science. One of the questionable elements in the above definition is that the concept 'society' is neither a static entity nor homogeneous in its structure, history, culture or topography. For this reason, the various sociological theories such as functionalism, Marxism, interactionsim and post-modernism are creations of time and place. Therefore, no single theory can aspire to explaining how all of society works, but can only address individual societies. Even then, as noted earlier in this book, even practitioners in the natural sciences are not without commitment to a particular world-view or paradigm. Theoretical perspectives, it can be argued, are not merely the creation of time and place but of personal beliefs and ideologies.

We referred in Chapter Six to a widely held view that evaluations should be not only useful but actually used. In this sense, it probably differs from sociological theory since, from our reading of the literature, there is no significant plea for the fruits of sociology to be of any great use for decision makers. The selection of theories listed above were not derived from major empirical work. Smelser (1994) makes a distinction between micro theories and macro theories in the field of sociology. The former focus on interpersonal interaction while the latter deal with organisations, structures and cultures. Just which of these categories evaluation theory would fit into, if either, is debateable. One clear hint is that discussion in the literature about evaluation theory is all about *program theory*. The fact that a good deal of evaluation practice is geared towards policy evaluation appears to have evaded the interest of those academics – predominantly in the USA – who espouse the cause of developing and applying theory to evaluations. Although Chen (1990) was one of the earlier writers on evaluation theory, perhaps the most influential work is that of Shadish et al (1991). They depicted three stages of evaluation theorising. Stage One focused on evaluation methods; Stage Two on values and Stage Three on users and use. These three stages were presented more visually by Alkin and Christie (2004) in their 'evaluation theory tree'. Further work by Mark (2005) and Stufflebeam and Shinkfield (2007) extended the corpus of literature emphasising the importance of program theory to carrying out worthwhile evaluations. The application of theory to practice was agreed by these authors as essential in order (a) to consolidate lessons learned from previous evaluations; (b) to avoid repeating past mistakes; (c) to make informed choices about data collection methods; and (d) to clarify how a program is expected to work and how to achieve its goals.

These claims inevitably lead to the question of how theory performs these functions. Rossi et al (1999) attempt to clarify how 'theory' can be interpreted. They accept that the word 'theory' sounds rather grand. They contend that most evaluators would be happy with one dictionary definition of theory as 'a particular conception or view of something to be done or of the method of doing it' (pp 98–99). Program theory, they continue, could also be called 'the program conceptualisation or, perhaps, the program plan, blueprint or design' (p 99) while Alkin et al (2004) write about 'Evaluation approaches, often referred to as evaluation theories or models ...' (p 398). However, in the volume edited by Shaw et al (2006), the text deals with numerous evaluation models, including empowerment, feminist, goal-oriented, participatory, quasi-experimental utilisation-focused models, that do not purport to be equivalent to theories. If, as its exponents claim, evaluation theory is to be valued because it provides a degree of scientific predictability as to how a program is likely to work (presumably meaning 'attain its goals'), then presumably this theory/approach/model/conceptualisation has been constructed as a result of data gathered from an overview, systematic review, narrative review, meta-analysis or meta-evaluation of many examples of reported evaluations that share some common features. Unfortunately, and rather tellingly, the literature does not provide us with such assurances. The statement by Dahler-Larsen in the collection of papers edited by Shaw et al (2006) strikes a salutary note of caution:

> The call for more research on evaluation and its effects is clearly justified ... evaluation may turn out to be oversold and its costs underestimated. (p 153)

Dahler-Larsen is not adopting a negative stance towards evaluation. He is suggesting that it would be of practical use to carry out scientific evaluations of evaluations.

A particularly detailed presentation of the principles and usefulness of program theory was delivered to a gathering at the African Evaluation Association in a trio of lectures by Anna Madison in 2002. Drawing substantially on the work of Shadish et al (1991) Madison lists three reasons why evaluation theory is important. These are:

- Theory of evaluation helps us to understand evaluation practice.
- Theory of social programming helps us to understand social problems and to select solutions and to measure their effectiveness.
- Theory-based evaluation helps us to understand the relationship between program theory, program processes and program outcomes. (Madison, 2002, p 1)

By way of further elucidation, Madison (2002) maintains that evaluation theory 'identifies and explains feasible practices that evaluators can use to construct knowledge of the value of social programs. Also, evaluation theory provides the conceptual framework for assessing the effectiveness of evaluation practice' (Madison, 2002, p 1).

Shadish et al (1991) – according to Madison – set out five components of evaluation or program theory. These are: *knowledge, value, use, social programming, and practice.* These are all defined as theories and they each pose key questions.

The theory of *knowledge* addresses the question: 'Is there anything special about the knowledge that evaluators construct and how do they construct such knowledge?'. In Madison's words: 'The theory of knowledge allows evaluators to place abstract epistemological debates into a practical context to reach conclusions about epistemological assumptions in their own work' (Madison, 2002, p 1).

Value theory raises the question 'How can evaluators make value problems explicit, deal with them openly and produce a sensitive analysis of the value implications of a program?'. Without a theory of value, it is not feasible for evaluators to decide and report whether a program is good or better than something else.

The third theory – the *theory of use* – prompts the question 'How can evaluators produce results that are useful for social problem solving?' Kinds of use include:

- *Instrumental use* – which leads to direct decision making about the program or project.
- *Conceptual use* – helps to clarify, hopefully changing thinking about the program.
- *Persuasive use* – leads to a change in position, particularly at the policy level.

Social programming theory asks the question 'How can social programs contribute to social problem solving and how can social programs be improved?'. The basic elements of a theory of social programming are:

- how programs are structured internally, what functions they fulfil, and how they operate;
- how the external context shapes and constrain (*sic*) the program; and
- how social change occurs, how programs change, and how program change contributes to social change. (Madison, 2002, p 2)

Finally, *practice theory* raises the question 'How should the practice of evaluation be conducted?'. Some of the elements of the theory of practice are:

- whether or not an evaluation should be done;
- what the purpose of the evaluation should be;
- what role the evaluator ought to play;
- what questions should be asked;
- what research design will be used; and
- what measures will be taken to facilitate use.

Having described the main features of each of the five evaluation theories, Madison goes on to detail the part each played in the three stages of the theory of evaluation, which, to an extent, reflects the three 'generations of evaluation' in the work of Guba and Lincoln (1985) which we referred to in Chapter Four. These three stages are delineated as:

- *Stage 1:* A commitment to using evaluation as a means of providing evidence of social program effectiveness in solving social problems. Stage 1 theorists strongly advocated the application of experimental and quasi-experimental designs to provide knowledge about programs.
- *Stage II:* Evaluators claimed that earlier practitioners failed to provide useful knowledge to improve programs. This stage sought to involve a range of stakeholders in the conduct of the evaluation; to use a range of data collection methods and to acknowledge that contextual issues are important considerations in evaluation.
- *Stage III:* Theorists asserted that incremental social change can be achieved by improving existing social programs; that multiple epistemologies, multiple methods and priorities characterise evaluation; that there will be a diversity of values among different stakeholders:

Madison concludes by providing an assessment of current trends in evaluation. These include:

- Evaluation sets out to promote specific policy agendas such as social justice.
- The perspectives and values of clients/consumers, the community and citizens in general are now deemed important.

- Multiple sources of knowledge are now accepted instead of a reliance on a positivist scientific methodology to reveal facts.
- Evaluations play a part in organisational development.
- The evaluator is not the only investigator but a partner in conducting evaluative work with stakeholders towards more collaborative, participatory and empowerment evaluation.

Some problems with theories

Setting aside the assortment of definitions attached to the word 'theory' in the evaluation literature, there are a number of potential and actual problems with the efforts to make evaluation more theory-driven. Chen (1990) and Weiss (1995) have both claimed that social programmes are based on theories about how and why the programme will work. The task of evaluation is to make explicit those theories, identify the inherent assumptions and test their validity. However, Sanderson (2002) regrets that:

> theory-based evaluation, while holding out considerable promise for the development of knowledge to underpin more effective policy making, nevertheless presents significant challenges in terms of articulating theories, measuring changes and effects, developing appropriate tests of theoretical assumptions, and in terms of the generalizability of results obtained in particular contexts. (p 18)

In a similar vein, Granger (1998) writes that it is virtually impossible to achieve precise and unequivocal causal attribution, particularly in the context of evaluating complex social interventions. The point is that many social interventions consist of a range of inputs directed towards achieving multiple outcomes.

Another possible cause for concern among evaluators is that all the relevant literature is confined to discussions about 'program theory'. No attention is given to policy or policy-making theory except, perhaps, implicitly in assuming that trying to explain 'how things work' and in what contexts could help to influence decisions not just on a single project or programme level but on a broader scale. This neglect of policy theory is both unexpected and predictable. It is unexpected in view of the many attempts over the past 60 years or more to describe the process of policy making. These have been discussed in Chapter Two. It is predictable, as we have also indicated in the same chapter, because the various 'theories' or explanations have amounted to little more than interpretations based more on supposition than on any research-derived information. There can be no single explanation that can predict what form the process of policy making will take because we live in a world that is not governed by social, political or even economic 'laws'.

A similar problem relates to program theory. There is nothing in the literature to suggest that there is any theory that can be used in order to predict or explain the dynamics or outcome of any project or programme. The issue of 'what works' is likely to be contingent on the unique characteristics of each project, programme or policy being evaluated. For this reason, while a 'theory' might emerge after the conclusion of a piece of evaluation, it cannot be relied on to act as a theoretical base for any other evaluations. If this reasoning is valid, perhaps evaluators should expend more effort in producing real-life examples of where program theory has had a positive effect on the evaluation and less time extolling the usefulness of theory in tracts whose content is, in itself, wholly theoretical.

However, we must acknowledge that (as noted in Chapter Four) the work of Pawson (2002a; 2002b) and Pawson and Tilley (1997) has been received very positively by evaluation theorists. They have, in a sense, revitalised academic discourses on the subject of evaluation theory. Yet some of those who have welcomed their *realistic evaluation* approach have discerned some weaknesses in it; weaknesses which are probably inherent in any attempt to construct evaluation theory. For example, Davis (2005) used a realist evaluation (RE) 'modelling' to appraise a sample of ten Best Value Reviews in one local authority n the UK between 1999 and early 2001. Davis points out that RE has focused on the evaluation of single projects and asserts that 'the extent to which findings from one context may be generalised to others remains problematical' (p 291). He further argues that:

> Emergent goals and process outcomes are not generally recognised or formally incorporated into any of the published realist research studies. (Davis, 2005, p 292)

Pedersen and Rieper (2008) first of all set out the main thesis of theory-driven evaluation. It was developed as an alternative to method-oriented approaches which were criticised for being 'unable and unwilling to open up the "black box": the space between actual input and expected outcome', that is, to reveal 'causal explanations' which they equate with 'theories'. They then define the role of the evaluator:

> It is the job of the evaluator to formulate and test hypotheses
> on how a programme generates social change and to identify
> the contexts influencing the operation of these in order to
> produce knowledge on what works, for whom, in what
> circumstances (p 272)

This is something of a contentious statement that goes to the heart
of our degree of scepticism about the value of theory building as the
primary purpose of formal evaluations. We shall return briefly to this
issue shortly. According to Pedersen and Rieper (2008), evaluation
theorists have had a limited horizon. They have attempted to build
what they describe as 'middle-range theories' rather than 'grand unified
theory'. In the RE literature, they add, the evaluand (the subject of the
evaluation) has been at the level of projects or programmes and not at
the level of large-scale public reforms – that is, at the policy evaluation
level. This is a fair summary of our view, not just of realist evaluation
but of theory-based or theory-driven evaluation theory as a whole.

It is, however, not a 'failing' as far as theory-building is concerned.
The central issue of evaluations is to do with attempting to excavate
cause or causes out of a mass of data involving real people in real-life
situations. In one sense, realist evaluation has laid to rest the possibility
of theory-driven evaluations ever presuming to generate theories
(*causal explanations*) other than at project and, perhaps, programme
levels. For Pawson and Tilley to insist quite rightly on much more
probing analysis of what works, for whom and in what circumstances
using the context–mechanism–outcome model, they emphasise the
contingent nature of community-based initiatives. Indeed, without
having recourse to the unfashionable experimental design framework,
the prospect of building a theory – as that term would be understood
in scientific research – is not likely.

To return to the statement from Pedersen and Rieper (2008)
concerning the definitive task of the evaluator, their interpretation
is open to debate. It is also relevant to the topic referred to earlier in
this chapter about the link between theory-driven evaluation and the
status of evaluation and of its practitioners. The desire to attach the
word 'theory' to 'evaluation' is arguably to do with raising the status of
both practice and practitioner to that of 'profession' and 'professional'.
Jacob and Boisvert (2010) have clearly catalogued the numerous
commentators who have argued for or against evaluation being regarded
as a profession. Those in favour outnumber those against. Donaldson
and Christie (2006) have also addressed this issue. Indeed, they refer to

evaluation as a science – a claim that even the most ardent of evaluation theorists would find difficulty supporting.

It is doubtful whether those who carry out project evaluations – many of them carried out by staff within an organisation – would be impressed by the maxim enunciated by Pedersen and Rieper (2008). One example of day-to-day, real-world evaluations is the compendium of evaluations reported in the Research and Evaluation Review published by the Health Promotion Agency for Northern Ireland. These are the titles of a sample of project evaluations included in the 2005–2006 edition, which appears to be the latest edition available:

- Evaluation of the Fresh Fruit in Schools pilot scheme 2005–2006.
- Evaluation of Work Well: a workplace health initiative for small businesses.
- Evaluation of No Smoking Day 2006.

The stated objectives of each of these projects' evaluation did not involve testing any hypotheses. It could be argued that certain implicit hypotheses were embedded in these projects in terms of a hope or supposition that certain actions would bring about certain results; that is, that a cause–effect nexus could be identified. It could also be argued that at the conclusion of a pilot project the findings can be useful in providing some evidence of how to organise and conduct a more far-reaching project in future. All three projects were modest in scope. As soon as a more ambitious version of them might be planned, the issue of comparability arises. Central to any attempt to establish guidelines, rules and criteria for how to carry out the more substantive evaluation will probably founder, just as research involving a comparison between different contexts, participants and time-scales is most likely to produce non-generalisable data.

Where is 'policy evaluation'?

By this we mean two things. First of all, to what extent does policy evaluation feature in the literature on evaluation? Secondly, what is the current state and status of policy evaluation as a topic of interest to those who study, write about, carry out and commission evaluations?

A substantial review of the evaluation literature from the 1960s onwards reveals three main strands:

- The 'how to' approach: texts setting out a range of evaluation research designs and data collection methods; for example, Weiss

(1972), Epstein and Tripodi (1977), Fitzgibbon and Morris (1987) and Patton (1987).

- Texts advocating certain frameworks for/approaches to evaluation such as *practical evaluation* (Patton, 1982); *naturalistic inquiry* (Guba and Lincoln, 1985); and *realistic evaluation* (Pawson and Tilley, 1997).
- The development and application of *evaluation theory*, for example, Chen (1990); Shadish et al (1991) and Rossi et al (1999).

All three strands include a percurrent theme in the literature of ways in which the use of evaluation findings might be enhanced and all three use as their reference point *program evaluation* which conceptually embraces both projects and programmes. The issue of *policy evaluation* is curiously absent. Of course, policy decisions will prompt, influence or determine the individual projects and programmes to be evaluated. Van der Knaap (1995) accepts that policy is enshrined in specific initiatives:

> … policy evaluation is concerned with a thorough investigation into the implementation and effects of public policy (for example, a program, a project). (p 200)

However, we would contend that evaluating a programme or project cannot be interpreted as a microcosmic assessment of a policy; only meta-analysis or systematic reviews of relatively large clusters of such projects/programmes can come near to discovering whether any policy is (a) being satisfactorily implemented and, if so, (b) whether the policy is having its intended effect.

It is relevant at this point to refer briefly to the reference in Chapter Two to the various connotations that surround the concept of 'policy'. The classifications offered by Hogwood (1987) are helpful in attempts to clarify what might be meant by the term 'policy evaluation'. He sets out a number of different interpretations of 'policy. These are:

- Policy as aspiration – as in, for example, 'our aim is to promote individual choice' or 'we stand for social equality'. These fall into the category of mission statements.
- Policy as a set of proposals. This involves refining aspirations into statements of intent, perhaps in the form of a White Paper or election manifesto.
- Policy as formal authorisation – when proposals are legitimated by means of an Act of Parliament.
- Policy as a programme – defined as a relatively specific sphere of government activity accompanied by an hypothecated budget.

- Policy as a process – that is, policy can be shaped at various stages of implementation. According to this interpretation, a statement of intent – to do or not to do something – need not be regarded as fixed, permanent or immutable.

While policy analysis is disposed towards predicting the ability of a policy – whatever form it might take – to achieve its objectives, policy evaluation is concerned with the implementation of policy – the process, outputs, outcomes or impact but not necessarily with all of these facets of policy in action or, indeed, of policy inaction.

One of the more searching and sustained discussions centring on the relationship between evaluation and policy is by Weiss (1999). As noted in Chapter Six, her pressing concern is with the problem of identifying whether or not policy makers are influenced by the results of evaluation studies. In her discussion, she does not deal exclusively with 'program evaluation'. She makes a salient point, a statement that underlines our own appraisal of the value in real-world terms of aspiring to devise theory-driven evaluation:

> A precondition for evaluation and its use by government has to be the availability of a sizeable group of social scientists who are interested in conducting policy-oriented research. Evaluation prospers where there is a critical mass of social scientists interested in empirical work, not just abstract theory-building. (p 482)

This apparent lack of 'empirical work', that defines the nature of much evaluation literature, is a major impediment to assessing whether evaluation findings have any impact on policy makers and their decisions. Weiss is honest enough to present her ideas about the use and non-use of evaluation research as 'conjectures' and 'hypotheses'. Yet, unfortunately, in most of the evaluation literature, such tentative suggestions all too often become cloaked in an aura of validated statements of fact.

In the UK, probably the first official recognition by the government of the need to evaluate policies appeared in a document produced by the Treasury Department (1988). A few years later, a report on the benefit of evaluating policy at a national level appeared in another government document, this time produced by the Department of the Environment (1992). This offers a rare insight into the value placed by the government at the time on the use of evaluation to assist and inform policy making at Cabinet level. The report cites a number of case studies aimed at evaluating national policies. These included a bus deregulation scheme and the Enterprise Allowance Scheme. The document lays down a number of principles and ground rules for carrying out policy evaluations. These are:

- Fundamental to any evaluation is an understanding of causality in the policy or system under study.
- Causality often involves a chain of events rather than a single direct cause and effect line.
- Sufficiently plausible explanations need to be highlighted in order to construct hypotheses for testing if no direct cause–effect relationship can be clearly established.
- Evaluation studies should not be embarked upon until policy objectives have been clearly defined. These may include short-term and long-term objectives.
- The research design should be capable of accommodating changes in policy direction and the setting of new objectives.
- There needs to be a shared perception of terminology.
- Evaluation should not only set out to answer the immediate questions but also pinpoint the issues which need monitoring and possible evaluation in the future.
- Both quantitative and qualitative data are used in most of the evaluations. The two designs complement each other.
- Where a large scale and expensive evaluation study is being planned, a feasibility or pilot phase must be included in the design.
- Evaluation is never value free and the same data can be variously interpreted.
- Often research for policy evaluation is not commissioned until the policy has started. operating and it is not possible to ascertain the 'before' situation to define a baseline from which to measure change.
- The appropriate level of resources to be devoted to an evaluation should be related to the likely scale of benefits to be achieved.
- A good customer–contractor relationship is important in order to ease the flow of information and informal feedback.

The virtue of all these statements is that the report relates each of them to actual case studies of evaluations carried out on various government initiatives ranging from a few months to ten years devoted to the evaluation research. One important message contained in the report is this:

> A distinction needs to be drawn between studies which evaluate national policies and those which evaluate the interpretation of those policies at the local level. (p 14)

As we shall see, the dominant form of evaluation contained in the literature corresponds to the second type in which projects and programmes, and not the policy at large, are the subject of formal evaluations. Another positive contribution to one of the three main themes in the literature referred to earlier in this section is that by stating what a government or government department expects from an evaluation, it is possible to infer why evaluation research findings are not apparently adopted by policy makers.

Walker (1997) refers to a comparatively rare example of policy evaluation at a national level instigated by the UK Department of Social Security. This initiative consisted of an evaluation of a number of new or modified programmes including supplementary benefit, housing benefit, jobseeker's allowance and the Social Fund. These were all pilot programmes carried out in relatively small geographical areas. In evaluating such 'social experiments', as Walker points out, 'there is no robust statistical means of generalizing to a national situation' (p 276).

In the search for texts dealing specifically with policy evaluation, the article by Geva-May and Pal (1999) looked promising but turned out to be disappointing. It purports to explore the difference between policy analysis and policy evaluation but deals with evaluation in general. Interestingly, nearly a decade after Walker's (1997) contribution to the meagre number of tracts on policy evaluation, Walker and Wiseman (2006), referring primarily to the UK, state that 'Only a minority of government policies have ever been formally evaluated' (p 362). Since 2006 we would argue that the situation has not changed. Walker and Wiseman date the UK government's interest in policy evaluation to be apparent from the 1990s when political support for evaluation emerged with the concern over excessive public expenditure and the introduction of private sector audit and management techniques. In 1997, the UK Labour government committed itself to piloting policies prior to full implementation and the Cabinet Office published handbooks for civil servants emphasising the importance of evaluation to policy design (Cabinet Office, 1999, 2004)

One possible reason for there being relatively few published accounts of empirical studies in the field of policy evaluation is that policies can be difficult to assess as far as successful outcomes are concerned. As Walker and Wiseman (2006) point out, policies are often complex with multiple objectives that are often imprecisely defined and which are tailored to different sub-groups. 'Such policies are difficult to evaluate and constrain the use of experimental and quasi-experimental designs' (p 363). The authors make a very useful distinction between policy-driven evaluation and evaluation-driven policy. In the first approach, the evaluators may come to their task with the policy already implemented and the research design decided on. This was, indeed, the scenario when we were commissioned to evaluate the two initiatives on care in the community mentioned in Chapter Four. On the other hand, with evaluation-driven policy, a policy experiment is designed to test what Walker and Wiseman call 'a nascent policy concept or strategy' (p 363). This, they claim, is an approach strongly represented in the USA but by only one fully worked evaluation in Britain. This was the cluster of projects included under the New Deal programme intended to improve employment prospects for young people, lone parents and disabled people. According to Walker and Wiseman, evaluation-driven policy 'increases the chances of obtaining precise estimates (*sic*) of impact by explicitly designing the policy and its implementation to be amenable to effective evaluation' (p 363). However, Walker and Wiseman introduce a qualifying statement, that 'the more politically important the policy, arguably the less it is shaped by evaluation' (p 367). This phenomenon, they maintain, can perhaps be explained by the fact that politicians and officials may hope to demonstrate that a policy works rather than to determine whether or not it does. If this is true, then it could account, at least to some extent, for the lack of attention to policy evaluation by academics/evaluators since governments might be apprehensive about commissioning the formal evaluation of policies that are not evaluation-driven but fervently ideology-driven.

If the UK government expressed such a commitment to submitting policies or 'nascent policies' to evaluation during the past 20 years or so, the question remains as to why so few examples have found their way into the evaluation literature. It is, of course, quite possible that the UK government and the devolved administrations in Northern Ireland, Scotland and Wales have commissioned a number of externally evaluated policies but the resulting reports have been confined to the scrutiny of civil servants and politicians or of various inspectorates and audit bodies. This possibility would become even more likely if the evaluation findings cast doubt on whether the policy was achieving its objectives. Whatever the reasons might be, there is no firm evidence that formal evaluations have had any impact on shaping, fine-tuning or modifying government policy.

Concluding comment

In this chapter we have drawn attention to a number of topics relating to the practice of evaluation. We would suggest that all but one of these aspects of evaluation have been relatively neglected. In the concluding chapter we shall discuss whether there could be an argument for enhancing their role. Systematic reviews, meta-analysis, meta-evaluation, experimental research designs, process evaluation and policy evaluation could possibly serve to enhance the status of formal evaluations and lead to a greater uptake of evaluation findings. On the other hand, we shall examine whether evaluation theory has played a significant part in the development of evaluation as a real-world activity.

References

Alkin, M.C. and Christie, C.A. (2004) 'An evaluation theory tree', in M.C. Alkin (ed) *Evaluation roots: Tracing theorists' views and influences*, Thousand Oaks, CA: Sage.

Alkin, M.C., Christie, C.A. and Rose, M. (2004) 'Communicating evaluation', in I.A. Shaw, J.C. Greene and M.M. Mark (eds) (2006) *Handbook of evaluation: Policies, programs and policies*, London: Sage.

Ashworth, K., Cebulla, A., Greenberg, D. and Walker, R. (2004) 'Meta-evaluation: discovering what works best in welfare provision', *Evaluation*, vol 10, no 2, pp 193-216.

Bickman, L. (1997) 'Evaluating evaluation: where do we go from here?', *Evaluation Practice*, vol 18, pp 1-16.

Boruch, K. (1997) *Randomized experiments for planning and evaluation*, Thousand Oaks, CA: Sage.

Cabinet Office (1999) *Professional policy making for the 21st century*, London: Cabinet Office Strategic Policy Making Team.

Cabinet Office (2004) *Trying it out: review of effectiveness of government pilots*, London Cabinet Office.

Campbell, D.T. (1969) 'Reforms as experiments', *American Psychologist*, vol 24 (April), pp 409-29.

Campbell, D.T. and Stanley, J.C. (1966) *Experimental and quasi-experimental designs for research*, Skokie IL: Rand-McNally.

Chelimsky, E. (1983) *The definition and measurement of quality as a management tool*, New Directions for Program Evaluation, Summer vol 18, pp 113-26.

Chelimsky, E. (1987) 'What have we learned about the politics of program evaluation?', *Evaluation Practice*, vol 8, no 1, pp 55-21.

Chen, H. (1990) *Theory-driven evaluation*, Beverly Hills, CA: Sage.

Chitty, C. (2000) 'Why pilot?', Paper presented to the Royal Statistical Society Conference, 'The evaluation of economic and social policies', RSS London, 4 July.

Chivers T. (2010) *The Telegraph*, 24 May. Available at http://blogs. telegraph.co.uk/culture/tomchivers/100008226/mmr-autism-scare-so-farewell-then-dr-andrew-wakefield/.

Clarke A. (1999) *Evaluation research: An introduction to principles, methods and practice*, London: Sage.

Cochrane, A.L. (1972) *Effectiveness and efficiency*, Nuffield Provincial Hospitals Trust.

Cook, T.D., Cooper, H., Cordray, D. and Hartman, H. (1992) *Meta-analysis for explanation: A casebook*, NY: Russell Sage.

Cooksy, L.J and Caracelli, V.J. (2005) 'Quality, context and use: issues in achieving the goals of evaluation', *American Journal of Evaluation*, vol 26, no 31, pp 31-42.

Datta, L.E. (2006) 'The practice of evaluation challenges and New Directions', in F. Shaw, J.C. Greene and M.M. Mark (eds) *The Sage handbook of evaluation,* Thousand Oaks, CA: Sage, pp 419-38.

Davis, P. (2005) 'The limits of realist evaluation: surfacing and exploring assumptions', *Evaluation*, vol 11, no 3, pp 275-96.

Department of the Environment (1992) *Policy evaluation: The role of social research*, London: HMSO.

Donaldson, S.I. and Christie. C.A. (2006) 'Emerging career opportunities in the transdiscipline of evaluation science', in S.I. Donaldson, D.E. Berger and K. Pezdak (eds) *Applied psychology: New frontiers and rewarding careers*, Mahwah N.J: Erlbaum Associates, pp 243-59.

Egger, M. and Smith, G.D. (1997) 'Meta-analysis: principles and procedures', *British Medical Journal,* vol 315, p 1533.

Epstein, I. and Tripodi, T. (1977) *Research techniques for program planning, monitoring and evaluation*, Columbia: University Press.

Fitzgibbon, C.T. and Morris, L.L. (1987) *How to design a program evaluation*, Beverly Hills, CA: Sage.

Fournier, D.M. and Smith, N.L. (1993) 'Clarifying the merits and argument in evaluation practice', *Evaluation and Program Planning*, vol 16, no 4, pp 315-23.

Georghiou, I. (1999) 'Meta-evaluation: evaluation of evaluations', *Scientometrics*, vol 45, no 3, pp 523-30.

Geva-May, I. and Pal, L.A. (1999) 'Good fences make good neighbours: policy evaluation and policy analysis – exploring the differences', *Evaluation*, vol 5, no 3, pp 259-77.

Goldacre, B. (2009) *Bad science,* London: Fourth Estate.

Gomby, D.S. and Larson, C.S. (1992) *The future of children*, NJ: Princeton University Publishers.

Gomm R and Davies C. (eds) (2000) *Using evidence in health and social care*, London: Sage/The Open University.

Gomm, R, Needham, G. and Bullman, A. (eds) (2000) *Evaluating research in health and social care,* London: Sage.

Granger, R.C. (1998) 'Establishing causality in evaluations of comprehensive community initiatives', in K. Fulbright-Anderson, A.C. Kubisch and J.C. Connell (eds) *New approaches to evaluating community initiatives,* vol 2, 'Theory, measurement and analysis', WA: Aspen Institute.

Green, J. and South. J. (2006) *Evaluation*, Maidenhead: Open University Press.

Greene, J.C. (1992) 'A case study of evaluation auditing as meta-evaluation', *Evaluation and Program Planning*, vol 15, pp 71-4.

Guba, E.G. and Lincoln, Y.S. (1985) *Naturalistic inquiry*, Thousand Oaks, CA: Sage.

Guba, E.G. and Lincoln, Y.S (1989) *Fourth generation evaluation*, San Francisco, CA: Jossey Bass.

Hansen, H.F. (2005) 'Choosing evaluation models', *Evaluation*, vol 11, pp 447-61.

Haralambos, M. and Holborn, M. (1995) *Sociology: Themes and perspectives*, London: Collins Educational.

Hattie, J.A and Hansford, B.C. (1984) 'Meta–analysis: a reflection on problems', *Australian Journal of Psychology*, vol 36, no 2, pp 239-54.

Hawe, P., Sheill, A. and Riley, T. (2004) 'Complex interventions: how "out of control" can a randomised trial be?', *BMJ* 328: 7455, pp 1561-63, 26 June.

Hogwood, B (1987) *From crisis to complacency*, Oxford: Oxford University Press.

House, E.R. (1980) *Stakeholder-based evaluation and value judgments,* Beverly Hills, CA; Sage.

HM Treasury (1988) *Policy evaluation: A guide for managers*, London: HMSO.

Hurteau, M., Houle, S. and Mongiat, S. (2009) 'How legitimate and justified are judgments in program evaluation?', *Evaluation*, vol 15, no 3. pp 307-19.

Kuhn, T.S. (1962) *The structure of scientific revolutions*, Chicago: University of Chicago Press.

Jacob, S. and Boisvert, Y. (2010) 'To be or not to be a profession: pros, cons and challenges for evaluation', *Evaluation*, vol 16, no 4, pp 349-69.

Lipsey, M.W., Crosse, S., Dunkle, J., Pollard, J. and Stobart, G. (1985) 'Evaluation: the state of the art and the sorry state of the science', in D.S. Cordray (ed) *Utilizing prior research in evaluation*, New Directions in Evaluation Planning No 27, San Francisco, CA: Jossey Bass, pp 7-28.

Madison, A. (2002) *Bridging evaluation theory and practice, Lecture to the African Evaluation Association*. Available at www.afrea.org/org/documents/Document.cfm?docID=130.

Mark M.M. (2005) 'Evaluation theory or what are evaluation methods for?', *The Evaluation Exchange*, vol 11, no 2, pp 2-3.

Morley S., Eccleston C. and Williams, A. (1999) *Systematic review and meta-analysis of randomized controlled trials of cognitive behaviour therapy and behaviour therapy for chronic pain in adults, excluding headache*, International Association for the Study of Pain Elsevier Science.

Moynihan, A. (2004) *Evaluating health services*, Milbank Memorial Fund New York.

Nutbeam, D. (1998) 'Evaluating health promotion: progress, problems and solutions', *Health Promotion International*, vol 13, pp 27-43.

Orr, L.L. (1999) *Social experiments: Evaluating public programs with experimental methods*, Thousand Oaks, CA: Sage.

Palfrey, C.F. and Thomas, P. (1996) 'Ethical issues in policy evaluation', *Policy & Politics*, vol 24, no 3, pp 277-86.

Patton, M.Q. (1982) *Practical evaluation*, NY: Sage.

Patton, M.Q. (1987) *How to use qualitative methods in evaluation,* NY: Sage.

Pawson, R. (2002a) 'Evidence-based policy: in search of a method', *Evaluation*, vol 8, no 2, pp 157-81.

Pawson, R. (2002b) 'Evidence-based policy: the promise of "realist synthesis"', *Evaluation*, vol 8, no 3, pp 340-58.

Pawson, R. and Tilley, N. (1997) *Realistic evaluation*, London: Sage.

Pedersen, L.H. and Rieper, O. (2008) 'Is realist evaluation a realistic approach to complex reforms?', *Evaluation*, vol 14, no 3, pp 271-94.

Rossi, P.H, Freeman, H.E. and Lipsey, M.W. (1999) *Evaluation: A systematic approach*, Newbury Park, CA: Sage.

Sanderson, I. (2002) 'Evaluation, policy learning and evidence-based policy', *Public Administration*, vol 80, no 1, pp 1-22.

Scriven, M. (1969) 'An introduction to meta-evaluation', *Educational Products Report*, vol 2, pp 36-8.

Scriven, M. (1995) 'The logic of evaluation and evaluation practice', in D.M. Fournier (ed) *Reasoning in evaluation: Inferential links and leaps*, New Directions for Evaluation No 68, San Francisco, CA: Jossey-Bass, pp 49-70.

Schwandt, T.A, and Halpern, E.S. (1988) *Linking auditing and metaevaluation*, Newbury Park, Beverly Hills, CA: Sage.

Shadish, W.R., Cook, T.D. and Leviton, L.D. (1991) *Foundations of program evaluation: Theories of practice*, Newbury Park, CA: Sage.

Shaw, I.A., Greene, J.C. and Mark, M.M. (eds) (2006) *Handbook of evaluation: Policies, programmes and practices*, London: Sage.

Smelser, N.J. (1994) *Sociology*, Cambridge, MA: Blackwell.

Stufflebeam D.L. (1981) 'Meta-evaluation: concepts, standards and uses', in R.A. Beck (ed) *Educational evaluation: The state of the art*, London: John Hopkins University Press.

Stufflebeam, D.L. (2001) 'The metaevaluation imperative', *American Journal of Evaluation,* vol 22, no 2, pp 183-209.

Stufflebeam D.L. and Shinkfield A.J. (2007) *Evaluation theory: Models and applications*, Boston: Kluwer-Nijhoff.

Tilley, N. and Clarke, A. (2006) 'Evaluation in criminal justice', in I.F. Shaw, J.C. Greener and M.M. Mark (eds) *Handbook of evaluation* London: Sage, pp 512-35.

Treasury Board of Canada Secretariat (2004) *Review of the quality of evaluations across departments and agencies.* Available at www.tbs-sct. gc.ca/cee/pubs/review-examen2004-eng.asp.

Van der Knaap, P. (1995) 'Policy evaluation and learning', *Evaluation,* vol 1, no 2, pp 189-216.

Vedung, E (1997) *Public policy and program evaluation*, New Brunswick, NJ: Transaction.

Walker, R. (1997) 'Public policy evaluation in a centralized state: a case study of social assistance in the United Kingdom', *Evaluation*, vol 3, no 5, pp 261-89.

Walker, R. and Wiseman, M. (2006) 'Managing evaluations', in I.A. Shaw, J.C. Greene and M.M. Mark (eds) (2006) *Handbook of evaluation: Policies, programmes and practices,* London: Sage.

Weiss, C. (1972) *Evaluation research: Methods for assessing program effectiveness*, NJ: Prentice-Hall.

Weiss, C. (1995) 'Nothing as practical as good theory', in J. Connell, A. Kubish, H. Schon and C. Weiss (eds) *New approaches in evaluating community initiatives*, NY: Aspen Institute.

Weiss, C. (1999) 'The interface between evaluation and public policy', *Evaluation*, vol 5, no 2, pp 468-86.

Wortman, P.M. (1994) 'Judging research quality', in H. Cooper and L.V. Hodges (eds) *The handbook of research synthesis*, NY: Russell Sage Foundation, pp 97-110.

EIGHT

Concluding thoughts

Under the broad aim of examining the development of evaluation and its impact on public policy, we set out in the Introduction to this book a set of key objectives, the first of which was to trace the emergence of evaluation in the political and academic worlds. As noted in Chapter One, evaluation in the UK and the USA emerged in the mid-20th century as a means of improving the performance of public sector organisations against a background of increasing fiscal pressures. In the case of the UK, much of the early work was crystallised in the early 1980s in the form of the Audit Commission, to which the government gave the role of evaluating performance in relation to effectiveness, efficiency and economy – the elements of what was seen at that time as 'value for money'.

Our second objective was to explore the concept of evaluation and its various interpretations. We have seen, largely in Chapter Two, that the range of interpretations is very wide, encompassing formal mechanisms such as performance indicators (PIs), audits, inspections and accreditations as well as a number of models and conceptions such as goal-oriented and goal-free evaluations, formative and summative evaluations, and evaluations that can be described as naturalistic, realistic, theory-driven and utilisation-focused. There can be no simple and comprehensive fix to the task of evaluation. Evaluators need to be explicit as to the 'version' of evaluation being used in any particular context.

The third objective was to identify the potential opportunities and problems in a range of data collection methods and in the analysis of data. We have seen that there are problems to be resolved when using any method of data collection – including interviews, observation, the scrutiny of documents and the use of questionnaires. Those planning and undertaking the collection of data for evaluations need to make many decisions about which methods to use and about exactly how to use the selected methods. The problems are deeply philosophical, in the case of ontology and epistemology, and operational as in the case, for example, of designing the questions to be asked in interviews. Evaluations which are not based on a careful consideration of these sets of issues need to be treated with considerable scepticism as they are likely to fail tests of validity and/or reliability.

The fourth objective was to trace the development of key evaluation frameworks. This exercise was inevitably selective. Our selection encompassed fourth generation evaluation (Guba and Lincoln, 1987), pluralistic evaluation (Smith and Cantley, 1985), participatory evaluation (Plottu and Plottu, 2009), realistic evaluation (Pawson and Tilley, 1997), evidence-based evaluation (Walshe, 2006), and the roles of power (Palfrey and Thomas, 1999) and of action research (Hart and Bond, 1995) in evaluations. There is, of course, no one 'best' framework for undertaking evaluations and we suspect there will never be such a thing. The challenge for evaluators is to select the most appropriate framework for the particular evaluation task being faced and the context in which it is to be carried out.

The fifth objective was to assess critically a range of criteria commonly used in evaluations. Including the issue of ethics we have identified 12 criteria which, in our experience, are the most commonly used and discussed in the evaluation literature. The boundaries between the criteria are often blurred and no criterion is a wholly satisfactory yardstick on its own. Each is useful in various contexts but also has the limitations to which we have drawn attention in Chapter Four. Different criteria are likely to be favoured by different stakeholders and the selection and use of criteria in any evaluation is therefore likely to depend on the distribution of power among the interested parties.

The sixth objective was to assess the role of economic evaluations. This was addressed in Chapter Five which entailed a consideration of the costs associated with public policies and services, the effects that policies are assumed to have, and the complexities involved in both costs and effects. We highlighted the importance of taking a systems-wide view rather than a narrow focus on any one element of the system. Evaluation is an activity in which blinkers need firmly to be left at home.

The seventh objective was to consider the extent to which academics have influenced the practice of evaluation. As noted in Chapter One, the starting point for evaluation research can be traced to the United States in the 1930s. There have been a number of contributions to the field which have had a major impact on what is widely regarded as good evaluation practice. A notable example is the work of Cochrane (1972) in relation to the evaluation of clinical practice. As discussed in Chapter Three, in more recent years the ideas of Smith and Cantley (1985), Guba and Lincoln (1989) and Pawson and Tilley (1989) have been particularly influential in the ways in which the theory and practice of evaluation have developed.

The eighth objective was to examine the nature of evidence and its use/non-use by decision makers. As well as the indicators of poor quality evaluations to which we drew attention in Chapter Seven, decisions about the extent to which evaluation evidence should be used will be based on a wide variety of factors. As shown in Chapter Six, these factors may be political in nature or may concern technical matters such as poorly presented reports, poor timing or poor communications. Perhaps the most difficult barrier to overcome in attempting to persuade decision makers to implement the recommendations of an evaluation report will often be lack of the right kind of resources at the right time in the right place.

The ninth objective was to assess the impact of evaluations on the formulation of policy. How can evaluators ensure that their work feeds back to policy-making processes and does not just end up on the shelf? This is an issue which has been analysed among others by Carol Weiss (1999). Evaluators are often disappointed with what they see as the failure of policy makers to give enough attention to their findings. But some research has suggested that the findings of evaluation research have indeed been influential in the longer run.

'In democracies, many people have a hand in defining the issues, identifying the perspective from which they should be addressed, proffering potential policy solutions and pressing for particular policy responses' (Weiss, 1999, p 471). The knowledge that evaluation researchers can add to that already available has to compete for a hearing with information from other sources, but what the evaluators can do is to contribute 'enlightenment' – 'the percolation of new information, ideas and perspectives into the arenas in which decisions are made' (Weiss, 1999, p 471).

Often social science findings generally, and evaluations in particular, are brought to the attention of civil servants, politicians and other policy makers by universities, policy think tanks, advisory bodies to ministers, staff developers and trainers, conferences, mass media, websites and friends. According to Weiss (1999), the reasons that policy makers may take notice of social science research include the following:

1. they may want to get a better sense of things so they can seek the best course of action;
2. they may distrust the information they are getting from other sources, such as pressure groups or sometimes the civil service;
3. to provide legitimacy for political action because of the apparent independence of researchers and their aura of integrity;

4. they may want to find evidence that supports their position;

5. they may want to appear to be up-to-date and well informed.

However, the information might arrive on the policy maker's desk in a truncated or distorted way. Furthermore, the version of it that arrives might be used merely to justify a policy decision that has been made on other grounds (Weiss, 1999, p 477).

What all this amounts to is that evaluators need to recognise the difficulties in achieving their aim of influencing the policy-making process. They need to be skilled communicators and aware of the political complexities. The relationship between evaluation and the worlds of public management and public policy is not simple. The ways in which evaluations might contribute to the improvement of public services can be tortuous and uncertain.

The final objective was to offer suggestions as to the directions in which evaluation needs to travel. In Chapter Seven we reported on our review of the literature relating to systematic reviews, meta-analysis, meta-evaluation, experimental research designs, process evaluation and policy evaluation. The boundaries between these schools are often blurred and in some cases it would seem that much more work is needed to develop them, especially in the case of meta-evaluation, process evaluation and policy evaluation, if evaluators are to have an increased influence on the formulation of public policies.

Locating evaluation in the real world

In tracing the development of evaluation as a potential source of evidence for decision making both at governmental and organisational levels, we have drawn attention to the concerns expressed in a good deal of the literature regarding the apparent reluctance of policy makers to act on the results of commissioned research. Since some authors have conjectured that the poor quality of some evaluation research might be the reason for the non-utilisation of the findings, we have cautioned against applying certain methods of data collection without taking into account their inherent limitations. We have also examined the issue of which criteria could be appropriate according to the key approaches to and purpose of evaluating projects, programmes and policies.

These considerations and the need to analyse what is meant by 'evidence' have provided a framework for examining what might be regarded as the deficiencies and defects in the corpus of evaluation literature over the past 50 years. In the light of our critical analysis of the literature, we offer below some suggestions about how evaluation and its supporting literature might be further developed and refined.

- Evaluations reported in various journals and books are dominated by attempts to discover whether the outcomes of policies – often implemented in specific projects and programmes – correspond with explicit policy objectives. It would appear that relatively little attention has been paid to the *process* involved in implementing the policy and in carrying out the evaluation. A clear focus on process could, for example, provide important information about why a project 'worked', did not 'work' or 'worked' for some people and not for others.
- In the real world, those who commission evaluation research are usually looking for a strictly time-limited piece of research that can deliver unequivocal answers to key questions about the value of a particular initiative. While academics might exert considerable energy in trying to develop theories and to extol the merits of this approach or that system, there is no evidence that such endeavours have had any impact on the likelihood of the results of evaluation being acted upon.
- This raises the question of whether those evaluators who complain about the non-utilisation of their findings have any grounds for doing so. In the first place, should they not accept the fact that policy makers and those such as civil servants and public sector executives who advise them are working on agendas relating to attracting votes, staying in power and managing finite resources? If the evaluation has been proved to have been carried out to a high standard of technical and ethical competence perhaps that is enough. The evaluator leaves any further action or inaction to those who make decisions and moves on. As Praestgaard (1999) argues, 'It is definitely demoralising if a political decision is contrary to the conclusion of an evaluation but that is politics' (p 531). For 'politics' read 'the real world'. Alternatively, in order both to satisfy their curiosity and to add a missing dimension to the academic literature, those who carry out evaluations could follow up their work by actually asking those who commissioned the research whether they intended to act, or – at a later stage – whether they had acted, on the evaluation findings and if not the reasons why they had not acted. However, in our view, it would hardly be advisable to adopt the suggestion from Georghiou (1995) that although there is no compulsion on managers and politicians to follow recommendations 'mandatory provision of reasons for not following them would ensure that full consideration

is given' (p 185). Discovering the eventual destination of evaluation findings is an uncharted area of social research and consequently has led to a welter of guesses, suppositions and hypotheses when academics could more usefully be actively seeking evidence. An example of this tendency to generalise without providing supporting evidence is the statement by Feinstein (2002) that 'It is generally recognized that evaluation activities generate knowledge that is significantly under-used' (p 437).

- Although there are journals published in the UK which are devoted to academic articles relating to evaluation, to aspects of public services and to government policy, very few reports of evaluations appear in media accessible to a wide readership. One reason for this might be that reports of evaluations remain available only to those who commissioned the research. It would be of benefit to everyone interested in evaluation if a new journal could be launched that managed to seek out and publish completed evaluation reports. These could be open to critical analysis and subjected to a meta-evaluation. In this way lessons could be learned about best practice and how to enhance the probability of evaluation contributing to policy.

- In seeking to raise the status of evaluation to that of a worthy academic discipline and field of study more attention needs to be paid to the issue of replication studies. We know that evaluation research is likely to be highly dependent for its data analysis and conclusions on contexts of time and place and, as Tilley (1996) has pointed out, strict replication of project research is hardly possible. Nevertheless, in spite of the difficulties involved in trying to match different evaluation studies in terms of sample populations and the unlikelihood of adequately controlling for intervening variables through randomised controlled trials, replication studies could be useful (a) in providing reasonably similar research projects that could be subjected to meta-evaluations and (b) in helping to clarify which factors led to differing results.

- Attempts to design and promote replication studies would help to offset the tendency among many academics to peddle their newly devised 'theories' and 'approaches' without any reference to empirical work that has generated or tested these purportedly innovative ideas. Of course, in the field of social research generally replication studies are probably less likely to be published than 'new' research, although this is in itself only an assumption which needs to be the subject of research.

- While there have been various debates about involving less empowered stakeholders in evaluations as subjects and even as co-evaluators (which we would support) it has to be recognised that the evaluator is clearly a stakeholder as well. The evaluator has an undeniable interest in how the evaluation is carried out and what results it produces. It is hopefully not stretching credibility too far to suggest that one of the reasons why so many evaluators are not happy that their efforts appear to have been in vain is that they perceive their own professional status and authority to have been undermined. They among all stakeholders might feel the least 'empowered'.

- As to the question of whether evaluators should take an overtly ideological stance we have not changed our view expressed elsewhere. We argued that 'there is no intrinsic value in evaluation espousing political causes *per se*. The *usefulness* of an inclusive, *open-ended* evaluation is to be judged not by its political impact on policy but by its capacity to produce robust and comprehensive data ... Evaluation takes place within a political context but it would be arrogant of those carrying out the evaluation to plead their own cause as primary amongst a variety of stakeholders' (Palfrey and Thomas, 1999, p 69).

- To date, the evaluation literature has been unconvincing about the evidence base on which the various approaches, systems and theories have been founded. We are not suggesting that the world of academia is divorced from reality. What we *are* saying is that the results of evaluations should be much more widely shared. Those at government level who commission evaluation research need to be encouraged – perhaps by the media and the public – to explain how cost-effective project, programme and policy evaluations have been. They should be made more accountable not just for the policies they determine but how they have come to their decisions.

To this end, evaluation research could play a crucial role in contributing to a more open political culture in which those who devise and modify policies explain how they have come to their decisions, including the extent to which the results of evaluations have proved influential.

References

Cochrane, A. (1972) *Effectiveness and efficiency*, London: Nuffield Provincial Hospital Trust.

Feinstein, O.N. (2002) 'Use of evaluations and evaluation of their use', *Evaluation*, vol 8, no 4, pp 433-39.

Georghiou, L. (1995) 'Assessing the framework programme', *Evaluation*, vol 1, no 2, pp 171-88.

Guba, E. and Lincoln, Y. (1987) 'The countenances of fourth-generation evaluation: description, judgment and negotiation', in D. Palumbo (ed) *The politics of program evaluation*, CA: Sage.

Guba, E. and Lincoln, Y. (1989) *Fourth generation evaluation*, Newbury Park, CA: Sage.

Hart, E. and Bond, M. (1995) *Action research for health and social care: A guide to practice*, Milton Keynes: Open University.

Palfrey, C. and Thomas, P. (1999) 'Politics and policy evaluation', *Public Policy and Administration*, vol 14, no 4, pp 58-70.

Palumbo, D. (1987) 'Politics and evaluation', in D. Palumbo (ed) *The politics of program evaluation*, California: Sage.

Pawson, R. and Tilley, N. (1989) 'What works in evaluation research?', *British Journal of Criminology*, vol 34, no 3, pp 291-306.

Pawson, R. and Tilley, N. (1997) *Realistic evaluation*, London: Sage.

Plottu, B. and Plottu, E. (2009) 'Approaches to participation in evaluation: some conditions for implementation', *Evaluation*, vol 15, no 3, pp 343-59.

Praestgaard, E. (1999) 'Meta-evaluation: evaluation of evaluations', *Scientometrics*, vol 43, no 3, pp 531-32.

Smith, G. and Cantley, C. (1985) *Assessing health care: A study in organisational evaluation*, Milton Keynes: Open University.

Tilley, N. (1996) 'Demonstration, exemplification, duplication and replication in evaluation research', *Evaluation*, vol 2, no 1, pp 35-50.

Walshe, K. (2006) 'Research, evaluation and evidence-based management', in K. Walshe and J. Smith (eds) *Healthcare management*, Milton Keynes: Open University Press.

Weiss, C. (1999) 'The interface between evaluation and public policy', *Evaluation*, vol 5, no 4, pp 468–86.

Index